HOLLY CLEGG

trim&TERRIFIC™

Freezer Friendly Meals

HOLLY CLEGG

trim&TERRIFIC™

Freezer Friendly Meals

Quick and Healthy Recipes You Can Make in Advance

By Holly Clegg

Photography by David Humphreys

RUNNING PRESS

PHILADELPHIA · LONDON

Library of Congress Control Number: 2006900798
ISBN-13: 978-0-7624-2597-6
ISBN-10: 0-7624-2597-0

Cover design by Bill Jones
Interior design by Maria Taffera Lewis
Edited by Diana C. von Glahn
Photography assistance by Wes Kroninger
Creative Consultant: Pamela Clegg Hill
Nutritional Analysis: Tammi Hancock, Hancock Nutrition
Typography: Berkeley Book and Formata

This book may be ordered by mail from the publisher.
Please include $2.50 for postage and handling.
But try your bookstore first!

Running Press Book Publishers
125 South Twenty-Second Street
Philadelphia, Pennsylvania 19103-4399

Visit us on the web!
www.runningpresscooks.com
www.runningpress.com
www.hollyclegg.com

Also by Holly Clegg*:
The New Holly Clegg Trim & Terrific Cookbook
Trim & Terrific Home Entertaining the Easy Way
Eating Well Through Cancer: Easy Recipes and Recommendations During and After Treatment
*To order these books, call 1-800-88HOLLY or visit her website, www.hollyclegg.com

Table of Contents

Acknowledgments

My entire family engaged in the creation of my *Trim & Terrific Freezer Friendly Cookbook* by testing, tasting, editing, or listening to my enthusiastic rambling.

My husband Mike, an attorney who doesn't cook and never is in the kitchen, tolerated my endless hours of cooking, and somewhat willingly sampled more new creations than he cared to. Mike was there for encouragement, representation, and support, but best of all, he is my husband of 27 years, which proves the way to a man's heart is through his stomach.

Haley, now at Geoprge Washington University in St. Louis, has been my kitchen sidekick, always willing to cook, test, and definitely taste with me. I miss "kitchen time" immensely with Haley as she continually questioned, analyzed, definitely critiqued, and truly cared and shared with me each endeavor in my cooking career.

Courtney, now in the working world, provides her valuable journalism skills, insightfulness, and incredible commitment to all my career opportunities. I think my shining moment was when she filled in for me on my local cooking television segment (hopefully only the beginning of her own shining career).

Todd, my oldest, prefers eating to cooking, often heads to the freezer for his favorite homemade meals when he is home. He works at a private equity firm, Onex, in New York City, but is close to my heart with his daily calls while walking to work—a mother's dream.

Robert, not only are you a successful builder, but you have your own talent in the kitchen. I enjoy your cooking calls. My dachshund, Elvis, is still by my side, following me from my office to the kitchen waiting for me to drop some food.

My parents, Ruth and Jerry, are the most incredible role models. Everyone asks, "Did you learn to cook from my mother?" The truth is, I did learn cooking from her, but the knowledge and values I gained from her just being my mother is my greatest gift. My father, the toughest and bravest man I know, is an inspiration on how to succeed in life. He even has more speaking engagements than I do! Best of all, there has never been a meal I prepared he hasn't liked. Of course, he is not partial at all!!

Mae Mae and Bella, our shared new dachshund, had the job of taking home freezer friendly recipes to cook, making sure the recipe tasted as good after being frozen, a tough job! Mae Mae wears many hats as she is my official taster, home sitter, and has done everything from cleaning, mailing books, or shopping for me. I can and do always depend on her.

Pam, my Clegg sis, made her trip here once again to run the kitchen for the photo shoot for the book. The beautiful photographs throughout the book would never be a reality without her. We spent endless days and nights cooking, but it was special and fun only because we did it together. I turn to Pam for recipe consultation and her caring, unconditional support. Cheers! And Jim, left alone in Boulder (thanks for sending me your beauty), had a Freezer Friendly freezer while she was away. Dr. Ilene, my sister, might not have a kitchen role, but her expertise in advice, mentoring, editing, and encouragement are what I depend on! Dr. Bart, thanks for the samples and for being only a phone call away. Michael and Kim, for the wine knowledge and my Ft. Worth representatives. Nana and Papa, food critics for years, supplied all my freezer containers. Aunt Garney, it's fun sharing my excitement and food with you when you are in town. Cannon, I'd gladly share my kitchen with you any time. Chuck and Barbara, my kitchen is always open.

To my friends: Francine, through sickness and health, you manage to keep tabs on me. I thank you for being my #1 supporter for too many years to count; and Doll, I appreciate your interest and fish. Louann and Ronnie, when it comes to being special, you two are the ones. No matter when or what I call about, I know you are there to share it with me. Gracie and Bill, I treasure our incredible friendship, all our getaways,

dinners, laughs, and times together. Karen, it is hard to imagine exercise in life without you. I value your friendship and no one knows the importance of our jaw movement—lots of problems solved, ideas created all in that one hour class giving you any title you want. Anthony, you know you are on retainer! Gail and Lewis, for a long-time friendship and catch up is great; Lynell, my groupie; and Jeff, Marti, and John (thanks for the blueberries); Mary and Rob; Louise and Jim; Melanie, started with that first book; the Ciffords (our extended family), the Sligars, and the Mocklers, neighbors but more importantly, life-long friends that can't be replaced. And to my college buddies— Amy (love my Amy jewelry), Jolie (began in your toaster oven), Leslie (my roommate, and shared memories), Lila (those Atlanta stops are my favorites, spending time with you), and Sherri (from make-up to Denver visits)—when we're together it is like we never were apart. What an incredible bond! Renate, thirty years later and even from England, you are a part of my life. And Marcia, Selma, and Joyce, my bridesmaids, I can count on ya'll for recipes, as family. It all began with y'all when I was a little girl.

To Diane Allen & Associates: Al, my mentor, for always taking time for me and keeping me focused, Diane and Nancy, you have been with me the whole ride. Thanks to the Louisiana Sweet Potato Commission for making me their national spokesperson for all these years, even though I still don't have a crown. To Baton Rouge Coca-Cola Bottling Company, I love being a part of your incredible team. Gary, thanks for your confidence; Melanie, I respect your business skills but really enjoy our friendship; Darin, thanks for keeping me on board; and Bob, always willing to help me. A big thank you to Missy, my hair surgeon (you know what that means) for coming over whether it is early in the morning or a last minute call. Mary, the cookbooks began with you so many years ago. Jill, my foodie turned friend who I still nag. And to the organization, Speaking of Women's Health, a dynamic group with a great message. I am proud to be your key note speaker.

David Humphreys, where do I begin? You are such a talented and gifted photographer exemplified by the stunning photography throughout my books. You are my dear friend who eternally keeps me smiling during these long and frequent photo shoots, and your creativity and dedication to my projects are most appreciated. Wes, even though lighting is your specialty, I thank you for willingly taking the time to be with me in my shoots doing whatever it takes!!!

With all my books, I depend on Tammi Hancock, of Hancock Nutrition, as I know her nutritional analysis is accurate. Thanks for your patience and for graciously analyzing that one more recipe I keep sending. To Gerald Miletello MD, the #1 oncologist and my

coauthor of *Eating Well Through Cancer,* you have been the perfect partner for an incredible book that only gets better with time; and to Melinda (we know who is the true cook of the family).

To everyone at Running Press: Diana, my superb editor, who is tops in her field. Your uplifting and committed attitude makes working together not a job but an enjoyable rewarding experience. Thanks for going way beyond the call of duty, but please know I appreciate the many hats you wear on my behalf. Bill Jones, you know I won't allow photo shoots without your presence. You have given the books life with your astute vision and creative design. And, we even saw some food styling talent! Seta, I appreciate your effort in organizing my tour, my life, and me. It is not an easy job, thanks so much. Craig, I look forward to working with you. Marge, you are the best for getting all those books out! Matty and Sarah, I know what an instrumental part you play in the success of my books. Jon, my commander in chief, you are why I am there, and I thank you for including me in the Running Press team.

Carlos, Diana, Emily, and those at Dezenhall Resources—working with you has been an unbelievable experience. I admire your talent, creativeness, and appreciate your attention. Thank you from the bottom of my heart for these new opportunities and I look forward to a long lasting relationship. To the Teflon/DuPont team, I am very passionate about using Teflon non-stick cookware. Teflon supports my Trim & Terrific philosophy keeping cooking healthier. I look forward to representing Teflon and sharing the healthy and safe cooking message with all the people who find themselves in the kitchen.

And thanks to all the television producers, magazine editors, and food editors who have graciously supported me through my Trim & Terrific years.

And to all those Trim & Terrific cooks, this book is for you. I hope these *Trim & Terrific Freezer Friendly* recipes are your cooking solution to preparing healthier meals without stressing about it all week. Thank you for allowing me to share my passion for cooking with you in so many different ways.

A Guide to the Symbols

Vegetarian recipe

A Note on the Recipes

❄ For all recipes that call for butter, an equal amount of margarine may be substituted.

❄ The nutritional analysis provided for each recipe is based on the larger portion size listed.

❄ Although most of the recipes in this book have diabetic exchanges, not all recipes are appropriate for diabetics. Follow your doctor's recommendations.

❄ Unless otherwise stated all eggs used should be large.

❄ Unless otherwise stated, onions and lemons are medium-sized.

❄ Many of the recipes suggest using non-stick pots, pans, and baking sheets. I always like the added protection of spraying my cookware and bakeware with non-stick cooking spray.

❄ Even those recipes that are slightly higher in fat are still healthier versions of classic recipes. So try them!

Introduction

"Making dishes ahead of time and freezing them takes the stress out of cooking."

Do you ever get home from work and crave a homemade meal ready in minutes? Many of us have a love-hate relationship with home-made food: we love to eat it, but hate the fact that we don't always have the time to make it. But we don't have to suffer from time constraints any longer. The next time you have the urge to cook, seize the moment (and this book!) and whip something up, *then* pop it in the freezer! You will soon become a huge fan of your freezer once you see how it allows you to make home-made meals on your own time frame. Let the freezer become your friendly, ready-made pantry.

In my new *Trim & Terrific Freezer Friendly Cookbook*, you'll have a great guide to solve your cooking dilemmas on those hectic days. These recipes were specifically designed to prepare as time permits, freeze, and then pull out when you need a delicious dish in a pinch. Use the freezer as your ultimate make-ahead strategy. Cook several meals when you have the time, then freeze them and you'll have food for days.

By cooking food ahead of time and freezing it for later, you make the most of your time, energy, and money. Frozen prepared meals add variety to your meal planning with nutritious pre-made options. The recipes in this book, as in all my books, can be prepared in less than thirty minutes, all using pantry friendly ingredients. You'll be surprised by how many of your favorite recipes freeze perfectly. Have Italian Pizza Rolls and Almond Glazed Brie to accent your entrée favorites like lasagnas, chilies, and casseroles by just pulling them out of your freezer. Let's not forget a heavenly frozen dessert for the late night hunger pains! Enjoy White Chocolate Cheesecake or Banana Split Pie, ready in your freezer. Stock your freezer with home prepared foods ranging from appetizers to desserts, then never again worry when company or extras pop in for dinner. Let your packed freezer be the perfect entertaining solution.

My *Trim & Terrific Freezer Friendly Cookbook* also serves as a time management tool. Whether it is the holidays, you're having a party, or just any night of the week, making dishes ahead of time and freezing them takes the stress out of cooking, giving you more time to spend with your friends and family. Freezing food gives home cooks a multitude of options. When preparing a recipe, prepare enough for the meal and freeze the extra for another time. If you live alone, freeze the prepared food in meal-size packages, creating your very own, home-made, one-person TV dinners. And if there are leftovers, just pack, label, and freeze. Plus, it's more economical to make your own supply of prepared dishes than to buy commercially prepared foods.

You'll find more than 200 tested recipes in this book, all chosen and designed for their ease of preparation, nutrition, and how well they freeze. Although my family saw my trips to the freezer to pull out a sampling of my latest tested creation as predictable, they loved the results! I insisted on tasting each recipe after freezing it to insure each meal retained its quality, in both taste and texture. At least, on these time-crunched days and when I was traveling, my freezer was full to pull out

dinners and my family had home cooked meals.

On the next few pages, you'll find the Freezer Guide section of this book, which is a complete guide to freezing. I tried to answer all the curiosities about what does and doesn't freeze, how long food freezes, and necessary information on how to freeze food. At the back of the book, I've provided a list of suggested menus, which has been popular in all my books. There, you'll find menu suggestions for all types of occasions and situations.

Best of all, my *Trim & Terrific Freezer Friendly Cookbook* is packed with easy, Trim & Terrific recipes that promise healthier meals that save you time. From now on, you don't have to worry about finding the time to make home-made meals on a weekly basis. With my *Trim & Terrific Freezer Friendly Cookbook,* you can cook on your own time and enjoy the benefits all week long.

Holly B. Clegg

Freezing Facts

❄ Freezing does not improve food quality—select only fresh, high-quality ingredients.

❄ Slightly undercook foods that will be frozen, as reheating will finish their cooking. This is especially true for pasta, rice, and vegetables.

❄ Food must be room temperature before freezing. Stirring will help cool food faster. Promptly freeze after the food reaches room temperature.

❄ Don't overload your freezer. It is best to freeze no more than 2 or 3 pounds per cubic foot of freezer capacity within a 24-hour period. Stack the food after it is frozen.

❄ The temperature of your freezer should not go above 0°F.

❄ If possible, thaw food in the refrigerator. It takes frozen food about 24 to 48 hours in the refrigerator to thaw completely. Eat thawed frozen food as soon as possible, since food spoils more quickly at this point than when it's fresh.

❄ Avoid freezing high sodium foods as salt lowers the freezing point of water.

❄ Do not put a cold dish in a hot oven—it can break the dish.

❄ For a timesaver, package foods to be reheated in a microwave oven in freezer/microwave safe containers.

❄ A casserole topping (cheese or bread) is best added when the dish is being heated to serve.

❄ Some spices may change flavor after they're frozen.

Foods That Do Not Freeze Well

❄ Cottage cheese

❄ Cheese

❄ Cream puddings and fillings

❄ Custard

❄ Fruits and vegetables with a high water content such as lettuce, tomatoes, cucumbers, and watermelon

❄ Gelatin salads

❄ Gravies, some

❄ Fried foods

❄ Mayonnaise

❄ Milk sauces

❄ Sour cream

❄ Whites of hard-cooked eggs and uncooked egg yolks

❄ Yogurt

Foods that Change After Being Thawed

❄ **Cheese**—may change in texture after freezing. Hard cheeses become crumbly

❄ **Soft cheese (cream cheese)**—becomes watery and may need to be beaten or combined with other ingredients once thawed

❄ **Cottage cheese**—separates and becomes mushy after freezing; stir after thawing

❄ **Gravies**—may thicken and need more liquid when reheating

❄ **Milk, yogurt, and sour cream**—may separate, stir after thawing

❄ **Sauces**—may separate. Whisk before reheating

❄ **Seasonings**—onions, herbs, and flavorings may change once they are frozen

❄ **Vegetables and pasta**—soften during freezing

Refreezing Thawed Food

❄ Foods may be refrozen if: they have only partially thawed, still have ice crystals in the package. Otherwise, refreezing can affect the quality.

❄ Meat, fish, poultry, prepared foods, vegetables, and fruits can be refrozen only if kept at temperature of 40 °F or below and if their color and odor is good.

❄ If ice cream is partially thawed, throw it out.

❄ When in doubt, it is best to throw out!

When the Power Goes Out

❄ If your freezer is unopened, it's full and well insulated, your foods will stay frozen longer.

❄ Depending on freezer size and how full it's loaded, food will stay frozen around two to four days.

❄ A half-filled freezer will keep food frozen only about 24 hours.

Freezing Guide

Biscuits and Muffins: Prepare according to directions. Cool to room temperature and freeze. Biscuits are recommended freezing for 2 to 3 months. Muffins are recommended freezing for 6 to 8 months.

Casseroles: Recommended freezing for 3 months.

Cheeses: Freezing cheese changes its consistency, making it more crumbly and mealy. When freezing cheese, if you plan to grate or melt the cheese, freezing won't make a difference.

Blue cheese, Roquefort, and Gorgonzola are usually served crumbly so they freeze well for about 6 months.

Firm cheeses such as Cheddar, Gouda, and Swiss, can be frozen for about 6 months. Hard cheeses, such as Parmesan, Asiago, and Romano, can be frozen up to 1 year.

Cookies, Cakes, and Frosting: Baked cookies can be frozen up to 6 months.

Frostings that freeze well: fudge frosting or confectioner's sugar icing. Do not freeze seven minute frosting, or frosting made with egg whites.

Frosted or filled cakes should be thawed in the refrigerator. Unfrosted cakes can be thawed in their wrapping at room temperature. Recommended freezing for 3 months.

Angel food cakes can be frozen 4 to 6 months.

Creamed meat, fish, and poultry: Recommended freezing for 2 to 4 months.

Herbs: Soft-leaved herbs like basil and parsley are best frozen. Freeze the leaves with a little water in ice-cube trays. Thaw them out in a colander before using.

Dressing: Recommended freezing for 1 month.

Fruit: Frozen fruit can be thawed partially at room temperature and is actually best when served with some ice crystals remaining. If the fruit is to be used in a cooked dish, use it directly from the freezer.

Fruits are 80% or more water. When frozen, the water expands, causing a change in the texture. When thawed, the texture will be mushy so defrosted fruit is best served in a recipe and not alone.

Save time thawing fruit or vegetables by running them under cool water in the sink.

Bananas: Overripe bananas can be peeled, broken into chunks, and stored in a freezer safe container or bag to help make creamy smoothies in no time

Smoothies make it easy to get extra fruit into your diet and are a great breakfast or snack in a hurry. Frozen bananas are great for this. Peel bananas, slice, and place on a cookie sheet. Put in freezer and freeze until solid. Remove from freezer and blend.

Fresh pineapple and fresh kiwi fruit should not be frozen because they contain an enzyme that prevents a gel from forming. Canned or frozen pineapple or kiwi fruit, however, can be frozen successfully because they have been heated in processing (heating destroys the enzyme).

Strawberries, Blueberries, Blackberries, and Raspberries: Wash and sort, adding sugar if desired. Freeze and label. Recommended freezing for up to one year at 0°F.

To freeze sweetened berries: Wash strawberries and drain in a colander. Remove stems and slice berries. Mix ¾ cup sugar to 4 cups sliced berries. Stir and let stand until sugar dissolves (just a few minutes), freeze.

Berries can also be crushed, sweetened, and then frozen.

Freezing whole berries for garnishes: Wash large, select berries, and drain on a paper towel. Flash freeze, transfer to a freezer bag.

Peaches: Make a simple syrup of 1¾ cups sugar boiled with 4 cups water and 2 tablespoons lemon juice. Cool. To get peels off easily, dip peaches in boiling water for 30 seconds, and then dip into ice water. Peel peaches and cut into chunks. Pour cooled syrup over cut peaches. Put peaches and syrup into plastic containers, allowing about ½ inch of headspace or freezer bags making sure peaches are completely covered by the syrup to prevent browning.

Meat: Trim excess fat from meat. The more saturated fat content the meat has (fish has less fat), the longer it will keep. Beef, lamb steaks, and roasts freeze up to 9 months wrapped properly. Prepare roast, trim fat and freeze in large pieces.

For long time storage: freeze meat and sliced meat with gravy or sauce to keep from drying out.

Meat should be thawed in the refrigerator (allow 1 day for every 5 pounds) and can take up to 48 hours, depending on the cut. Alternately, it can be defrosted in the microwave. If you're using the microwave, make sure you cook the meat immediately as meat has already started the cooking process.

Only freeze meat in its supermarket wrapping for a short time (1 month). For longer storage, wrap properly or place in airtight freezer containers.

Turkey and other large fowl should be cut from bones to save freezer space.

Pork will last about 6 to 8 months and sausage for about 3 months. Ham and other cured meats lose color and may become rancid quicker than other meats.

Meatloaf: Prepare as usual. Do not put bacon strips on top. Can be frozen baked or unbaked. Recommended freezing for 3 to 4 months.

Pasta: Baked pasta dishes may be put directly from the freezer into the oven.

Remove any plastic wrap and cover with foil. Bake at 350°F until hot in the center.

Pies: Unbaked fruit pies have a better fresh fruit flavor than frozen baked pies, but the bottom crust tends to get soggy. If freezing, the filling should be slightly thicker than usual (can use extra 1 tablespoon flour, ½ tablespoon cornstarch). Do not cut vents in top crust. Bake without thawing, cut slits in upper crust and bake at 375°F. for 40 to 50 minutes or until top crust is brown. Recommended freezing baked fruit pies, mince pies, nut pies for 3 to 4 months. Custard pies recommended for 2 months.

Pie dough freezes well, make some extra to have when needed. For added convenience, freeze pie crusts in the pan.

Pie dough keeps well in the freezer. Wrap tightly in heavy-duty aluminum foil or freezer-weight plastic wrap and seal in a freezer bag. It should keep for up to 6 months.

Prepare and bake pastry as usual. Cool, package, and freeze. Thaw in wrapping at room temperature. Recommended freezing for 2 to 3 months.

Pizza: Prepare as usual, but do not bake. Recommended freezing for 1 month.

Potatoes (sweet): Bake sweet potatoes, wrap, label, and freeze. Recommended freezing 3 months.

Sauces: Tomato sauces freeze well. Mayonnaise based sauces don't freeze well because they separate.

Seafood: Always start with high quality seafood.

A good rule of thumb: don't buy prepackaged products.

Check for freshness by using sight, smell, and touch.

Oxidation is especially a problem in the storage of the high-fat species of fish like salmon, trout, and whitefish.

To best eliminate air in freezer bags, place the seafood into the bags, seal and freeze it. After a few days, remove the frozen product from the freezer, open the package and add a small amount of cold tap water to eliminate any air, and freeze. Use as little water as possible. It is best to not add water to the bag before freezing to keep the seafood from absorbing water until it is frozen, which can affect flavor and texture.

Fish may be frozen in waxed paper milk cartons. The fish are placed in half-gallon or quart-size cartons, and water is added until the fish are covered to remove air, seal and freeze. Although this method works, the seafood product will absorb water during freezing, which will eventually affect its flavor and texture.

It is best to freeze fish and seafood products rapidly. Properly packed and frozen fatty fish (salmon, trout) can be frozen for at least three months and twice that for lean fish.

As a rule, seafood should be thawed as quickly as possible, but never in hot water or at room temperature. Cold running water remains the fastest and best means of thawing seafood. With thin packages, such as individual fillets, the thawing process should take no longer than 5 to 10 minutes. The thawing process will take longer with thicker packages.

Seafood can also be taken directly from the freezer and cooked. But it will take longer to cook.

Soups and purees: Cream-based soups may be heated without thawing on a very low heat, watching and stirring frequently for a smooth texture. Recommended freezing for 4 to 6 months.

Tomatoes: For extra tomatoes, puree and de-seed raw tomatoes in a juicer or a food mill so you'll be able to make sauce all year long. After pureeing, chill in the refrigerator to ensure that it will freeze evenly and then store in a resealable bag in the freezer.

Veggies: Frozen vegetables may be cooked directly from the freezer but cooking times should be only one-half to two thirds as long as fresh. Don't overcook. Cooked, creamed vegetables lose flavor rapidly and are not recommended for freezer storage

Waffles: Prepare waffles according to directions. Cool to room temperature. Wrap, label, and freeze. Recommended freezing 1 to 2 months.

Freezer Guide for Properly Stored Food

Bacon:	1 month
Beef:	6 months to 1 year
Butter or Margarine:	9 months
Cheese:	4 months
Chicken pieces:	3 months
Cooked chicken with gravy:	6 months
Cooked chicken with no gravy:	1 month
Cookies, baked:	1 month
Egg whites or egg substitute:	6 months
Fish or shellfish:	**Fatty fish:** 3 months, **Lean fish:** 6 months
Shellfish:	3 months

Frozen fruits, commercial:	1 year
Frozen veggies, commercial:	8 months
Fruits (except citrus):	8 to 12 months
Fruits and juices:	4 to 6 months
Layer cakes, baked:	1 month
Meats, cooked:	3 months
Meat, ground:	3 to 4 months
Milk:	1 to 3 months
Muffins, baked:	1 month
Nuts:	6 to 12 months
Pork:	3 to 6 months
Pound cakes, baked:	1 month
Quick breads, baked:	1 month
Soups and Stews (without potatoes):	1 month
Turkey:	6 months
Veal, Lamb:	6 to 9 months
Vegetables:	8 to 12 months
Whole chicken:	3 to 6 months
Yeast bread, baked:	1 month

Freezing Containers: What Not to Use

Air and moisture are the two main elements that can cause freezer burn. Freezer storage must be moisture proof and airtight. The following list includes containers that should not be used to freeze food.

❄ Milk or juice cartons, or plastic jugs

❄ Ricotta, cottage cheese, or yogurt containers

❄ Butter/margarine tubs

❄ Glass jars that don't have "Ball" or "Kerr" on them

❄ Glass jars with narrow mouths (even if they're Ball or Kerr jars)

❄ Plastic zip-top storage bags (as opposed to plastic zip-top freezer bags)

❄ Plastic sandwich bags

❄ Plastic produce or bread bags

Packaging Hints

Proper packaging protects frozen food's flavor, color, moisture content, and nutritional value.

Use freezer containers or wrappings of moisture and vapor-resistant material.

Pack food compactly into the container to reduce air in the package.

Allow room for food to expand as the food freezes and try to make sure excess air is pressed from freezer bags.

Leave enough headspace (space between the packed food and closure) to allow for expansion when freezing.

Freeze the prepared foods in your favorite casserole baking dish for food to thaw and cook without changing dishes.

For microwave reheating, make sure containers are microwaveable.

Food should be placed in a single layer on freezer shelves until frozen.

Use only containers with wide top openings so food can be removed without thawing, if desired.

The containers or packaging should be moisture proof, airtight, and odorless.

Recommended containers for freezer packaging: zip-top plastic freezer bag, plastic coated freezer paper, plastic or glass containers with wide mouths and tight-fitting lids, heavy-duty aluminum foil, heavy-duty plastic wrap.

Appetizers

Freezing, Thawing, and Preparing Appetizers

❄ Freeze appetizers in single layers on trays and then transfer to shallow, airtight containers for storage, separating layers with a double layer of freezer wrap. Package toast and other crisp appetizers separately.

❄ To Prepare After Freezing: About one hour before serving, arrange frozen appetizers on serving trays and cover. Let thaw at room temperature.

❄ Appetizers containing perishable foods such as meat, fish, poultry, or dairy products should not be left at room temperature for more than two hours because of the possibility of food poisoning. Length of freezer storage: 3 to 4 weeks.

Smoked Salmon Tortilla Bites

These salmon-stuffed pinwheels are packed with flavor and flair and make a great pick up snack. Arrange cut side up on platter for an outstanding presentation.

MAKES 4 TO 5 DOZEN

1	(5-ounce) package reduced-fat garlic and herb spreadable cheese
1	(8-ounce) package reduced-fat cream cheese
¼	cup chopped red onion
¼	cup capers, drained
2	teaspoons lemon juice
4	ounces smoked salmon, cut into pieces
8	(6- to 8-inch) flour tortillas

In a mixing bowl, blend together both cheeses until creamy. Stir in red onion, capers, lemon juice, and smoked salmon. Divide and spread filling to cover each tortilla and roll up like a jelly roll. Place seam down on a tray and secure each roll with a toothpick. Refrigerate until well chilled or pop in the freezer to make easier to cut. Cut each roll into pinwheels about ⅜-inch thick

Note:

Use different color flavored tortillas for an attractive presentation.

To Prepare and Eat Now: Refrigerate until serving. Serve with or without toothpicks.

To Freeze: Freeze cut tortilla bites on a tray for one hour. Transfer bites to zip-top freezer bags, label, and freeze. Recommended freezing time: up to 1 to 2 months.

To Prepare After Freezing: Defrost in the refrigerator in single layer and serve.

Nutritional information per 2 pieces: Calories 59, Protein (g) 3, Carbohydrate (g) 6, Fat (g) 2, Calories from Fat (%) 37, Saturated Fat (g) 1, Dietary Fiber (g) 0, Cholesterol (mg) 9, Sodium (mg) 244, Diabetic Exchanges: 0.5 starch, 0.5 fat

Almond-Glazed Brie 🥕

Brie baked in an almond and brown sugar sauce wrapped in phyllo dough melts in your mouth with each bite.

MAKES 8 TO 10 SERVINGS

1	(8- to 10-ounce) Brie round
2	tablespoons light brown sugar
2	tablespoons almond liqueur
¼	cup sliced almonds, toasted
12	sheets phyllo dough

Slice a thin slice off the top of the Brie, removing the rind.

In a microwaveable bowl, microwave the brown sugar and almond liqueur for 30 seconds. Spread brown sugar mixture on top of the Brie and sprinkle with the sliced almonds.

On a piece of wax paper, lay one sheet of phyllo dough. Spray with non-stick cooking spray and repeat with each sheet, layering on top of each other. Lay Brie in center of phyllo dough and wrap phyllo around the Brie to seal.

To Prepare and Eat Now: Preheat the oven to 350°F. Place Brie in pie plate or baking dish coated with non-stick cooking spray. Bake for 30 to 35 minutes or until phyllo dough is light brown and cheese is melted. Let sit for 10 minutes before serving.

To Freeze: Coat with non-stick cooking spray, wrap in plastic wrap, label, and freeze. Recommended freezing time: up to 2 to 3 months.

To Prepare After Freezing: Preheat the oven to 350°F. Remove Brie directly from the freezer and place Brie in pie plate or baking dish coated with non-stick cooking spray. Bake for 40 to 45 minutes or until phyllo dough is light brown and cheese is melted. Let sit for 10 minutes before serving.

NUTRITIONAL INFORMATION PER SERVING: *Calories 129, Protein (g) 6, Carbohydrate (g) 5, Fat (g) 9, Calories from Fat (%) 62, Saturated Fat (g) 5, Dietary Fiber (g) 0, Cholesterol (mg) 28, Sodium (mg) 180, Diabetic Exchanges: 1 high-fat meat, 0.5 other carbohydrate, 0.5 fat*

Baked Garlic Brie with Honey

Oozing warm Brie laced with garlic and a slightly sweet honey taste wrapped in phyllo dough makes an amazing appetizer.

MAKES 20 TO 24 SERVINGS

12 sheets phyllo dough

1 teaspoon minced garlic

1 (14- to 16-ounce) round Brie cheese

3 tablespoons honey

Lay a sheet of phyllo dough on waxed paper and coat with non-stick cooking spray. Repeat with remaining phyllo sheets until all 12 sheets are stacked.

In a small non-stick skillet coated with non-stick cooking spray, sauté the garlic for about a minute; do not brown. Lay the Brie on top the stack of phyllo dough, and carefully slice off a thin layer from the top. Spread the Brie with the garlic and honey. Wrap Brie by folding up the dough over the cheese to seal.

To Prepare and Eat Now: Preheat the oven to 350°F. and place Brie in pie plate or baking dish coated with non-stick cooking spray. Bake for about 35 to 40 minutes or until phyllo dough is browned.

To Freeze: Coat with non-stick cooking spray, wrap in plastic wrap, label, and freeze. Recommended freezing time: up to 2 to 3 months.

To Prepare After Freezing: Preheat the oven to 350°F. Remove Brie directly from the freezer and place in a pie plate or baking dish coated with non-stick cooking spray in the oven. Bake for 40 to 45 minutes or until phyllo dough is light brown and cheese is melted. Let sit for 10 minutes before serving.

NUTRITIONAL INFORMATION PER SERVING: *Calories 107, Protein (g) 5, Carbohydrate (g) 10, Fat (g) 6, Calories from Fat (%) 46, Saturated Fat (g) 3, Dietary Fiber (g) 0, Cholesterol (mg) 19, Sodium (mg) 165, Diabetic Exchanges: 1 high-fat meat, 0.5 starch*

Baked Herb Brie with Grapes

A savory herb topping with sweet grapes wrapped in phyllo dough makes an enticing appetizer. Garnish Brie with grapes to serve.

MAKES 8 TO 10 SERVINGS

1	(8-ounce) Brie cheese
¼	cup sliced green or red seedless grapes
¼	teaspoon dried thyme leaves
¼	teaspoon dried rosemary leaves
12	sheets phyllo dough

Slice Brie in half horizontally. Cover bottom half with sliced grapes and sprinkle with thyme and rosemary. Replace the top of the Brie and press together; set aside. On a piece of wax paper, lay one sheet of phyllo dough. Spray with non-stick cooking spray and repeat with each sheet, layering on top of each other, until finished. Lay Brie in center of phyllo dough and wrap dough around Brie to seal.

To Prepare and Eat Now: Preheat the oven to 350°F. Place Brie in pie plate or baking dish coated with non-stick cooking spray. Bake for about 35 to 40 minutes or until phyllo dough is browned. Let sit for 10 minutes before serving.

To Freeze: Coat with non-stick cooking spray, wrap in plastic wrap, label, and freeze. Recommended freezing time: up to 2 to 3 months.

To Prepare After Freezing: Preheat the oven to 350°F. Remove the Brie directly from the freezer and place in a pie plate or baking sheet coated with non-stick cooking spray. Bake for 40 to 45 minutes or until the phyllo dough is light brown and the cheese is melted. Let sit for 10 minutes before serving.

NUTRITIONAL INFORMATION PER SERVING: *Calories 151, Protein (g) 6, Carbohydrate (g) 16, Fat (g) 7, Calories from Fat (%) 41, Saturated Fat (g) 4, Dietary Fiber (g) 0, Cholesterol (mg) 23, Sodium (mg) 235, Diabetic Exchanges: 1 high-fat meat, 1 starch*

Caramelized Onion Cheesecake

This savory cheesecake laced with caramelized onion and topped with peppery jalapeño jelly turns cheesecake into a terrific appetizer. Serve with crackers or a thin slice with a fork. May be served warm or chilled.

MAKES 20 TO 25 SERVINGS

3	tablespoons butter, divided
1	onion, thinly sliced
1	tablespoon light brown sugar
½	cup Italian bread crumbs
2	(8-ounce) packages reduced-fat cream cheese
1	egg
2	egg whites
¼	cup evaporated fat-free milk
1	tablespoon cornstarch
	Salt and pepper to taste
½	teaspoon dried thyme leaves
1	tablespoon Dijon mustard
	Dash cayenne pepper
1	(10-ounce) jar jalapeño pepper jelly

Preheat the oven to 350°F.

In a heavy non-stick pot, melt 1 tablespoon of the butter and sauté onion over medium heat, stirring occasionally for 10 minutes or until it begins to turn golden brown. Stir in brown sugar and cook for 2 minutes longer, set aside.

Meanwhile, melt the remaining butter and combine with the bread crumbs. Press into the bottom of a non-stick 9-inch springform pan coated with non-stick cooking spray. Bake for 5 minutes.

In a mixing bowl, mix together the cream cheese, egg, egg whites, evaporated milk, cornstarch, salt and pepper, thyme, mustard, and cayenne until creamy. Stir in caramelized onions and carefully transfer filling to partially baked crust. Bake about 35 to 45 minutes or until filling is set.

To Prepare and Eat Now: Eat when ready warm or chilled. Spread with jalapeño pepper jelly and serve.

To Freeze: Cool to room temperature, then wrap, label, and freeze. Recommended freezing time: up to 2 to 3 months.

To Prepare After Freezing: Defrost in refrigerator and serve. If you want to serve cheesecake warm, reheat in an oven set at 350°F. for about 10 to 15 minutes to remove the chill. Spread the jalapeño pepper jelly over the cheesecake before serving.

NUTRITIONAL INFORMATION PER SERVING: *Calories 109, Protein (g) 3, Carbohydrate (g) 11, Fat (g) 6, Calories from Fat (%) 47, Saturated Fat (g) 4, Dietary Fiber (g) 0, Cholesterol (mg) 25, Sodium (mg) 147, Diabetic Exchanges: 1 other carbohydrate, 1 fat*

Shrimp and Sausage Cheesecake

This make-ahead appetizer cheesecake with smoked Gouda, shrimp, and sausage is a unique and amazing combination.

MAKES 20 TO 25 SERVINGS

Note:

Cook the sausage in a non-stick pan coated with non-stick cooking spray until it is crispy. Shrimp may be cooked this way, too.

1   cup crushed, reduced-fat baked whole grain wheat crackers

2   tablespoons butter, melted

1   onion, chopped

½   cup chopped green bell pepper

½   cup chopped red bell pepper

1   tablespoon minced garlic

2   (8-ounce) packages reduced fat cream cheese

1   egg

2   egg whites

⅓   cup fat free half and half

    Dash hot sauce

1   pound small peeled shrimp, cooked

½   cup diced, smoked reduced fat sausage, cooked

1   cup shredded, smoked Gouda cheese

1   bunch green onions (scallions), chopped

Preheat the oven to 350°F.

Coat a 9-inch springform pan with non-stick cooking spray. In a mixing bowl, mix together the crushed crackers and butter, and press into bottom of the prepared pan.

In a medium non-stick skillet coated with non-stick cooking spray, sauté the onion, green pepper, red pepper, and garlic over medium heat until tender, about 5 minutes; set aside.

In a mixing bowl, mix together the cream cheese, egg, and egg whites until creamy. Add the half and half and hot sauce, mixing well. Stir in the cooked vegetables, shrimp, sausage, Gouda, and green onions. Carefully pour over the crust. Bake for 40 to 50 minutes or until mixture is set. Remove from oven, and let cool in pan 10 minutes. Run knife around inside edge to loosen, and remove the sides from the pan.

To Prepare and Eat Now: Eat when ready warm or refrigerate until ready to serve.

To Freeze: Cool in refrigerator then wrap, label, and freeze. Recommended freezing time: up to 2 to 3 months.

To Prepare After Freezing: Defrost in refrigerator and serve with crackers.

NUTRITIONAL INFORMATION PER SERVING: *Calories 118, Protein (g) 8, Carbohydrate (g) 5, Fat (g) 7, Calories from Fat (%) 53, Saturated Fat (g) 4, Dietary Fiber (g) 1, Cholesterol (mg) 65, Sodium (mg) 220, Diabetic Exchanges: 1 lean meat, 0.5 starch, 1 fat*

Chili Rolls

Chili and cheese baked in miniature rolls makes a hearty party pick-up or snack. Keep in your freezer to pull out as needed.

MAKES 40

2   (12-ounce) packages soft party rolls or miniature rolls (20 to a package)

1   (15-ounce) can turkey chili without beans

2   cups shredded, reduced-fat sharp Cheddar cheese

Split the rolls in half and indent the bottoms with your fingertips making a small impression. Put about 1 teaspoon of chili and a little shredded cheese in the bottom half of the roll. Cover with the top of the roll. Store in refrigerator or freeze until ready to use.

To Prepare and Eat Now: Preheat the oven to 350°F. Place rolls on a non-stick baking sheet and bake for 15 minutes or until the cheese is melted.

To Freeze: Wrap, label, and freeze. Recommended freezing time: up to 3 months.

To Prepare After Freezing: Defrost in the refrigerator or cook directly from the freezer. Preheat the oven to 350°F. Place rolls on a non-stick baking sheet and bake for 15 to 20 minutes or until cheese is melted.

NUTRITIONAL INFORMATION PER SERVING: *Calories 76, Protein (g) 4, Carbohydrate (g) 9, Fat (g) 2, Calories from Fat (%) 29, Saturated Fat (g) 1, Dietary Fiber (g) 1, Cholesterol (mg) 7, Sodium (mg) 181, Diabetic Exchanges: 0.5 lean meat, 0.5 starch*

Crab and Goat Cheese Empanadas with Mango Salsa

Won ton wrappers are a simple and quick tool to make speedy crab empanadas. For another option, the filling may be used as a dip with crackers. The Mango Salsa, sweet and spicy, is the ideal sauce for these cheesy crab empanadas.

MAKES 3 1/2 TO 4 DOZEN

1   red onion, chopped

1/2 teaspoon minced garlic

1   tablespoon minced habañero pepper

1/3 cup chopped flat leaf (Italian) parsley

2   (4-ounce) packages goat cheese, softened

    Salt and pepper to taste

1   pound lump crabmeat, picked for shells

48 won ton wrappers

    Mango Salsa (recipe follows)

In a small non-stick skillet coated with non-stick cooking spray, sauté the onion, garlic, and habañero over medium heat until tender, about 5 to 7 minutes. Cool slightly.

In a mixing bowl, combine the sautéed vegetables, parsley, and goat cheese. Season with salt and pepper and carefully fold in the crabmeat. Place a heaping teaspoon of the filling into the center of each won ton square and fold ends together, forming a triangle. To make the ends stick, use your finger to dab a little water along the edges of the won ton wrapper.

Note:

did you know that mangoes are full of nutrients, including vita- mins A and C? No wonder they're called the "King of Fruits!"

NUTRITIONAL INFORMATION PER SERVING: *Calories 48, Protein (g) 4, Carbohydrate (g) 5, Fat (g) 1, Calories from Fat (%) 24, Saturated Fat (g) 1, Dietary Fiber (g) 0, Cholesterol (mg) 10, Sodium (mg) 58, Diabetic Exchanges: 0.5 very lean meat, 0.5 starch*

To Prepare and Eat Now: Preheat the oven to 350°F. Place empanadas on a non-stick baking sheet coated with non-stick cooking spray and bake for 15 minutes or until lightly browned. Serve with Mango Salsa (recipe follows).

To Freeze: Place empanadas on a baking sheet to flash freeze. Once frozen, transfer to zip-top freezer bags to store in freezer. Recommended freezing time: up to 2 months.

To Prepare After Freezing: Preheat the oven to 350°F. Take empanadas directly from the freezer and place on a non-stick baking sheet coated with non-stick cooking spray. Bake for 15 to 20 minutes or until lightly browned. Serve with Mango Salsa.

Mango Salsa

This is so superb, you could eat it with a spoon. Fresh, canned, or jarred mangos work well for the recipe. This salsa compliments grilled fish or chicken.

MAKES 3 CUPS (48 SERVINGS OF 1 TABLESPOON EACH)

2½ cups chopped mangos

1 teaspoon freshly grated ginger

⅓ cup chopped red onion

1 tablespoon lime juice

1 tablespoon brown sugar, optional

In a bowl, combine the mangos, ginger, red onion, lime juice, and brown sugar.

NUTRITIONAL INFORMATION PER SERVING: *Calories 6, Protein (g) 0, Carbohydrate (g) 2, Fat (g) 0, Calories from Fat (%) 0, Saturated Fat (g) 0, Dietary Fiber (g) 0, Cholesterol (mg) 0, Sodium (mg) 0, Diabetic Exchanges: Free*

Empanadas

I spent lots of time coming up with an easy and tasty version of this Spanish meat pie. Packed with an abundance of flavors with a faint sweet touch, these meat pies quickly disappeared right out of the oven!

MAKES 40

1	pound ground sirloin
¼	pound ground lean pork
1	onion, finely chopped
1	teaspoon minced garlic
1½	teaspoons chili powder
1	teaspoon ground cumin
⅓	cup finely chopped green olives
¼	cup finely chopped golden raisins
½	cup chipotle salsa
3	tablespoons fat-free sour cream
	Salt and pepper to taste
2	(10-biscuit) cans refrigerated flaky biscuits

Preheat the oven to 350°F.

In a medium non-stick skillet, cook the sirloin, pork, onion, and garlic over medium heat until done, about 8 to 10 minutes. Drain any excess grease. Add the chili powder, cumin, olives, raisins, salsa, sour cream, and salt and pepper. Remove from heat.

Separate each biscuit in half by tearing apart the layers to make 40 rounds. With a rolling pin, roll out each biscuit half on a lightly floured surface or press with hands into a 4-inch circle. Spoon meat mixture evenly in center of each biscuit circle. Fold dough over filling to form a half, pressing edges with a fork to seal. Place filled biscuits on a non-stick baking sheet coated with non-stick cooking spray. Bake for 17 to 20 minutes or until golden.

To Prepare and Eat Now: Eat when ready after baking.

To Freeze: Let the baked Empanadas cool, and then transfer to freezer zip-top bags, label, and freeze. Recommended freezing time: up to 2 to 3 months.

To Prepare After Freezing: Preheat the oven to 350°F. Place Empanadas directly from the freezer on a non-stick baking sheet coated with non-stick cooking spray and bake for 15 to 20 minutes or until heated through.

NUTRITIONAL INFORMATION PER SERVING: *Calories 49, Protein (g) 3, Carbohydrate (g) 6, Fat (g) 1, Calories from Fat (%) 26, Saturated Fat (g) 0, Dietary Fiber (g) 0, Cholesterol (mg) 6, Sodium (mg) 128, Diabetic Exchanges: 0.5 very lean meat, 0.5 starch*

Italian Pizza Rolls

These tasty meat sensations quickly disappeared as I pulled them from the oven. My kids and the adults were both grabbing for seconds.

MAKES 18 TO 20 HALF ROLLS

⅓ cup finely chopped carrots

⅓ cup finely chopped onion

⅓ cup finely chopped green pepper

1 teaspoon minced garlic

½ pound ground sirloin

½ cup tomato sauce

½ teaspoon dried oregano leaves

½ teaspoon dried basil leaves

½ cup shredded, part-skim Mozzarella cheese

9 to 10 egg roll wrappers

In a non-stick skillet coated with non-stick cooking spray, sauté the carrots, onion, green pepper, and garlic for 5 to 7 minutes over medium heat until tender. Add the sirloin, cooking until browned. Remove from heat and stir in tomato sauce, oregano, basil, and Mozzarella cheese.

Place about 2 tablespoons in the middle of each egg roll wrapper. Fold the lower bottom third up, fold the 2 sides toward the center, and then roll up.

To Prepare and Eat Now: Preheat the oven to 425°F. Place pizza rolls on a non-stick baking sheet coated with non-stick cooking spray. Bake for 9 minutes, turn the rolls over and continue baking for another 4 to 6 minutes or until crispy and browned. Cut each roll in half and serve.

To Freeze: Do not bake prepared rolls before freezing. Freeze on a baking sheet, then transfer to freezer zip-top bags, label, and freeze. Recommended freezing time: up to 2 to 3 months.

To Prepare After Freezing: Preheat the oven to 425°F. Remove rolls directly from the freezer and place on a non-stick baking sheet coated with non-stick cooking spray. Bake for 10 to 12 minutes, turn the rolls over and continue baking for another 5 to 6 minutes or until crispy and browned. Cut each roll in half and serve.

NUTRITIONAL INFORMATION PER SERVING: *Calories 72, Protein (g) 7, Carbohydrate (g) 7, Fat (g) 2, Calories from Fat (%) 25, Saturated Fat (g) 1, Dietary Fiber (g) 0, Cholesterol (mg) 16, Sodium (mg) 128, Diabetic Exchanges: 1 very lean meat, 0.5 starch*

Meaty Biscuit Cups

These few simple ingredients, ground meat, barbecue sauce, and corn, make these hearty meaty pick-ups. They're also great for a light lunch.

MAKES 20

1	pound ground sirloin
⅓	cup finely chopped red onion
⅓	cup barbecue sauce
½	cup frozen corn, thawed
1	(10-count) can flaky biscuits
½	cup shredded, reduced-fat sharp Cheddar cheese

Preheat the oven to 400°F.

In a medium non-stick skillet, cook the sirloin and red onion over medium heat, about 5 minutes or until meat is done. Drain any excess grease. Remove from heat and add the barbecue sauce and corn, mixing well.

Divide each biscuit in half by pulling apart the layers. Press each half into non-stick muffin tins coated with non-stick cooking spray. Divide the meat evenly into the prepared muffin tins. Bake for 10 minutes.

To Prepare and Eat Now: Preheat the oven to 400°F. After baking 10 minutes, remove from the oven and sprinkle with cheese. Return to the oven for one minute or until cheese melts.

To Freeze: Cool baked cups to room temperature. Do not sprinkle with the cheese. Freeze on a baking sheet, then transfer to zip-top freezer bags. Recommended freezing time: up to 2 months.

To Prepare After Freezing: Preheat the oven to 350°F. Defrost cups or place them frozen on a non-stick baking sheet. Bake for 10 to 15 minutes or until heated through, sprinkle with cheese and return to the oven for one minute or until cheese melts.

NUTRITIONAL INFORMATION PER SERVING: *Calories 74, Protein (g) 6, Carbohydrate (g) 7, Fat (g) 2, Calories from Fat (%) 28, Saturated Fat (g) 1, Dietary Fiber (g) 0, Cholesterol (mg) 13, Sodium (mg) 146, Diabetic Exchanges: 1 very lean meat, 0.5 starch*

Pork Steamed Dumplings

No need to order Chinese take-out when you have these mouth-watering homemade dumplings to pull out of your own freezer. As the dumplings must be filled, be sure to allow enough time to prepare. Then you can freeze them to pull out later as an impressive appetizer pick-up.

MAKES 60

1 pound pork tenderloin, trimmed and cut into chunks

½ pound ground pork

1 (5-ounce) can sliced water chestnuts, drained

⅓ cup cornstarch

2 tablespoons minced fresh ginger

1 teaspoon minced garlic

2 tablespoons reduced-sodium soy sauce

2 tablespoons sugar

1 teaspoon sesame oil

½ cup chopped green onions (scallions)

60 won ton wrappers

In a food processor, process pork tenderloin chunks until finely chopped. Add the ground pork, water chestnuts, cornstarch, ginger, garlic, soy sauce, sugar, sesame oil, and green onions, pulsing only until mixed and the water chestnuts are chopped.

Place about 1 teaspoon of the pork mixture in the center of each won ton wrapper and gather up the corners, pinching them together at the top. Pat the edges with water to make them stick.

To Prepare and Eat Now: Bring a pot of water to boil and arrange dumplings in steamer basket over the boiling water. Cover and steam about 20 to 25 minutes or until the pork mixture is entirely cooked.

To Freeze: Arrange uncooked dumplings on baking sheet and freeze for one hour. Transfer to freezer zip-top bag, label, and freeze. Recommended freezing time: up to 3 months.

To Prepare After Freezing: Bring a pot of water to boil and arrange dumplings directly from the freezer in the steamer basket over the boiling water. Cover and steam about 25 to 28 minutes or until the pork mixture is entirely cooked.

NUTRITIONAL INFORMATION PER SERVING: *Calories 49, Protein (g) 3, Carbohydrate (g) 6, Fat (g) 1, Calories from Fat (%) 24, Saturated Fat (g) 0, Dietary Fiber (g) 0, Cholesterol (mg) 8, Sodium (mg) 32, Diabetic Exchanges: 0.5 very lean meat, 0.5 starch*

Shrimp and Portabella

This quick and elegant creation of portabella mushrooms and shrimp in a light sauce works wonders over toast points or in pastry shells.

MAKES 4 SERVINGS

1	tablespoon butter
⅓	cup finely chopped onions
1	tablespoon minced garlic
½	pound sliced baby portabella mushrooms
1½	pounds medium shrimp, peeled
2	tablespoons brandy, optional
½	cup fat-free half and half
⅓	cup chopped green onion stems
	Salt and pepper to taste
	Chopped parsley for garnish

In a large non-stick skillet, melt butter over medium heat and sauté onions for several minutes. Add garlic and portabellas, continuing to sauté for 3 minutes. Add shrimp and continue cooking over medium heat until shrimp are done, about 4 minutes. Add brandy and shake in pan for 1 minute. Add the half and half, heating thoroughly. Add green onion stems, and salt and pepper, cooking for about 2 minutes.

To Prepare and Eat Now: Garnish with parsley and serve warm.

To Freeze: Cool to room temperature. Place in a freezer container, label, and freeze. Recommended freezing time: up to 1 month.

To Prepare After Freezing: Defrost in the refrigerator, then cook in a non-stick pan over low heat until thoroughly heated.

NUTRITIONAL INFORMATION PER SERVING: *Calories 199, Protein (g) 31, Carbohydrate (g) 9, Fat (g) 4, Calories from Fat (%) 20, Saturated Fat (g) 2, Dietary Fiber (g) 1, Cholesterol (mg) 260, Sodium (mg) 346, Diabetic Exchanges: 0.5 other carbohydrate, 1 fat*

Seafood Toast

This simple appetizer of crabmeat, shrimp, green chilies, and cheese spread baked on top of cocktail bread makes a marvelous choice.

MAKES 36

5   ounces reduced-fat cream cheese

2   tablespoons butter, softened

1   (4-ounce) can chopped green chilies, drained

1   (4.25-ounce) can small shrimp, drained

1   (4.25-ounce) can crabmeat, drained

Several dashes hot pepper sauce

1   cup shredded, reduced-fat sharp Cheddar cheese, divided

36 slices cocktail bread (honey grain wheat)

$\frac{2}{3}$ cup fat-free sour cream

Salt to taste

Paprika

In a bowl, blend together the cream cheese and butter. Stir in green chilies, shrimp, crabmeat, hot pepper sauce, and $\frac{1}{2}$ cup cheese. Spread on top of the cocktail bread.

To Prepare and Eat Now: Preheat the oven to 350°F. Arrange toasts on a non-stick baking sheet. In a small bowl, mix together the sour cream, remaining $\frac{1}{2}$ cup cheese, and salt. Top with a dollop of sour cream mixture on top of the seafood mixture on the bread. Sprinkle with paprika. Bake for 15 to 20 minutes or until bubbly.

To Freeze: Freeze unbaked prepared toasts in single layer on baking sheet. Once frozen, transfer to freezer zip-top plastic bags, label, and freeze. Recommended freezing time: up to 2 months.

To Prepare After Freezing: Preheat the oven to 350°F. Remove toasts from the freezer and arrange on a non-stick baking sheet. In a small bowl, mix together the sour cream, remaining $\frac{1}{2}$ cup cheese, and salt. Top with a dollop of sour cream mixture on top of the seafood mixture on the bread. Sprinkle with paprika. Bake for 20 to 25 minutes or until bubbly.

NUTRITIONAL INFORMATION PER SERVING: *Calories 62, Protein (g) 4, Carbohydrate (g) 6, Fat (g) 2, Calories from Fat (%) 37, Saturated Fat (g) 1, Dietary Fiber (g) 1, Cholesterol (mg) 18, Sodium (mg) 155, Diabetic Exchanges: 0.5 very lean meat, 0.5 starch*

Black-Eyed Pea Dip 🥕

This quick dip is simply black-eyed peas in a zippy sauce with cheese and a touch of jalapeños. Don't save this dip only for New Year's good luck, as it will entice your family and friends year-round.

MAKES 20 (¼ CUP) SERVINGS

1	onion, chopped
⅓	cup chopped green bell pepper
1	tablespoon chopped pickled jalapeños
2	(15-ounce) cans black-eyed peas, drained
2	tablespoons all-purpose flour
1	(10-ounce) can diced tomatoes and green chilies
4	ounces shredded, reduced-fat Monterey Jack cheese

In a non-stick pot coated with non-stick cooking spray, sauté the onion, green pepper, and jalapeños over medium-low heat until tender, about 5 minutes. Add the black-eyed peas and stir in the flour. Gradually add the tomatoes and cheese, stirring until melted and heated throughout.

To Prepare and Eat Now: Eat when ready warm with crackers or chips.

To Freeze: Cool to room temperature, place in a freezer container, label, and freeze. Recommended freezing time: up to 2 to 3 months.

To Prepare After Freezing: Defrost in refrigerator and heat in a non-stick pot over low heat, stirring, until thoroughly heated. May be reheated in the microwave.

NUTRITIONAL INFORMATION PER SERVING: *Calories 58, Protein (g) 4, Carbohydrate (g) 8, Fat (g) 1, Calories from Fat (%) 17, Saturated Fat (g) 1, Dietary Fiber (g) 2, Cholesterol (mg) 3, Sodium (mg) 237, Diabetic Exchanges: 0.5 very lean meat, 0.5 starch*

Quick Spinach Dip

These five ingredients create a quick and spunky spinach dip without any effort! The salsa has all the seasonings, which keeps this recipe simple.

MAKES 4 CUPS

2   (10-ounce) packages frozen chopped spinach

2   tablespoons all-purpose flour

1   cup skim milk

1   cup picante sauce or salsa

1   cup shredded, reduced-fat Monterey Jack cheese

Prepare spinach according to package directions; drain very well.

In a non-stick saucepan, combine the flour and milk and heat over medium heat for 3 to 5 minutes or until bubbly and thickened. Add the cooked spinach, picante sauce, and cheese, cooking until the cheese is melted.

Note:

Spinach is an excellent source of vitamins A & C and fiber.

To Prepare and Eat Now: Eat when ready warm with crackers.

To Freeze: Cool to room temperature, then transfer to freezer container, label, and freeze. Recommended freezing time: up to 2 to 3 months.

To Prepare After Freezing: Defrost in the refrigerator. Heat in a non-stick saucepan over low heat until thoroughly heated. May be reheated in the microwave.

NUTRITIONAL INFORMATION PER SERVING: *Calories 45, Protein (g) 4, Carbohydrate (g) 4, Fat (g) 2, Calories from Fat (%) 30, Saturated Fat (g) 1, Dietary Fiber (g) 1, Cholesterol (mg) 4, Sodium (mg) 135, Diabetic Exchanges: 0.5 lean meat, 1 vegetable*

Spinach and Brie Dip

Bacon adds a crunchy saltiness to this dip, complimenting the mild creamy Brie.

MAKES 5 CUPS

1   onion, chopped

⅓   cup all-purpose flour

2   cups skim milk

1   teaspoon minced garlic

2   (10-ounce) boxes frozen chopped spinach, thawed and drained

2   teaspoons lemon juice

6   ounces Brie cheese, rind removed and cubed

⅓   cup grated Parmesan cheese

4   strips center cut bacon, cooked and broken into pieces

     Salt and pepper to taste

     Dash cayenne

In a medium non-stick pot coated with non-stick cooking spray, sauté onion until very tender. Add flour and gradually stir in milk cooking until bubbly and thickened. Add garlic, spinach, lemon juice, Brie, and Parmesan cheese, stirring until cheese is melted. Stir in bacon. Season with salt, pepper, and cayenne.

Note:

Make the dip ahead of time and bake it in a hollowed out round bread in the oven for a grand effect. Using a serrated knife, cut a thin slice off the top of the bread. Hollow out the center leaving a 1-inch shell. Discard the center portion or cut into squares and toast to serve with dip. Place the bread shell on a non-stick baking dish. Transfer the dip into the bread shell. Bake for about 20 to 25 minutes or until heated. If bread browns too quickly, cover with foil.

To Prepare and Eat Now:

Eat warm in a serving dish or in bread (see Note) and with crackers.

To Freeze: Cool to room temperature, transfer to a freezer container, label, and freeze. Recommended freezing time: up to 2 to 3 months.

To Prepare After Freezing:

Defrost in the refrigerator or microwave. Heat in a non-stick pot over low heat or bake at 350°F. in the bread until thoroughly heated and bread is crispy. Serve in the bread and with crackers. May be reheated in the microwave and served in the bread.

NUTRITIONAL INFORMATION PER SERVING: *Calories 68, Protein (g) 5, Carbohydrate (g) 5, Fat (g) 3, Calories from Fat (%) 44, Saturated Fat (g) 2, Dietary Fiber (g) 1, Cholesterol (mg) 11, Sodium (mg) 131, Diabetic Exchanges: 0.5 medium-fat meat, 1 vegetable*

Spinach and Artichoke Dip

My readers will notice this isn't the first time I've included Spinach and Artichoke dip in one of my books. However, this combination is one of our new favorites, as I am always testing for innovative recipes. The red pepper and wine in this version give the dip a slightly sweet flavor that we LOVED! This dip also is great served in a hollowed out bread with bread chunks alongside to dip with.

MAKES 4 CUPS, 16 (¼ CUP) SERVINGS

½ teaspoon minced garlic

½ cup chopped onion

½ cup chopped red bell pepper

2 tablespoons all-purpose flour

1 (12-ounce) can evaporated fat-free milk

½ cup dry white wine (milk may be substituted)

1 (15-ounce) can artichoke hearts, drained and coarsely chopped

2 (10-ounce) boxes chopped frozen spinach, defrosted and squeezed dry

1½ cups shredded Italian four-cheese blend (provolone, Parmesan, Mozzarella, and Asiago)

Salt and freshly ground black pepper

In a medium non-stick saucepan coated with non-stick cooking spray, sauté the garlic, onion, and red bell pepper over medium heat, about 5 minutes, until tender. Gradually add flour, stirring to coat vegetables, for one minute. Gradually add milk and wine, cooking over medium heat until mixture comes to a boil and thickens, stirring constantly. Stir in artichokes, spinach, and cheeses, stirring until cheese melts. Season with salt and pepper.

To Prepare and Eat Now: Eat when warm in a serving dish or in hollowed out bread with crackers.

To Freeze: Cool to room temperature, then transfer to freezer container, label, and freeze. Recommended freezing time: up to 2 to 3 months.

To Prepare After Freezing: Defrost in the refrigerator or in the microwave. Heat in a non-stick pot over a low heat until thoroughly heated. May be reheated in the microwave.

NUTRITIONAL INFORMATION PER SERVING: *Calories 83, Protein (g) 6, Carbohydrate (g) 7, Fat (g) 3, Calories from Fat (%) 32, Saturated Fat (g) 2, Dietary Fiber (g) 1, Cholesterol (mg) 8, Sodium (mg) 159, Diabetic Exchanges: 1 lean meat, 1.5 vegetable*

Chili Dip

This easy yet hearty meat dip boasts corn, salsa, and a chili essence. Chili Dip is a guaranteed hit, especially while watching sports on television.

MAKES 21 (¼ CUP) SERVINGS

1	pound ground sirloin
1	onion, chopped
1	teaspoon minced garlic
2	teaspoons chili powder
½	teaspoon ground cumin
1	(16-ounce) jar salsa (chipotle salsa if available)
1	cup frozen corn
½	pound light, pasteurized, processed cheese spread, cut into chunks

In a large non-stick pot, cook the sirloin, onion, and garlic over medium heat for about 5 to 7 minutes or until done. Drain any excess liquid. Add the chili powder, cumin, salsa, corn, and cheese, stirring until the cheese is melted.

To Prepare and Eat Now: Eat when ready with chips.

To Freeze: Cool to room temperature, then transfer to freezer container, label, and freeze. Recommended freezing time: up to 3 months.

To Prepare After Freezing: Defrost in the refrigerator or place immediately in a non-stick medium pot on low heat to thaw and heat. May also be reheated in the microwave.

NUTRITIONAL INFORMATION PER SERVING: *Calories 71, Protein (g) 7, Carbohydrate (g) 6, Fat (g) 2, Calories from Fat (%) 30, Saturated Fat (g) 1, Dietary Fiber (g) 0, Cholesterol (mg) 17, Sodium (mg) 172, Diabetic Exchanges: 1 very lean meat, 0.5 starch*

Stuffed Crab Poblano Peppers

The poblano pepper has a mild, slightly sweet heat. Don't let peppers intimidate you as this recipe took minutes to prepare and was fabulous! Makes a nice light lunch, evening meal, or even an appetizer.

MAKES 8

½   cup fat-free sour cream

¼   cup Italian or seasoned bread crumbs

½   cup chopped red onion

⅓   cup finely chopped roasted red peppers (from jar)

1   pound white crabmeat, picked for shells

⅓   cup shredded, reduced-fat sharp Cheddar cheese

   Salt and pepper to taste

4   poblano peppers, halved and seeded

In a medium bowl, combine the sour cream, bread crumbs, onion, and red peppers. Carefully fold in crabmeat and cheese. Season with salt and pepper. Spoon crab mixture into halved peppers.

Note:

Fresh poblanos measure about 4 to 5 inches long and about 2½ inches wide. Select rich green peppers without bruises, wrinkles, or soft spots. These peppers provide great health benefits in the capsaicin that give them their punch, and that is also a potent antioxidant that may help prevent cancer.

To Prepare and Eat Now: Preheat the oven to 375°F. Place filled peppers on a non-stick baking sheet coated with non-stick cooking spray. Cover with foil and bake for 25 to 30 minutes or until peppers are tender. Remove foil and continue baking for 5 to 7 minutes longer or until the tops are lightly browned.

To Freeze: Cool uncooked peppers to room temperature, then wrap, label, and freeze. Recommended freezing time: up to 2 to 3 months.

To Prepare After Freezing: Defrost peppers in the refrigerator. Preheat the oven to 375°F. Place filled peppers on a non-stick baking sheet coated with non-stick cooking spray. Cover with foil and bake for 25 to 35 minutes or until peppers are tender. Remove foil and continue baking for 5 to 7 minutes longer or until the tops are lightly browned.

NUTRITIONAL INFORMATION PER SERVING: *Calories 132, Protein (g) 14, Carbohydrate (g) 8, Fat (g) 5, Calories from Fat (%) 33, Saturated Fat (g) 1, Dietary Fiber (g) 1, Cholesterol (mg) 58, Sodium (mg) 259, Diabetic Exchanges: 2 lean meat, 0.5 starch*

Stuffed Mushrooms with Crawfish

Crawfish, sautéed veggies, and a touch of sherry perk up this stuffed mushroom recipe. Crabmeat, cooked small peeled shrimp, or a combination may be substituted for the crawfish.

MAKES ABOUT 30 SERVINGS (2 MUSHROOMS PER SERVING)

2	pounds fresh mushrooms, medium-sized
1	onion, chopped
1	teaspoon minced garlic
½	cup chopped green bell pepper
1	pound crawfish tails, rinsed and drained (or preferred seafood)
1	cup breadcrumbs
	Dash cayenne
½	cup chopped green onions (scallions)
	Salt and pepper to taste
2	tablespoons olive oil
3	tablespoons sherry

Clean the mushrooms and remove the stems, leaving the caps whole. Chop the stems.

In a large non-stick skillet coated with non-stick cooking spray, sauté the mushroom stems, onion, garlic, and green pepper over medium heat until tender, about 5 to 7 minutes. Add crawfish tails or preferred seafood, stirring for one minute. Remove from heat and add breadcrumbs, cayenne, green onions, salt and pepper, olive oil, and sherry. Stir until combined.

Meanwhile, place the mushrooms in a metal colander or steaming container over a pot of boiling water, cover, and steam for about 5 minutes. You can also put the mushrooms in the microwave for about 3 to 5 minutes.

Stuff the mushrooms with the filling

To Prepare and Eat Now: Preheat the oven to 350°F. Place filled mushrooms on a non-stick baking sheet and bake for 15 minutes or until well heated.

To Freeze: Cool uncooked mushrooms to room temperature, then wrap, label, and freeze. Recommended freezing time: up to 2 to 3 months.

To Prepare After Freezing: Defrost in the refrigerator or place frozen on a non-stick baking sheet. Bake at 350°F. for 20 to 30 minutes or until thoroughly heated.

NUTRITIONAL INFORMATION PER 2 MUSHROOMS (30 SERVINGS): *Calories 44, Protein (g) 4, Carbohydrate (g) 4, Fat (g) 1, Calories from Fat (%) 27, Saturated Fat (g) 0, Dietary Fiber (g) 1, Cholesterol (mg) 16, Sodium (mg) 38, Diabetic Exchanges: 0.5 very lean meat, 0.5 starch*

Muffins, Breads, and Brunch

Freezing, Thawing, and Preparing Muffins, Breads, and Brunch

❄ **Biscuits and Muffins:** Prepare according to directions. Cool to room temperature and freeze. Biscuits are recommended freezing for 6 to 8 months.

❄ **Waffles:** Prepare waffles according to directions. Cool to room temperature. Wrap, label and freeze. Recommended freezing 1 to 2 months.

Banana Blueberry Muffins

I had ripe bananas and fresh blueberries and created this wonderful not-too-sweet muffin with a touch of cinnamon and a burst of blueberries. Pecans or walnuts add a nice touch also.

MAKES 12

1 cup mashed ripe bananas (about 2 bananas)

$1/3$ cup light brown sugar

2 tablespoons canola oil

1 egg, slightly beaten

1 teaspoon vanilla extract

$1 3/4$ cup all-purpose flour

2 teaspoons baking powder

$1/4$ teaspoon baking soda

1 teaspoon ground cinnamon

$1/2$ cup buttermilk

1 cup fresh or frozen blueberries (unthawed if frozen)

Preheat the oven to 375°F. Line muffin tins with paper cups.

In a bowl, mix together the bananas, brown sugar, and oil. Gradually stir in the egg and vanilla.

In a small bowl, combine flour, baking powder, baking soda, and cinnamon. Stir flour mixture into banana mixture alternately with buttermilk, stirring until the mixture is just moist. Fold in blueberries and spoon into the muffin pan. Bake for 20 minutes or until muffins spring back when touched lightly in the center.

Note:
Frozen blueberries may be substituted for fresh. No need to defrost before using.

To Prepare and Eat Now: Eat when ready.

To Freeze: Cool to room temperature and transfer to freezer zip-top bags, label, and freeze. Recommended freezing time: up to 4 to 6 months.

To Prepare After Freezing: Remove from freezer to defrost or pop in the microwave directly from the freezer to heat.

NUTRITIONAL INFORMATION PER SERVING: *Calories 145, Protein (g) 3, Carbohydrate (g) 27, Fat (g) 3, Calories from Fat (%) 19, Saturated Fat (g) 0, Dietary Fiber (g) 1, Cholesterol (mg) 18, Sodium (mg) 113, Diabetic Exchanges: 1.5 starch, 0.5 fruit, 0.5 fat*

Raspberry Surprise Bran Muffins

Bran flakes give this incredible muffin a crunch while raspberry jam provides a burst of fruit surprise with every bite.

MAKES 24

2½ cups all-purpose flour

1 cup sugar

2 teaspoons baking powder

½ teaspoon baking soda

1½ cups buttermilk

⅓ cup canola oil

2 eggs

1 teaspoon vanilla

4 cups bran flakes cereal

1 cup fresh raspberries

1 cup seedless raspberry jam

Preheat the oven to 400°F. Line muffin tins with paper cups.

In a bowl, combine the flour, sugar, baking powder, and baking soda; set aside.

In another large bowl whisk together the buttermilk, oil, eggs, and vanilla. Add flour mixture and bran flakes to the egg mixture, stirring only until blended. Carefully stir in raspberries. Spoon a little batter into each muffin cup, make a well in the center to fit about 1 teaspoon of raspberry jam, and cover with batter, filling about three-fourths full. Bake for 20 to 25 minutes or until the muffin tops are lightly browned.

To Prepare and Eat Now: Eat when ready.

To Freeze: Cool to room temperature and transfer to freezer zip-top bags, label, and freeze. Recommended freezing time: up to 4 to 6 months

To Prepare After Freezing: Remove from freezer to defrost or pop in the microwave directly from the freezer to heat.

NUTRITIONAL INFORMATION PER SERVING: *Calories 177, Protein (g) 3, Carbohydrate (g) 34, Fat (g) 4, Calories from Fat (%) 20, Saturated Fat (g) 0, Dietary Fiber (g) 2, Cholesterol (mg) 18, Sodium (mg) 131, Diabetic Exchanges: 2 starch, 0.5 fruit, 0.5 fat*

Banana Orange Bran Muffins

Use whatever bran flakes cereal you have in your pantry—I like the fruit and bran variety adding extra fruit. The bran flakes give this terrific muffin fiber and texture while the fruit adds that sweet bite. Any dried fruit may be used instead of cranberries.

MAKES 18

1	cup mashed bananas
½	cup frozen orange juice concentrate, thawed
½	cup light brown sugar
1	egg
¼	cup canola oil
1½	cups bran flakes cereal
1	cup all-purpose flour
2	teaspoons baking powder
¼	teaspoon baking soda
½	teaspoon ground cinnamon
½	cup dried cranberries
⅓	cup chopped walnuts, optional

Preheat the oven to 400°F. Lightly coat a 12-cup muffin tin with non-stick cooking spray or line with paper cups; set aside.

In a large bowl, beat together the bananas, orange juice concentrate, brown sugar, egg, and oil. Stir in the bran flakes. Let stand for about 5 to 7 minutes for cereal to soften.

In another bowl, combine the flour, baking powder, baking soda, and cinnamon. Add the dry ingredients to the cereal mixture, stirring just until combined. Gently fold in the dried cranberries and walnuts.

Fill the muffin cups two-thirds full with the batter. Bake for 20 minutes or until muffins spring back when lightly touched in the center.

To Prepare and Eat Now: Eat when ready.

To Freeze: Cool to room temperature and transfer to freezer zip-top bags, label, and freeze. Recommended freezing time: up to 4 to 6 months.

To Prepare After Freezing: Remove from freezer to defrost or pop in the microwave directly from the freezer to heat.

NUTRITIONAL INFORMATION PER SERVING: *Calories 125, Protein (g) 2, Carbohydrate (g) 23, Fat (g) 4, Calories from Fat (%) 25, Saturated Fat (g) 0, Dietary Fiber (g) 1, Cholesterol (mg) 12, Sodium (mg) 93, Diabetic Exchanges: 1 starch, 0.5 fruit, 0.5 fat*

Refrigerated Bran Oatmeal Muffins 🥕

This great basic batter keeps in the refrigerator for six weeks so you can have hot muffins whenever you want. Toss in nuts, raisins, or dried fruit for added flavor.

MAKES 5 TO 6 DOZEN

½	cups old-fashioned oatmeal
2	cups bran cereal
2	cups shredded wheat
2	cups boiling water
⅔	cup canola oil
1	cup light brown sugar
1	cup sugar
4	eggs
5	cups all-purpose flour
5	teaspoons baking soda
1	tablespoon ground cinnamon
1	quart buttermilk

Preheat the oven to 400°F. Line muffin tins with paper cups.

In a large bowl, combine the oatmeal, bran cereal, and shredded wheat. Add the boiling water; set aside to cool.

In a mixing bowl, mix together the oil, brown sugar, and sugar. Add the eggs, beating well after each addition. Stir in the cereal mixture.

In a small bowl, combine the flour, baking soda, and cinnamon. Add to the oatmeal mixture alternately with the buttermilk, stirring only until combined. Pour batter into muffin tin. Bake for 20 minutes or until lightly browned. This batter keeps in the refrigerator in covered container up to six weeks.

To Prepare and Eat Now: Eat when ready.

To Freeze: Cool to room temperature and transfer to freezer zip-top bags, label, and freeze. Recommended freezing time: up to 3 months.

To Prepare After Freezing: Remove from freezer to defrost or pop in the microwave directly from the freezer to heat.

NUTRITIONAL INFORMATION PER SERVING: *Calories 101, Protein (g) 2, Carbohydrate (g) 17, Fat (g) 3, Calories from Fat (%) 25, Saturated Fat (g) 0, Dietary Fiber (g) 1, Cholesterol (mg) 12, Sodium (mg) 111, Diabetic Exchanges: 1 starch, 0.5 fat*

Upside Down
Apple Corn Muffins

The apple pie topping smothering these light cornmeal muffins make them an irresistible breakfast or any time snack.

MAKES 12

2	tablespoons butter
½	cup light brown sugar
½	teaspoon ground cinnamon
1	pound baking apples, peeled, cored, and sliced
1	cup yellow cornmeal
1	cup all-purpose flour
3	tablespoons sugar
1	teaspoon baking soda
1	cup buttermilk
1	egg
3	tablespoons canola oil

Preheat the oven to 350°F.

In a non-stick skillet, melt the butter and stir in the brown sugar until dissolved and bubbly. Stir in the cinnamon and apples, cooking over medium heat about 5 minutes or until just tender. Divide the apple mixture equally among 12 non-stick muffin cups coated with non-stick cooking spray.

In a bowl, mix together the cornmeal, flour, sugar, and baking soda. In another bowl, mix the butter-milk, egg, and oil to blend. Stir into cornmeal mixture just until moistened. Spoon batter evenly into muffin cups over apple mixture. Bake for 15 to 17 minutes or until firm to touch.

Immediately run a knife between each muffin and cup and invert on a baking sheet to remove muffins.

To Prepare and Eat Now:
Eat when ready.

To Freeze: Cool to room temperature and transfer to freezer zip-top bags, label, and freeze. Recommended freezing time: up to 2 months.

To Prepare After Freezing:
Remove from freezer to defrost or pop in the microwave directly from the freezer to heat.

NUTRITIONAL INFORMATION PER SERVING: *Calories 203, Protein (g) 3, Carbohydrate (g) 35, Fat (g) 6, Calories from Fat (%) 27, Saturated Fat (g) 2, Dietary Fiber (g) 1, Cholesterol (mg) 23, Sodium (mg) 150, Diabetic Exchanges: 2 starch, 0.5 fruit, 1 fat*

Yam Spice Muffins with Crumble Topping

These spicy sweet potato muffins with a crumbly oatmeal walnut topping will garner rave reviews.

MAKES 12 TO 14

1¾ cups all-purpose flour

½ cup sugar

1 teaspoon baking powder

½ teaspoon baking soda

1 teaspoon ground cinnamon

½ teaspoon ground nutmeg

1 egg

1 egg white

1 (15-ounce) can sweet potatoes (yams), drained and mashed or 1 cup mashed sweet potatoes

2 tablespoons dark molasses

½ cup buttermilk

Crumble Topping (recipe follows)

Preheat the oven to 400°F. Line muffin tins with paper cups.

In a large bowl, combine the flour, sugar, baking powder, baking soda, cinnamon, and nutmeg.

In a small bowl, mix together the egg, egg white, sweet potatoes, molasses, and buttermilk. Make a well in the center of the dry ingredients and add the egg mixture, stirring just until moistened. Transfer batter to muffin tins and top with Crumble Topping (recipe follows). Bake for 15 to 20 minutes or until muffins are lightly browned.

To Prepare and Eat Now: Eat when ready.

To Freeze: Cool to room temperature and transfer to freezer zip-top bags, label, and freeze. Recommended freezing time: up to 4 to 6 months.

To Prepare After Freezing: Remove from freezer to defrost or pop in the microwave directly from the freezer to heat.

NUTRITIONAL INFORMATION PER SERVING: Calories 189, Protein (g) 4, Carbohydrate (g) 34, Fat (g) 4, Calories from Fat (%) 21, Saturated Fat (g) 1, Dietary Fiber (g) 1, Cholesterol (mg) 18, Sodium (mg) 106, Diabetic Exchanges: 2.5 starch, 0.5 fat

It's a Fact!

Did you know that one serving of sweet potatoes has 327% of your daily requirements for Vitamin A? Even carrots don't have that much! In fact, sweet potatoes are one of the most nutritious vegetables you can eat.

Crumble Topping

¼ cup light brown sugar

2 tablespoons all-purpose flour

1 tablespoon butter, melted

⅓ cup old fashioned oatmeal

1 teaspoon vanilla extract

½ cup chopped walnuts

In a bowl, mix together the brown sugar, flour, butter, oatmeal, vanilla, and walnuts until crumbly.

Quick Lemon Blueberry Bread ✏

When fresh blueberries are available, this luscious lemon bread with a mouthful of blueberries is so good it could pass for cake. If you need a quick homemade gift, this bread is sure to be remembered.

MAKES 16 SERVINGS

1   (8-ounce) package reduced-fat cream cheese

1 ⅓ cups sugar, divided

2   eggs

2   tablespoons lemon extract

1 ½ cups biscuit baking mix

1   tablespoon grated lemon rind

1 ½ cups fresh blueberries

⅓   cup lemon juice

Preheat the oven to 350°F. Coat a non-stick 9 x 5 x 3-inch loaf pan with non-stick cooking spray.

In a large mixing bowl, beat the cream cheese and 1 cup sugar until light and fluffy. Add the eggs and lemon extract. Stir in the baking mix and lemon rind just until blended. Carefully stir in the blueberries.

Note:

If you're using frozen blueberries, do not thaw them before using, or they will be too mushy.

Bake for 45 minutes to 1 hour or until a toothpick inserted in the center comes out clean. Immediately poke holes in 1-inch intervals on the top of the bread with a toothpick.

In a small non-stick saucepan over medium heat or in the microwave oven, combine the remaining ⅓ cup sugar and lemon juice, heating until the sugar is dissolved. Pour evenly over the top of the bread. Cool and slice.

To Prepare and Eat Now: Eat when ready.

To Freeze: Cool to room temperature, then wrap, label, and freeze. Recommended freezing time: up to 4 to 6 months.

To Prepare After Freezing: Remove from freezer to defrost.

NUTRITIONAL INFORMATION PER SERVING: *Calories 169, Protein (g) 3, Carbohydrate (g) 27, Fat (g) 5, Calories from Fat (%) 28, Saturated Fat (g) 3, Dietary Fiber (g) 1, Cholesterol (mg) 36, Sodium (mg) 211, Diabetic Exchanges: 2 starch, 0.5 fat*

Banana Bread

Basic banana bread is hard to beat. Be creative and add nuts, chocolate chips, or cranberries for the holiday season.

MAKES 16 SLICES

2   large or 3 small bananas

¼   cup sugar

½   cup light brown sugar

¼   cup canola oil

2   eggs

1   teaspoon vanilla extract

1½   cups all-purpose flour

1   teaspoon baking soda

¼   cup buttermilk

Heat oven to 350°F. Coat a 9 x 5 x 3-inch non-stick loaf pan with non-stick cooking spray.

In a mixer, beat the bananas until pureed. Add sugar, brown sugar, oil, eggs, and vanilla and continue beating until creamy.

In a small bowl, combine the flour and baking soda. Stir in the flour mixture alternately with the buttermilk beginning and ending with the flour, mixing only until combined.

Transfer batter into the prepared pan. Bake for 40 to 45 minutes, or until a toothpick inserted in the center comes out almost clean.

Note:

When bananas start to get too ripe, place in the freezer until ready to use.

To Prepare and Eat Now: Eat when ready.

To Freeze: Cool to room temperature, then wrap, label, and freeze. Recommended freezing time: up to 4 to 6 months.

To Prepare After Freezing: Remove from freezer to defrost.

NUTRITIONAL INFORMATION PER SERVING: *Calories 136, Protein (g) 2, Carbohydrate (g) 22, Fat (g) 4, Calories from Fat (%) 28, Saturated Fat (g) 0, Dietary Fiber (g) 1, Cholesterol (mg) 27, Sodium (mg) 95, Diabetic Exchanges: 1.5 starch, 0.5 fat*

Butterscotch Banana Bread 🥕

Dark brown sugar gives this bread a rich caramel flavor, which pairs perfectly with the butterscotch chips.

MAKES 16 SLICES

¼ cup canola oil

1 cup dark brown sugar

2 eggs

1 cup mashed bananas (about 2 bananas)

1 teaspoon vanilla extract

1¾ cups all-purpose flour

1 teaspoon baking soda

1 teaspoon baking powder

1 teaspoon ground cinnamon

¼ cup skim milk

½ cup butterscotch chips

½ cup chopped pecans, optional

Preheat the oven to 350°F. Coat a non-stick 9 x 5 x 3-inch loaf pan with non-stick cooking spray.

In a large bowl, beat together the oil and brown sugar. Add the eggs, bananas, and vanilla, stirring well.

In another bowl, combine the flour, baking soda, baking powder, and cinnamon. Gradually combine the dry ingredients and the milk with the banana mixture, stirring only until combined.

Pour batter into the prepared loaf pan and bake 45 to 50 minutes or until a toothpick inserted in the center comes out clean.

To Prepare and Eat Now: Eat when ready.

To Freeze: Cool to room temperature, wrap, label, and freeze. Recommended freezing time: up to 4 to 6 months.

To Prepare After Freezing: Remove from freezer to defrost.

NUTRITIONAL INFORMATION PER SERVING: *Calories 197, Protein (g) 2, Carbohydrate (g) 32, Fat (g) 6, Calories from Fat (%) 29, Saturated Fat (g) 2, Dietary Fiber (g) 1, Cholesterol (mg) 27, Sodium (mg) 127, Diabetic Exchanges: 2 starch, 1 fat*

Nutty Yam Banana Bread 🥕

Sweet potatoes, bananas, and walnuts are the star ingredients for this incredibly tasty moist bread packed with flavor and nutrition.

MAKES 16 SERVINGS

½ cup mashed bananas (about 1 banana)

1 cup mashed sweet potatoes (yams)

¾ cup light brown sugar

¼ cup canola oil

1 teaspoon vanilla extract

2 eggs

1 cup all-purpose flour

1 teaspoon baking soda

½ teaspoon baking powder

1 teaspoon ground cinnamon

½ cup chopped walnuts

Preheat the oven to 350°F. Coat a non-stick 9 x 5 x 3-inch loaf pan with non-stick cooking spray.

In a large bowl, mix together the bananas, sweet potatoes, brown sugar, oil, vanilla, and eggs. In a separate bowl, combine the flour, baking soda, baking powder, and cinnamon. Stir the flour mixture into the banana mixture, mixing only until combined. Stir in the walnuts. Bake for 40 to 45 minutes, or until toothpick inserted in the center comes out clean.

To Prepare and Eat Now: Eat when ready.

To Freeze: Cool to room temperature, then wrap, label, and freeze. Recommended freezing time: up to 4 to 6 months.

To Prepare After Freezing: Remove from freezer to defrost.

NUTRITIONAL INFORMATION PER SERVING: *Calories 154, Protein (g) 3, Carbohydrate (g) 22, Fat (g) 7, Calories from Fat (%) 38, Saturated Fat (g) 1, Dietary Fiber (g) 1, Cholesterol (mg) 26, Sodium (mg) 113, Diabetic Exchanges: 1.5 starch, 1 fat*

Peanut Butter Bread 🥕

All you need is preserves with this not too sweet, yet, fabulously light peanut butter bread. In between a yeast bread and a sweet bread, this simple recipe makes a good snack or morning breakfast.

MAKES 16 SERVINGS

2	cups all-purpose flour
⅓	cup sugar
4	teaspoons baking powder
1½	cups skim milk
½	cup reduced-fat crunchy peanut butter

Preheat the oven to 350°F. Coat a non-stick 9 x 5 x 3-inch loaf pan with non-stick cooking spray.

In a large bowl, combine the flour, sugar, and baking powder. Stir in the milk and peanut butter. Transfer batter to the loaf pan and bake for 35 minutes.

To Prepare and Eat Now: Eat when ready.

To Freeze: Cool to room temperature, then wrap, label, and freeze. Recommended freezing time: up to 4 to 6 months.

To Prepare After Freezing: Remove from freezer to defrost.

NUTRITIONAL INFORMATION PER SERVING: *Calories 128, Protein (g) 4, Carbohydrate (g) 21, Fat (g) 3, Calories from Fat (%) 22, Saturated Fat (g) 1, Dietary Fiber (g) 1, Cholesterol (mg) 0, Sodium (mg) 172, Diabetic Exchanges: 1.5 starch, 0.5 fat*

It's a Fact!

Peanuts are naturally cholestorol-free!!

Toasted Coconut Banana Bread 🥕

Toasted coconut and bananas team up for this terrific tropic bread. I like to toss in toasted walnuts or pecans too.

MAKES 16 SLICES

1	egg
⅔	cup light brown sugar
¼	cup canola oil
1	teaspoon vanilla extract
2	bananas, mashed
1	cup light coconut milk, shake before opening
2	cups all-purpose flour
1	teaspoon ground cinnamon
1	teaspoon baking powder
½	teaspoon baking soda
½	cup flaked coconut, toasted

Preheat the oven to 350°F. Coat a 9-inch non-stick loaf pan with non-stick cooking spray.

In a bowl, mix together the egg, brown sugar, oil, and vanilla. Add the mashed banana and coconut milk. Combine the flour, cinnamon, baking powder, and baking soda in a small bowl. Gradually stir in the flour mixture into the banana mixture just until moist. Add half the coconut and transfer batter into the prepared pan. Sprinkle with remaining coconut and press into top of batter. Bake for 45 to 55 minutes, or until a toothpick inserted in the center comes out almost clean.

> **Note:**
> Slow down the ripening of bananas by putting them in the fridge. The skin may brown, but the bananas on the inside will keep from getting overripe.

To Prepare and Eat Now: Eat when ready.

To Freeze: Cool to room temperature, then wrap, label, and freeze. Recommended freezing time: up to 4 to 6 months.

To Prepare After Freezing: Remove from freezer to defrost.

NUTRITIONAL INFORMATION PER SERVING: *Calories 161, Protein (g) 2, Carbohydrate (g) 26, Fat (g) 6, Calories from Fat (%) 30, Saturated Fat (g) 2, Dietary Fiber (g) 1, Cholesterol (mg) 13, Sodium (mg) 84, Diabetic Exchanges: 1.5 starch, 1 fat*

Sweet Potato Praline Coffee Cake

Hot out of the oven, this scrumptious melt-in-your mouth cake is hard to beat. Best of all, this personal favorite, tastes equally as good after being frozen. The sensational Praline topping makes every bite a yummy one.

MAKES 12 SERVINGS

4	tablespoons butter
⅔	cup plus 3 tablespoons light brown sugar, divided
2	tablespoons light corn syrup
½	cup chopped pecans
2½	cups biscuit baking mix
1	(15-ounce) can sweet potatoes (yams), drained and mashed or 1 cup mashed sweet potatoes
⅓	cup skim milk
¼	cup dried cranberries

Preheat the oven to 400°F.

In a 9 x 9 x 2-square non-stick baking pan, melt the butter in the oven. Stir in ⅔ cup brown sugar and corn syrup and spread the mixture evenly in the pan. Sprinkle with pecans.

In a large mixing bowl, beat together the biscuit baking mix, sweet potatoes, and milk until the dough forms a ball. Turn dough onto a surface dusted with baking mix, knead several times and roll or pat into a 12-inch rectangle. Sprinkle with the remaining 3 tablespoons brown sugar and cranberries. Roll up the dough jellyroll style from the longer side. Cut crosswise into one-inch pieces and arrange sitting on top of the pecan mixture in pan. The dough will spread when baking. Bake for 25 to 30 minutes or until golden brown. Immediately turn upside down onto a serving plate.

To Prepare and Eat Now: Eat when ready.

To Freeze: Cool to room temperature, then wrap, label, and freeze. Recommended freezing time: up to 4 to 6 months.

To Prepare After Freezing: Thaw to room temperature and serve. The coffee cake may be reheated in the oven at 350°F. or in the microwave.

NUTRITIONAL INFORMATION PER SERVING: *Calories 276, Protein (g) 2, Carbohydrate (g) 43, Fat (g) 11, Calories from Fat (%) 36, Saturated Fat (g) 4, Dietary Fiber (g) 1, Cholesterol (mg) 10, Sodium (mg) 360, Diabetic Exchanges: 3 starch, 2 fat*

Quick Breakfast Swirl Cake 🥕

This scrumptious coffee cake begins with baking mix. The cake is not too sweet with a tad of chocolate crunch making it a super morning treat, and a good afternoon snack too, if there is any left!

MAKES 16 SERVINGS

2	cups all-purpose baking mix
¾	cup skim milk
⅓	cup sugar
1	egg
1	teaspoon vanilla extract
4	tablespoons butter, melted, divided
1	tablespoon cocoa
⅓	light brown sugar
⅓	cup chopped pecans
⅓	cup flaked coconut, optional

Preheat the oven to 350°F. Coat a non-stick 9 x 9 x 2-inch baking pan with non-stick cooking spray.

In a large bowl, stir together baking mix, milk, sugar, egg, vanilla, and 2 tablespoons melted butter, until combined. Transfer to prepared pan.

In a small bowl, mix together the cocoa, brown sugar, pecans, and coconut. Sprinkle on top of batter and swirl through batter with a knife. Bake for 20 to 25 minutes or until done in center. Do not over bake.

To Prepare and Eat Now: Eat when ready.

To Freeze: Cool to room temperature, then wrap, label, and freeze. Recommended freezing time: up to 4 to 6 months.

To Prepare After Freezing: Remove from freezer to defrost to room temperature or heat in the oven wrapped in foil.

NUTRITIONAL INFORMATION PER SERVING: *Calories 148, Protein (g) 2, Carbohydrate (g) 19, Fat (g) 7, Calories from Fat (%) 43, Saturated Fat (g) 1, Dietary Fiber (g) 1, Cholesterol (mg) 13, Sodium (mg) 233, Diabetic Exchanges: 1.5 starch, 1 fat*

Mini Sticky Cinnamon Rolls 🥕

These simple mouthfuls of decadence begin with refrigerated crescent rolls. Pull them out of the freezer for breakfast or serve them to guests for brunch. No one will believe these were made with canned dinner rolls!

MAKES 48

6	tablespoons butter
½	cup light brown sugar
1	teaspoon ground cinnamon
¼	cup raisins
¼	cup chopped pecans, optional
2	(8-ounce) cans reduced-fat crescent dinner rolls

Preheat the oven to 375°F. Coat a non-stick mini muffin tin with non-stick cooking spray.

In a microwaveable dish, microwave the butter and brown sugar until melted, about 30 to 45 seconds. Stir in the cinnamon, raisins, and pecans.

Unroll the crescent roll dough, keeping 2 triangles together to form a rectangle. Divide the butter mixture evenly on each rectangle and spread. Work quickly as the dough gets soft. Roll up the rectangle from the short side and cut each roll into 6 slices. Place the cut rolls in the prepared muffin cups. Bake for 10 to 12 minutes.

To Prepare and Eat Now: Eat when ready.

To Freeze: Cool to room temperature and transfer to freezer zip-top bags, label, and freeze. Recommended freezing time: up to 4 to 6 months.

To Prepare After Freezing: Remove from freezer to defrost or pop in the microwave directly from the freezer to heat.

NUTRITIONAL INFORMATION PER SERVING: *Calories 58, Protein (g) 1, Carbohydrate (g) 7, Fat (g) 3, Calories from Fat (%) 46, Saturated Fat (g) 1, Dietary Fiber (g) 0, Cholesterol (mg) 4, Sodium (mg) 89, Diabetic Exchanges: 0.5 starch, 0.5 fat*

Oatmeal Pancakes

Oatmeal adds great texture and flavor to these homemade pancakes. We keep these pancakes in the freezer, microwave, and serve for a speedy breakfast. Serve with syrup and try slicing bananas on top. Whole wheat flour can also be used for great-tasting pancakes.

MAKES 16

1   cup old-fashioned oatmeal

2   cups buttermilk

1   tablespoon canola oil

1   egg

2   egg whites

3   tablespoons light brown sugar

1   teaspoon vanilla extract

1½ cups all-purpose or whole wheat flour

1   teaspoon ground cinnamon

1   teaspoon baking powder

1   teaspoon baking soda

1   tablespoon butter, optional

In a large bowl, combine oatmeal and buttermilk and let stand for 2 minutes. Beat in oil, egg, egg whites, sugar, and vanilla.

In a small bowl, combine the flour, cinnamon, baking powder, and baking soda. Add dry ingredients to oatmeal, stirring only until combined.

In a large non-stick skillet coated with non-stick cooking spray, melt the butter and heat over medium heat. Pour about ¼ cup batter for each pancake into the skillet and cook about 1 to 2 minutes on each side or until lightly browned and bubbly, then flip.

To Prepare and Eat Now: Eat when ready when ready.

To Freeze: Cool to room temperature and transfer to freezer zip-top bags, label, and freeze. Recommended freezing time: up to 2 months.

To Prepare After Freezing: Remove from freezer to defrost. Reheat in the microwave or in a skillet coated with non-stick cooking spray over low heat until warm.

NUTRITIONAL INFORMATION PER SERVING: *Calories 99, Protein (g) 4, Carbohydrate (g) 17, Fat (g) 2, Calories from Fat (%) 18, Saturated Fat (g) 0, Dietary Fiber (g) 1, Cholesterol (mg) 14, Sodium (mg) 149, Diabetic Exchanges: 1 starch*

Breakfast Crepes

Buying pre-made crepes makes this a simple recipe. The combination of meat, sausage, and cheese wrapped in a crepe will start any day off right. The sausage mixture may also be mixed with grits, put in a casserole dish and topped with cheese for another breakfast option.

MAKES 8 SERVINGS

½   pound reduced-fat bulk sausage

½   pound ground sirloin

½   cup chopped onion

2   ounces reduced-fat cream cheese

3   ounces reduced-fat, pasteurized, processed cheese spread

⅔   cup fat-free sour cream

     Paprika

8   (7-inch) crepes

In a large non-stick skillet, cook the sausage, sirloin, and onion until the meat is done; drain any excess grease. Add the cream cheese and processed cheese, stirring until the cheese is melted and the mixture blended. Divide the mixture among the crepes and roll up. Place filled crepes in an oblong baking dish coated with non-stick cooking spray.

To Prepare and Eat Now: Preheat the oven to 350°F. and bake, covered, for 20 to 30 minutes. Remove foil and spread with sour cream and sprinkle with paprika. Continue baking, uncovered, for 5 more minutes.

To Freeze: Filling may be frozen separately and later used to fill crepes when ready to serve. Alternately, after filling crepes, cool to room temperature, then wrap, label, and freeze. Recommended freezing time: up to 2 months.

To Prepare After Freezing: Remove from freezer to defrost. Preheat the oven to 350°F. and bake, covered with foil, for 30 to 40 minutes. Remove foil and spread with sour cream and sprinkle with paprika. Continue baking, uncovered, for 5 more minutes.

NUTRITIONAL INFORMATION PER SERVING: *Calories 167, Protein (g) 15, Carbohydrate (g) 12, Fat (g) 5, Calories from Fat (%) 31, Saturated Fat (g) 2, Dietary Fiber (g) 0, Cholesterol (mg) 48, Sodium (mg) 349, Diabetic Exchanges: 2 lean meat, 1 starch*

Florentine English Muffins

Creamed spinach and Mozzarella on muffin halves make a quick breakfast. Top with fresh tomato slices, if desired.

MAKES 10 SERVINGS

2   (10-ounce) packages frozen chopped spinach

1   tablespoon all-purpose flour

1   cup skim milk

    Dash ground nutmeg

    Salt and pepper to taste

5   English muffins, cut in half

1   cup shredded, part-skim Mozzarella cheese

Cook the spinach according to package directions, drain very well.

In a non-stick saucepan, mix the flour and milk over medium heat, stirring until thickened, about 5 minutes. Stir in the spinach, nutmeg, and salt and pepper. Lay the English muffin halves on a baking sheet. Divide the spinach mixture evenly on top of the muffins. Top each muffin with the Mozzarella.

To Prepare and Eat Now: Preheat the broiler. Place under the broiler for 2 minutes, or until the cheese is melted and the muffin begins to brown. Watch carefully.

To Freeze: Cool and wrap muffins individually and place in freezer zip-top bags, label, and freeze. Recommended freezing time: up to 1 to 2 months.

To Prepare After Freezing: Remove from freezer to defrost. Preheat the broiler. Place under the broiler for 2 minutes, or until the cheese is melted and the muffin begins to brown. Watch carefully.

NUTRITIONAL INFORMATION PER SERVING: *Calories 123, Protein (g) 8, Carbohydrate (g) 18, Fat (g) 3, Calories from Fat (%) 19, Saturated Fat (g) 1, Dietary Fiber (g) 2, Cholesterol (mg) 8, Sodium (mg) 227, Diabetic Exchanges: 0.5 lean meat, 1 starch, 1 vegetable*

Mini Muffin Rancheros

Everyday ingredients create these quick breakfast pick-ups. Pull out of the freezer for a nutritious and satisfying breakfast.

MAKES 8

¼ cup chopped red onions

2 eggs

5 egg whites

2 tablespoons chopped green chilies

¾ cup salsa

½ cup shredded, reduced-fat Cheddar cheese

4 English muffins, halved

In a non-stick skillet coated with non-stick cooking spray, sauté the onion until tender, about 3 to 4 minutes.

In a small bowl, whisk together the eggs and egg whites. Add to the cooked onion and scramble the eggs until done. Divide the egg mixture to top the muffin halves. Top each muffin with salsa and sprinkle with cheese.

To Prepare and Eat Now: Preheat the oven to 350°F. Place muffins on a non-stick baking sheet and bake for 5 to 10 minutes or until thoroughly heated.

To Freeze: Cool to room temperature, then wrap, label individually, and freeze. Recommended freezing time: up to 1 to 2 months.

To Prepare After Freezing: Remove from freezer to defrost. Microwave or preheat the oven to 350°F and bake for 5 to 10 minutes or until thoroughly heated.

NUTRITIONAL INFORMATION PER SERVING: *Calories 125, Protein (g) 8, Carbohydrate (g) 15, Fat (g) 3, Calories from Fat (%) 22, Saturated Fat (g) 1, Dietary Fiber (g) 0, Cholesterol (mg) 57, Sodium (mg) 302, Diabetic Exchanges: 1 lean meat, 1 starch*

Baked Blintz Casserole

This sweet and satisfying cake-like dish has a touch of orange and a rich cheese filling inside. Cut it into squares and serve with fresh berries and a dollop of fat-free sour cream.

MAKES 10 TO 12 SERVINGS

4   tablespoons butter

⅓   cup sugar

2   eggs

2   egg whites

½   cup orange juice

1   cup all-purpose flour

2   teaspoons baking powder

1   cup fat-free sour cream

       Cheese Filling (recipe follows)

Cheese Filling

1   (8-ounce) package reduced-fat cream cheese

1   cup fat-free cottage cheese

1   teaspoon grated orange rind

1   egg

3   tablespoons sugar

1   tablespoon vanilla extract

In a mixing bowl, beat together the cream cheese, cottage cheese, orange rind, egg, sugar, and vanilla until smooth and creamy.

Preheat the oven to 350°F. Coat a 2-quart oblong casserole with non-stick cooking spray.

In a mixing bowl, beat together the butter and sugar until creamy. Add eggs and egg whites, one at a time, beating well after each addition. Add orange juice.

Combine flour and baking powder in small bowl and add alternately with sour cream to sugar mixture, ending with flour. Pour half of the mixture into the prepared pan and top with Cheese Filling (see recipe below). Spoon remaining batter on top of Cheese Filling to cover, being careful not to mix. Bake for 45 minutes or until golden brown and set.

To Prepare and Eat Now: Eat when ready immediately.

To Freeze: Cool to room temperature, then wrap, label, and freeze. Recommended freezing time: up to 1 to 2 months.

To Prepare After Freezing: Remove from freezer to defrost. Preheat the oven to 350° and bake, covered, for about 25 to 35 minutes or until thoroughly heated. If you have frozen leftovers or individual portions, it heats up well in the microwave.

NUTRITIONAL INFORMATION PER SERVING: *Calories 215, Protein (g) 9, Carbohydrate (g) 23, Fat (g) 9, Calories from Fat (%) 39, Saturated Fat (g) 6, Dietary Fiber (g) 0, Cholesterol (mg) 81, Sodium (mg) 290, Diabetic Exchanges: 1 lean meat, 1.5 starch, 1 fat*

Shrimp and Cheese Grits

Easy to prepare shrimp with cheesy seasoned grits and ham is an easy fulfilling breakfast. The shrimp may be omitted.

MAKES 4 TO 6 SERVINGS

1   cup quick grits

3   cups water

½   cup skim milk

1½ cups shredded, reduced-fat sharp Cheddar cheese, divided

¼   cup freshly grated Parmesan cheese

½   teaspoon paprika

    Dash cayenne pepper

⅓   cup diced Canadian bacon

1   pound medium shrimp, peeled

1   teaspoon minced garlic

1   tablespoon lemon juice

    Salt and pepper, to taste

½   cup chopped green onions (scallions)

Cook grits in the water and milk according to instructions on package. When the grits are ready, stir in 1 cup Cheddar cheese, the Parmesan cheese, paprika, and cayenne and stir until the cheese is melted.

Coat a large non-stick skillet with non-stick cooking spray and set over medium heat. Add the Canadian bacon and sauté until it begins to brown. Add the shrimp and garlic and cook, stirring until the shrimp are fully pink and almost done, 3 to 5 minutes. Add the lemon juice. Remove from the heat and stir in the grits mixture. Season with salt and pepper and add the green onions.

Coat a 2-quart casserole dish with non-stick cooking spray. Transfer the grits and shrimp mixture to the prepared dish. Sprinkle the dish with the remaining ½ cup Cheddar cheese.

To Prepare and Eat Now: Eat when ready immediately or preheat the oven to 350°F and bake for 10 minutes or until cheese is melted.

To Freeze: Cool to room temperature, then wrap, label, and freeze. Recommended freezing time: up to 1 to 2 months.

To Prepare After Freezing: Remove from freezer to defrost. Preheat the oven to 350°F. Bake for 30 minutes, covered, or until thoroughly heated.

NUTRITIONAL INFORMATION PER SERVING: *Calories 268, Protein (g) 26, Carbohydrate (g) 23, Fat (g) 7, Calories from Fat (%) 25, Saturated Fat (g) 4, Dietary Fiber (g) 1, Cholesterol (mg) 134, Sodium (mg) 470, Diabetic Exchanges: 3 lean meat, 1.5 starch*

Cornbread 🥕

Salsa and cheese are the secret ingredients giving this cornbread some spunk. This recipe is for two pans, as I love having a pan of cornbread to pull out of the freezer whenever I serve chili. One pan for now and save the other for later.

MAKES 2 PANS (16 SERVINGS PER PAN)

3	cups yellow cornmeal
1	cup all-purpose flour
4	tablespoons sugar
4	teaspoons baking powder
2	teaspoons baking soda
	Salt to taste
3	cups buttermilk
2	eggs
3	egg whites
4	tablespoons butter, melted
2	cups shredded, reduced-fat sharp Cheddar cheese
1/3	cup salsa

Preheat the oven to 400°F. Coat two 9-inch cake or square pans with non-stick cooking spray.

In a mixing bowl, combine the cornmeal, flour, sugar, baking powder, baking soda, and salt. In another bowl, whisk together the buttermilk, eggs, egg whites, and butter. Mix the buttermilk mixture into the dry ingredients, stirring until combined. Fold in the cheese and salsa. Divide the mixture into the two pans. Bake for 25 to 30 minutes or until golden brown.

To Prepare and Eat Now: Slice and serve.

To Freeze: Cool to room temperature, then wrap, label, and freeze. Recommended freezing time: up to 1 to 2 months.

To Prepare After Freezing: Remove from freezer to defrost.

NUTRITIONAL INFORMATION PER SERVING: *Calories 115, Protein (g) 5, Carbohydrate (g) 17, Fat (g) 3, Calories from Fat (%) 27, Saturated Fat (g) 2, Dietary Fiber (g) 1, Cholesterol (mg) 22, Sodium (mg) 227, Diabetic Exchanges: 1 starch, 0.5 fat*

Sun-Dried Tomato Bread 🥕

Forget about yeast or the bread-maker with this simple sensational, savory homemade bread packed with sun-dried tomatoes, basil, and Parmesan.

MAKES 10 TO 12 SERVINGS

⅔   cup sun-dried tomatoes, coarsely chopped

1½   cups all-purpose flour

1   teaspoon baking powder

½   teaspoon baking soda

1   teaspoon sugar

1   teaspoon minced garlic

1   teaspoon dried basil leaves

2   tablespoons chopped parsley

¼   cup grated Parmesan cheese

1   egg

¾   cup skim milk

2   tablespoons olive oil

Preheat the oven to 350°F. Coat an 8½ x 4½ x 2½-inch non-stick loaf pan with non-stick cooking spray.

Pour boiling water over the tomatoes and let sit for 10 minutes. Drain water; set aside.

In a large bowl, combine the flour, baking powder, baking soda, sugar, garlic, basil, parsley, and cheese.

In a small bowl, whisk together the egg, milk, and olive oil and stir into the flour mixture, just until combined. Fold in the tomatoes. Transfer batter into the prepared pan and bake for 35 to 40 minutes or until the top is crispy.

To Prepare and Eat Now: Eat when ready.

To Freeze: Cool to room temperature, then wrap, label, and freeze. Recommended freezing time: up to 4 to 6 months.

To Prepare After Freezing: Remove from freezer to defrost. Serve room temperature or wrap in foil and bake at 350°F. for about 15 to 20 minutes or until thoroughly heated.

NUTRITIONAL INFORMATION PER SERVING: *Calories 107, Protein (g) 4, Carbohydrate (g) 15, Fat (g) 3, Calories from Fat (%) 29, Saturated Fat (g) 1, Dietary Fiber (g) 1, Cholesterol (mg) 19, Sodium (mg) 125, Diabetic Exchanges: 1 starch, 0.5 fat*

Spinach Bread

This creamed spinach topped bread has more versatility, serve as a bread, appetizer, or with soup to complete the meal.

MAKES 16 SLICES

2   (10-ounce) packages frozen chopped spinach

1   teaspoon minced garlic

2   tablespoons all-purpose flour

1   (12-ounce) can evaporated fat-free milk

¼   teaspoon hot sauce

    Salt and pepper to taste

1   loaf French bread, sliced in half lengthwise

1½ cups shredded, part-skim Mozzarella cheese

Prepare the spinach according to package directions; drain well.

In a small non-stick saucepan coated with non-stick cooking spray, sauté the garlic and stir in the spinach and flour. Gradually stir in the milk, hot sauce, and season to taste. Cook over medium heat until thickened and bubbly. Spread the spinach mixture on each cut half of the French bread.

To Prepare and Eat Now: Preheat the oven to 350°F. Sprinkle bread with Mozzarella cheese. Place bread halves on a non-stick baking sheet and bake for 10 minutes or until the cheese is melted and the bread is crispy.

To Freeze: After spreading spinach on bread, let cool to room temperature, then wrap, label each half separately, and freeze. Recommended freezing time: up to 2 months.

To Prepare After Freezing: Remove from freezer to defrost. Preheat the oven to 350°F. and place each bread half on a baking sheet. Bake for 7 minutes, sprinkle with cheese, and return to oven and continue baking until the cheese is melted. If baking directly from the freezer, add extra cooking time.

NUTRITIONAL INFORMATION PER SERVING: *Calories 132, Protein (g) 8, Carbohydrate (g) 19, Fat (g) 3, Calories from Fat (%) 19, Saturated Fat (g) 1, Dietary Fiber (g) 2, Cholesterol (mg) 8, Sodium (mg) 289, Diabetic Exchanges: 0.5 lean meat, 1.5 starch*

Italian Stuffed Bread 🥕

Mozzarella cheese, Dijon mustard, and poppy seeds are key ingredients in this make-ahead bread, which takes minutes to prepare, and is a guaranteed success.

MAKES 14 TO 16 SLICES

1	loaf Italian bread
6	tablespoons butter, melted
	Dash hot sauce
2	teaspoons Dijon mustard
1	teaspoon poppy seeds
1	cup shredded, part-skim Mozzarella cheese

Slice the bread diagonally in 1-inch slices, being careful not to cut through the bottom crust. In a small bowl, stir together the butter, hot sauce, mustard, and poppy seeds. Divide mixture between slices of bread. Sprinkle cheese between each slice and a little on top.

To Prepare and Eat Now: Preheat the oven to 350°F. Bake bread, wrapped in foil, for about 15 to 20 minutes or until the cheese is melted. Unwrap foil last 5 minutes in the oven to let bread get crispy and brown.

To Freeze: Wrap, label, and freeze. Recommended freezing time: up to 2 months.

To Prepare After Freezing: Remove from freezer to defrost or bake directly from the freezer. Wrap bread in foil and bake at 350°F. for about 20 to 30 minutes or until cheese is melted and bread is fully heated. Unwrap foil last 5 minutes in the oven to let bread get crispy and brown.

NUTRITIONAL INFORMATION PER SERVING: *Calories 134, Protein (g) 4, Carbohydrate (g) 15, Fat (g) 7, Calories from Fat (%) 44, Saturated Fat (g) 4, Dietary Fiber (g) 1, Cholesterol (mg) 16, Sodium (mg) 252, Diabetic Exchanges: 1 starch, 1 fat*

Green Chili Cheese Bread 🥕

The simple combination of green chilies, garlic, and cheese turn a slice of bread into a slice of heaven.

MAKES 12 TO 16 SLICES

4   tablespoons butter, softened

2   (4-ounce) cans chopped green chilies, drained

1   tablespoon minced garlic

2   tablespoons light mayonnaise

1½   cups shredded, reduced-fat Monterey Jack cheese

1   (16-ounce) French bread, cut in half lengthwise

In a bowl, combine the butter, chilies, garlic, mayonnaise, and cheese. Spread the mixture on top of each bread half.

To Prepare and Eat Now: Preheat the oven to 350°F. Place bread halves on a non-stick baking sheet and bake for 10 to 15 minutes or until the cheese is melted and bread is crispy. Alternately, you can broil the bread for about one minute, but be sure to watch it carefully.

To Freeze: Wrap bread, label, and freeze. Recommended freezing time: up to 2 months.

To Prepare After Freezing: Remove from freezer to defrost. Preheat the oven to 350°F. Bake for 10 to 15 minutes or until the cheese is melted and bread is crispy. Alternately, you can broil it for one minute, but be sure to watch it carefully.

NUTRITIONAL INFORMATION PER SERVING: *Calories 143, Protein (g) 6, Carbohydrate (g) 15, Fat (g) 6, Calories from Fat (%) 40, Saturated Fat (g) 3, Dietary Fiber (g) 1, Cholesterol (mg) 14, Sodium (mg) 326, Diabetic Exchanges: 0.5 lean meat, 1 starch, 1 fat*

Artichoke Cheese Toast 🥕

Versatile, tasty, and satisfying, this toast can be served as a side, snack, or even an appetizer.

MAKES 16 SLICES

1	medium loaf Italian bread
⅔	cup fat-free sour cream
½	teaspoon minced garlic
1	(14.5-ounce) can artichoke hearts, drained and coarsely chopped
½	cup shredded, reduced-fat Cheddar cheese
½	cup shredded, reduced-fat Monterey Jack cheese
½	cup chopped green onions (scallions)
	Dash hot sauce
	Salt and pepper to taste
2	tablespoons grated Parmesan cheese

Slice the bread in half lengthwise and carefully scoop out the center with your fingers, cutting into small pieces. Toast 2 cups of the small pieces until light brown; cool and set aside.

In a bowl, combine the sour cream, garlic, artichokes, Cheddar and Monterey Jack cheeses, green onions, hot sauce, and salt and pepper. Fold in toasted bread pieces. Spoon mixture into bread shells. Sprinkle each half with Parmesan cheese.

To Prepare and Eat Now: Preheat the oven to 350°F. Bake for 18 to 20 minutes or until the cheese is melted. Cut into slices.

To Freeze: Wrap, label, and freeze before baking. Recommended freezing time: up to 2 months.

To Prepare After Freezing: Remove from freezer, wrap in foil and bake directly from the freezer at 350°F. for about 20 minutes. Unwrap foil and bake about 5 to 10 minutes longer or until cheese is melted and bubbly.

NUTRITIONAL INFORMATION PER SERVING: *Calories 95, Protein (g) 5, Carbohydrate (g) 13, Fat (g) 2, Calories from Fat (%) 21, Saturated Fat (g) 1, Dietary Fiber (g) 1, Cholesterol (mg) 6, Sodium (mg) 230, Diabetic Exchanges: 0.5 very lean meat, 1 starch*

Chilies, Stews, and Soups

Freezing, Thawing, and Preparing Chilies, Stews, and Soups

❄ **Soups and Purées:** Cream-based soups may be heated without thawing on a very low heat, watching and stirring frequently for a smooth texture. Recommended freezing for 4 to 6 months.

❄ Avoid freezing soups or stews with potatoes in them. The potatoes get mushy with freezing.

❄ Bring our soups, stews, and chilies to room temperature before putting them in the freezer. That way, the heat won't affect other food in your freezer.

Best Chili

Everyone seems to have their secret for the perfect chili, so I put all those secrets in one pot to create the best chili ever. This is a time saver recipe as you throw it all together and cook on the stove. I like serving with chopped red onions, cheese, and chips.

MAKES 12 CUPS

2	green bell peppers, seeded and chopped
2	onions, chopped
4	pounds ground sirloin or ground sirloin chili meat
1	tablespoon minced garlic
1	(15-ounce) can tomato sauce
2	tablespoons molasses
1	tablespoon cocoa
½	cup chili powder
1	tablespoon ground cumin
1	teaspoon dried oregano leaves
1	(12-ounce) bottle light Mexican beer
2	(14-ounce) cans beef broth
2	(15-ounce) cans pinto beans, drained and rinsed

In a large pot coated with non-stick cooking spray, sauté the bell peppers and onion until tender, about 5 to 7 minutes. Add the ground meat and garlic, and stir until the meat is done, about 7 minutes. Add the tomato sauce, molasses, cocoa, chili powder, cumin, oregano, beer, and beef broth. Bring to a boil, reduce heat, and simmer for one hour. Add beans, cooking 10 minutes longer and serve.

To Prepare and Eat Now: Eat when ready.

To Freeze: Cool to room temperature, then transfer to freezer containers, label, and freeze. Recommended freezing time: up to 3 months.

To Prepare After Freezing: Remove from freezer to defrost. Reheat in a non-stick pot over a low heat. Alternately, you can reheat in the microwave.

NUTRITIONAL INFORMATION PER SERVING: *Calories 306, Protein (g) 37, Carbohydrate (g) 22, Fat (g) 9, Calories from Fat (%) 24, Saturated Fat (g) 3, Dietary Fiber (g) 7, Cholesterol (mg) 80, Sodium (mg) 775, Diabetic Exchanges: 4.5 lean meat, 1 starch, 1.5 vegetable*

Black Bean Chili

The squash and corn add a nice dimension to this flavorful chili.

MAKES 8 SERVINGS

2   cups dried black beans, rinsed

1   cup chopped red onion

1   cup diced carrot

½   cup chopped red bell pepper

½   cup chopped green bell pepper

1   tablespoon minced garlic

2   tablespoons chili powder

2   teaspoons ground cumin

¼   teaspoon cayenne pepper

1   bay leaf

6   cups water

1   (10.5-ounce) can diced tomatoes and green chilies

    Salt and pepper to taste

1   cup diced zucchini

1   cup diced yellow squash

1   cup frozen corn

1   tablespoon seeded and finely chopped jalapeño peppers

NUTRITIONAL INFORMATION PER SERVING: *Calories 221, Protein (g) 12, Carbohydrate (g) 43, Fat (g) 1, Calories from Fat (%) 3, Saturated Fat (g) 0, Dietary Fiber (g) 7, Cholesterol (mg) 0, Sodium (mg) 188, Diabetic Exchanges: 0.5 very lean meat, 2.5 starch, 1.5 vegetable*

Place the beans in a large bowl and cover with cold water. Let stand at least 4 hours or overnight. Drain.

In a large non-stick pot coated with non-stick cooking spray, sauté the onion, about 5 minutes. Add the carrot, peppers, garlic, chili powder, cumin, cayenne, and bay leaf. Continue cooking, stirring often, until the vegetables are tender, about 10 minutes. Add the black beans and the 6 cups of water. Bring to a boil, reduce heat, cover and simmer 1 hour. Add the tomatoes and chilies, salt and pepper, and continue cooking, uncovered, until the beans are tender and the mixture is thick, 45 to 60 minutes. Add the zucchini, yellow squash, corn and jalapeños, cooking about 10 to 12 minutes or until the vegetables are tender.

To Prepare and Eat Now: Eat when ready. Serve over rice, if desired.

To Freeze: Cool to room temperature, then transfer to freezer containers, label, and freeze. Recommended freezing time: up to 3 months.

To Prepare After Freezing: Remove from freezer to defrost. Reheat in a non-stick pot over low heat. Alternately, you can reheat in the microwave. Serve over rice, if desired.

Chicken Lentil Chili

If you've never had lentils, here is your chance. I bought a bag of red lentils at our local farmer's market and created this easy and great-tasting chili packed with flavors and textures. For a shortcut, use rotisserie or leftover chicken. For a vegetarian version, substitute a can of white beans for the chicken. I serve my chili loaded with Monterey Jack cheese, chopped avocado, and chopped red onion.

MAKES 6 (1 ¼ CUP) SERVINGS

1	cup red lentils or any variety lentils, washed
2	(14.5-ounce) cans chicken broth
1	(28-ounce) can diced tomatoes and juice
1	onion, finely chopped
1	green bell pepper, seeded and chopped
1	red bell pepper, seeded and chopped
1	teaspoon minced garlic
1	tablespoon chili powder
½	teaspoon ground cumin
1	(4-ounce) can diced green chilies, drained
3	cups coarsely chopped, cooked chicken breasts
	Salt and pepper to taste
	Shredded Monterey Jack cheese, optional for serving
	Chopped avocado, optional for serving
	Chopped red onion, optional for serving

In a large non-stick pot, combine the lentils and chicken broth. Bring to a boil, reduce heat, cover and cook for 30 minutes. Add the tomatoes, onion, peppers, garlic, chili powder, cumin, and green chilies. Bring to another boil over medium heat, reduce heat, cover and continue cooking for 20 minutes longer or until lentils are tender. Add chicken, season with salt and pepper, and cook 5 minutes longer.

To Prepare and Eat Now: Eat when ready.

To Freeze: Cool to room temperature, then transfer to freezer containers, label, and freeze. Recommended freezing time: up to 2 to 3 months.

To Prepare After Freezing: Remove from freezer to defrost. Reheat in a non-stick pot over a low heat. Alternately, you can reheat in the microwave.

NUTRITIONAL INFORMATION PER SERVING:
Calories 288, Protein (g) 34, Carbohydrate (g) 31, Fat (g) 4, Calories from Fat (%) 11, Saturated Fat (g) 1, Dietary Fiber (g) 8, Cholesterol (mg) 60, Sodium (mg) 717, Diabetic Exchanges: 4 very lean meat, 1.5 starch, 2 vegetable

Southwestern Shrimp and Black Bean Chili

Shrimp, black beans, and corn team together with southwestern seasonings for a show-stopping chili.

MAKES 4 TO 6 SERVINGS

1   green bell pepper, seeded and chopped

1   red bell pepper, seeded and chopped

1   large onion, chopped

1   cup shredded carrots

1   tablespoon finely chopped jalapeño pepper

½   teaspoon minced garlic

1   tablespoon chili powder

1½   teaspoons dried cumin

1   (16-ounce) can chopped tomatoes, with their juices

1   (16-ounce) can black beans, drained and rinsed

½   cup water

1   pound medium shrimp, peeled

1½   cups frozen corn

In a large non-stick pot coated with non-stick cooking spray, sauté the green and red peppers, onion, carrot, jalapeño, and garlic until tender, about 6 to 8 minutes. Stir in the chili powder, cumin, tomatoes, black beans, water, and shrimp and bring to a boil. Reduce the heat and cook for 5 to 7 minutes, or until the shrimp are pink. Add the corn and continue cooking 5 minutes longer.

To Prepare and Eat Now: Eat when ready.

To Freeze: Cool to room temperature, then transfer to freezer containers, label, and freeze. Recommended freezing time: up to 2 to 3 months.

To Prepare After Freezing: Remove from freezer to defrost. Reheat in a non-stick pot over a low heat. Alternately, you can reheat in the microwave.

NUTRITIONAL INFORMATION PER SERVING: *Calories 218, Protein (g) 20, Carbohydrate (g) 32, Fat (g) 2, Calories from Fat (%) 8, Saturated Fat (g) 0, Dietary Fiber (g) 8, Cholesterol (mg) 112, Sodium (mg) 599, Diabetic Exchanges: 2 very lean meat, 1.5 starch, 1.5 vegetable*

Pulled Pork Chili

Pulled pork and chili combine to create this rich full-bodied flavored chili with a twist. Serve with fat-free sour cream, sliced jalapeños, and reduced-fat shredded Cheddar cheese.

MAKES 12 CUPS

3   pounds boneless pork loin, trimmed of excess fat and cut into 2-inch cubes

Salt and pepper

1   red onion, chopped

1   teaspoon minced garlic

2   red bell peppers, seeded and chopped

2   tablespoons dark brown sugar

2   tablespoons chili powder

2   tablespoons ground cumin

3   tablespoons cilantro, chopped, optional

1   (28-ounce) can diced tomatoes with juice

1   (10-ounce) can diced tomatoes and green chilies

4   tablespoons honey

½   cup prepared black coffee

½   cup bourbon, optional

1   (15-ounce) can black beans, rinsed and drained

1   (15-ounce) can kidney beans, rinsed and drained

Season the pork heavily with salt and pepper and brown in batches in a large, heavy non-stick pot coated with non-stick cooking spray over medium heat. Remove the pork from the pot and set aside.

In the same pot, coated with non-stick cooking spray, sauté the onion, garlic, and bell pepper until tender, about 7 minutes. Add the brown sugar, chili powder, cumin, and cilantro. Add the pork back to the pot along with both cans of tomatoes, honey, coffee, and bourbon. Let simmer, covered, on low heat for 2 to 3 hours or, until the pork is juicy and buttery soft. After 2 hours, add the beans, stir well, and continue cooking until the meat pulls into shreds. Using a fork, shred some of the pork while it's still in the pot.

To Prepare and Eat Now: Eat when ready with condiments.

To Freeze: Cool to room temperature, then transfer to freezer containers, label, and freeze. Recommended freezing time: up to 3 months.

To Prepare After Freezing: Remove from freezer to defrost. Reheat in a non-stick pot over low heat. Alternately, you can reheat in the microwave.

NUTRITIONAL INFORMATION PER SERVING: Calories 294, Protein (g) 28, Carbohydrate (g) 26, Fat (g) 9, Calories from Fat (%) 27, Saturated Fat (g) 3, Dietary Fiber (g) 5, Cholesterol (mg) 64, Sodium (mg) 518, Diabetic Exchanges: 3 lean meat, 1 starch, 2 vegetable

White Chili with Tomato Salsa

Outstanding selection! I had to have seconds of this one. Rotisserie chicken and canned chicken broth may be used when you're in a hurry. A dollop of the Tomato Salsa and a sprinkle of reduced-fat Cheddar cheese will kick the chili up a notch.

MAKES 6 TO 8 SERVINGS

1½ pounds boneless, skinless chicken breasts, cut into pieces

1 onion, quartered

8 cups water

1 onion, chopped

1 teaspoon minced garlic

2 (15.5-ounce) cans great Northern beans, rinsed and drained, divided

4 cups chicken broth, reserved from cooking the chicken, divided

1 teaspoon chili powder

1 teaspoon ground cumin

½ teaspoon dried oregano leaves

1 (4-ounce) can diced green chilies, drained

1 (14.5-ounce) can white sweet corn, drained

Tomato Salsa (recipe follows), optional

NUTRITIONAL INFORMATION PER SERVING: *Calories 231, Protein (g) 27, Carbohydrate (g) 25, Fat (g) 2, Calories from Fat (%) 8, Saturated Fat (g) 0, Dietary Fiber (g) 8, Cholesterol (mg) 49, Sodium (mg) 578*

In a large pot, place the chicken pieces and the quartered onion. Cover with 8 cups of water and bring to a boil. Cook at a low boil for 20 to 30 minutes or until the chicken is tender. Reserve the broth, and cut the chicken into bite-size pieces. Discard the onion.

In a large non-stick pot coated with non-stick cooking spray, sauté the chopped onion and garlic over a medium heat for 3 to 5 minutes or until tender, stirring constantly.

In a food processor, place 1 can great Northern beans with 1 cup of the chicken broth and process until smooth. Add the smooth bean mixture, remaining can great Northern beans, remaining 3 cups chicken broth, chili powder, cumin, oregano, green chilies, and corn to the pot with onion. Bring to a boil, reduce heat, add chicken and cook for 20 to 30 minutes.

To Prepare and Eat Now: Eat when ready with a dollop of Tomato Salsa.

To Freeze: Cool to room temperature, then transfer to freezer containers, label, and freeze. Recommended freezing time: up to 3 months.

To Prepare After Freezing: Remove from freezer to defrost. Reheat in a non-stick pot over low heat. Alternately, you can reheat in the microwave. Prepare salsa and serve with chili.

It's a Fact!

Canned tomatoes are a quick solution for a quick salsa.

Tomato Salsa

This salsa is best when you make it right before serving the chili.

1 ½   cups chopped tomato

2   tablespoons chopped fresh cilantro

½   teaspoon minced garlic

¼   cup chopped red onion

½   teaspoon sugar

When ready to serve chili, in a bowl mix together the tomato, cilantro, garlic, red onion, and sugar. Cover and refrigerate until ready to use.

NUTRITIONAL INFORMATION PER SERVING: *Calories 10, Protein (g) 0, Carbohydrate (g) 2, Fat (g) 0, Calories from Fat (%) 0, Saturated Fat (g) 0, Dietary Fiber (g) 0, Cholesterol (mg) 0, Sodium (mg) 2, Diabetic Exchanges: Free*

Basic Beef Stew

This mild stew with carrots and mushrooms in a savory brown gravy is great with rice or mashed potatoes.

MAKES 4 TO 6 SERVINGS

1½ pounds lean beef stew meat

Salt and pepper to taste

¼ cup all-purpose flour

1 (14.5-ounce) can seasoned onion beef broth

2 tablespoons currant jelly

2 cups baby carrots

½ pound mushrooms, halved

Season the meat with the salt and pepper. In a large non-stick pot coated with non-stick cooking spray, cook the meat over medium heat until browned on all sides, about 5 to 7 minutes. Stir in the flour, mixing to coat. Gradually stir in the beef broth and jelly, mixing well. Bring the mixture to a boil, lower the heat, cover, and simmer for 15 minutes. Add the carrots and mushrooms and continue cooking, covered, about 45 minutes, or until the meat is tender, stirring occasionally.

To Prepare and Eat Now: Eat when ready.

To Freeze: Cool to room temperature, then transfer to freezer containers, label, and freeze. Recommended freezing time: up to 3 months.

To Prepare After Freezing: Remove from freezer to defrost. Reheat in a non-stick pot over a low heat. Alternately, you can reheat in the microwave.

NUTRITIONAL INFORMATION PER SERVING: *Calories 232, Protein (g) 24, Carbohydrate (g) 14, Fat (g) 8, Calories from Fat (%) 33, Saturated Fat (g) 3, Dietary Fiber (g) 1, Cholesterol (mg) 70, Sodium (mg) 352, Diabetic Exchanges: 3 lean meat, 0.5 starch, 1 vegetable*

Beef Stew with Dumplings

Dumplings add a heap of fun and flavor to this basic beef stew.

MAKES 10 SERVINGS

2½ pounds beef top round, trimmed of excess fat cut into 1 inch pieces

Salt and pepper to taste

½ cup all-purpose flour

2 cups sliced carrots

1 cup chopped celery

1 cup chopped onion

1 teaspoon minced garlic

1 tablespoon dried thyme leaves

2 tablespoons chopped parsley

2 cups tomato juice

4 cups beef broth

Dumplings (recipe follows)

Dumplings

1½ cups all-purpose flour

3 teaspoons baking powder

Salt and pepper to taste

¾ cup skim milk

2 tablespoons butter, melted

In a bowl, combine the flour, baking powder, and salt and pepper. Combine the milk and butter and add to the dry ingredients, mixing well.

Season the meat with salt and pepper and toss with flour. In a large non-stick pot coated with non-stick cooking spray, cook the meat over a medium heat until browned, about 8 minutes. Add the carrots, celery, onion, garlic, thyme, parsley, tomato juice, and beef broth. Bring to a boil, scraping the bottom of the pan, reduce heat, cover and simmer for 50 to 60 minutes or until meat is tender.

Meanwhile, prepare and add the dumplings (see recipe) to the stew, one heaping tablespoon at a time. Cover the pan tightly, and continue cooking until the dumplings are done, 12 to 15 minutes.

To Prepare and Eat Now: Eat when ready.

To Freeze: Cool to room temperature, then transfer to freezer containers, label, and freeze. Recommended freezing time: up to 3 months.

To Prepare After Freezing: Remove from freezer to defrost. Reheat in a non-stick pot over a low heat. Alternately, you can reheat in the microwave.

NUTRITIONAL INFORMATION PER SERVING:
Calories 298, Protein (g) 31, Carbohydrate (g) 27, Fat (g) 7, Calories from Fat (%) 20, Saturated Fat (g) 3, Dietary Fiber (g) 2, Cholesterol (mg) 70, Sodium (mg) 714, Diabetic Exchanges: 3.5 lean meat, 1.5 starch, 1 vegetable

Different Twist Pork Stew

This adventurous stew made with pork, sweet potatoes, and corn makes an awesome twist on traditional stew. This is great with corn bread.

MAKES 6 TO 8 SERVINGS

2   pounds pork tenderloin, trimmed of fat and cut into 1½-inch cubes

1   large onion, chopped

1   (28-ounce) can diced tomatoes, with their juices

1   (14.5-ounce) can fat-free chicken broth

1½ pounds sweet potatoes (yams) (about 3 sweet potatoes), peeled and cut into 1-inch cubes

1   (16-ounce) package frozen corn

2   bay leaves

    Salt and pepper to taste

In a large non-stick pot coated with non-stick cooking spray, brown the pork over medium heat, about 5 to 7 minutes. Add the onion and cook until tender. Add the tomatoes, chicken broth, sweet potatoes, corn, bay leaves, and salt and pepper. Bring to a boil, lower heat, and simmer until the pork and sweet potatoes are tender, about 45 minutes to 1 hour. Remove the bay leaves and discard.

To Prepare and Eat Now: Eat when ready.

To Freeze: Cool to room temperature, then transfer to freezer containers, label, and freeze. Recommended freezing time: up to 2 months.

To Prepare After Freezing: Remove from freezer to defrost. Reheat in a non-stick pot over a low heat. Alternately, you can reheat in the microwave.

NUTRITIONAL INFORMATION PER SERVING: *Calories 308, Protein (g) 28, Carbohydrate (g) 39, Fat (g) 4, Calories from Fat (%) 13, Saturated Fat (g) 1, Dietary Fiber (g) 5, Cholesterol (mg) 74, Sodium (mg) 440, Diabetic Exchanges: 3 very lean meat, 2 starch, 2 vegetable*

Chicken Stew

The chicken in this stew is cooked in seasoned broth, which tenderizes and flavors it, creating a heartier, full-flavored version of chicken soup.

MAKES 8 CUPS

2   stalks celery, chopped

½   cup coarsely chopped carrots

1   onion, chopped

1   (14.5-ounce) can chopped tomatoes and juice

3   cups canned chicken broth, divided

1   teaspoon dried basil leaves

½   teaspoon dried thyme leaves

1   bay leaf

1½   pounds boneless, skinless chicken breasts

1   (15-ounce) can white navy beans, drained and rinsed

   Salt and pepper to taste

In a large non-stick pot coated with non-stick cooking spray, sauté the celery, carrot, and onion over medium heat until the onion is tender, about 5 minutes. Stir in the tomatoes with their juice, 2 cups chicken broth, basil, thyme, and bay leaf. Add the chicken breasts and bring mixture to a boil. Reduce the heat and simmer, until the chicken is cooked through and liquid is reduced, turning the chicken breasts over and stirring the mixture occasionally, about 25 to 35 minutes. Remove chicken and shred or cut into bite size pieces. Return to the pot. Remove and discard the bay leaf. Add the beans to the pot and cook until thoroughly heated. Add remaining broth to a desired stew consistency. Season with salt and pepper.

To Prepare and Eat Now: Eat when ready.

To Freeze: Cool to room temperature, then transfer to freezer containers, label, and freeze. Recommended freezing time: up to 2 months.

To Prepare After Freezing: Remove from freezer to defrost. Reheat in a non-stick pot over a low heat. Alternately, you can reheat in the microwave.

NUTRITIONAL INFORMATION PER SERVING: *Calories 181, Protein (g) 25, Carbohydrate (g) 16, Fat (g) 1, Calories from Fat (%) 7, Saturated Fat (g) 0, Dietary Fiber (g) 4, Cholesterol (mg) 49, Sodium (mg) 574, Diabetic Exchanges: 3 very lean meat, 1 starch*

Meatball Stew

These fantastic little meatballs, seasoned with Italian seasonings and doused in rich tomato gravy, provide a hearty one-dish meal.

MAKES 6 SERVINGS

2   pounds ground sirloin

2   large egg whites, lightly beaten

⅓   cup dry bread crumbs

2   teaspoons minced garlic

    Salt and pepper to taste

1   teaspoon dried basil leaves

1   teaspoon dried thyme leaves

1   onion, finely chopped

1   green bell pepper, seeded and chopped

2   (14.5-ounce) cans diced tomatoes, with their juices

1   (10.75-ounce) can tomato puree

1¼ cups canned beef broth

⅔   cup long-grain rice

1¼ cups frozen green peas

Preheat the broiler.

In a bowl, combine the meat, egg whites, bread crumbs, garlic, salt and pepper, basil, and thyme. Shape into balls about 1½ inches in diameter. Place the meatballs on a non-stick baking sheet coated with non-stick cooking spray. Broil in the oven for 4 to 5 minutes, turn the meatballs, and continue broiling for 4 minutes longer, or until done. Remove from the broiler and set aside.

In a large non-stick pot coated with non-stick cooking spray, sauté the onion and green pepper over medium heat until tender, about 5 minutes. Add the tomatoes, tomato puree, and beef broth. Bring to a boil and add the meatballs. Mix in the rice, cover, reduce the heat, and continue cooking for 20 minutes, or until rice is done. Stir in the peas, cover, and continue cooking for 5 minutes, or until the peas are tender.

To Prepare and Eat Now: Eat when ready.

To Freeze: Cool to room temperature, then transfer to freezer containers, label, and freeze. Recommended freezing time: up to 3 months.

To Prepare After Freezing: Remove from freezer to defrost. Reheat in a non-stick pot over a low heat. Alternately, you can reheat in the microwave.

NUTRITIONAL INFORMATION PER SERVING: *Calories 327, Protein (g) 38, Carbohydrate (g) 29, Fat (g) 8, Calories from Fat (%) 20, Saturated Fat (g) 3, Dietary Fiber (g) 4, Cholesterol (mg) 80, Sodium (mg) 807, Diabetic Exchanges: 4 lean meat, 1 starch, 3 vegetable*

Meatball Soup

This family pleaser combines two favorites, chicken soup and meatballs.

MAKES 8 SERVINGS

½   cup chopped carrots

½   cup chopped celery

1   onion, chopped

1   teaspoon minced garlic

2   bay leaves

8   cups chicken broth

2   (14.5-ounce) cans diced tomatoes and juice

    Meatballs (recipe follows)

4   ounces fettuccine or spaghetti, broken into thirds

1   (6-ounce) bag fresh spinach

    Salt and pepper to taste

In a large non-stick pot coated with non-stick cooking spray, sauté the carrots, celery, onion, and garlic for 5 to 7 minutes or until tender. Add the bay leaves, chicken broth, and tomatoes and bring to a boil.

Meanwhile make the Meatballs (see recipe). When the mixture boils, add the pasta and meatballs, cover, reduce heat and cook for about 12 minutes or until the meatballs are done. Add the spinach, stirring until wilted. Season with salt and pepper.

To Prepare and Eat Now: Eat when ready.

To Freeze: Cool to room temperature, then transfer to freezer containers, label, and freeze. Recommended freezing time: up to 3 to 4 months.

To Prepare After Freezing: Remove from freezer to defrost. Reheat in a non-stick pot over a low heat. Alternately, you can reheat in the microwave.

Meatballs

1   pound ground sirloin

½   pound ground pork

1   egg white, beaten

1   teaspoon minced garlic

⅓   cup grated Parmesan cheese

½   cup Italian breadcrumbs

½   teaspoon ground nutmeg

    Salt and pepper to taste

In a bowl, combine the sirloin, pork, egg white, garlic, Parmesan cheese, breadcrumbs, nutmeg, and salt and pepper. Form into meatballs.

NUTRITIONAL INFORMATION PER SERVING: *Calories 288, Protein (g) 25, Carbohydrate (g) 25, Fat (g) 10, Calories from Fat (%) 32, Saturated Fat (g) 4, Dietary Fiber (g) 3, Cholesterol (mg) 53, Sodium (mg) 853, Diabetic Exchanges: 3 lean meat, 1 starch, 2 vegetable*

Veal, Mushroom, and Barley Soup

A touch of dill gives this thick, rich, soup amazing flavor. It's perfect for cold days. Beef may be used instead of veal.

MAKES 6 SERVINGS

1	pound lean stewing veal, trimmed and cut into 2-inch chunks
1	large onion, finely chopped
½	cup finely chopped, peeled carrots
⅓	cup finely chopped celery
2	cups sliced mushrooms
8	cups canned fat-free chicken broth, plus more as needed
¾	cup pearl barley
1	teaspoon minced garlic
1	teaspoon dried dill leaves
	Salt and pepper to taste

Coat a large non-stick pot with non-stick cooking spray and brown the veal on all sides over medium heat, about 8 minutes. Remove the veal and set aside.

Add the onion, carrots, celery, and mushrooms and sauté until tender, about 5 to 7 minutes. Add the chicken broth, veal, and barley to the pot and bring to a boil. Cover loosely, reduce the heat, and simmer about 45 minutes. Add the garlic, dill leaves, and salt and pepper and continue simmering until the barley is tender, about 10 to 15 minutes. If the soup gets too thick, add more chicken broth.

To Prepare and Eat Now: Eat when ready.

To Freeze: Cool to room temperature, then transfer to freezer containers, label, and freeze. Recommended freezing time: up to 2 months.

To Prepare After Freezing: Remove from freezer to defrost. Reheat in a non-stick pot over a low heat. Alternately, you can reheat in the microwave.

NUTRITIONAL INFORMATION PER SERVING: *Calories 221, Protein (g) 22, Carbohydrate (g) 26, Fat (g) 3, Calories from Fat (%) 12, Saturated Fat (g) 1, Dietary Fiber (g) 7, Cholesterol (mg) 63, Sodium (mg) 599, Diabetic Exchanges: 2.5 very lean meat, 1.5 starch, 1 vegetable*

Black Bean Soup

Four ingredients make an excellent soup without any fuss. Serve with finely chopped red onion, cheese, and a dollop of fat-free sour cream, if desired.

MAKES 5 CUPS

2 (15-ounce) cans black beans, drained and rinsed

1½ cups vegetable broth

1 cup chunky salsa

1 teaspoon ground cumin

Combine the black beans, broth, salsa, and cumin in a blender and pulse until blended to the desired consistency.

Note:

Drain and rinse canned beans to reduce the sodium content.

To Prepare and Eat Now: Heat in the microwave or a non-stick pot over a low heat.

To Freeze: Transfer to freezer containers, label, and freeze. Recommended freezing time: up to 3 months.

To Prepare After Freezing: Remove from freezer to defrost. Heat in a non-stick pot over a low heat. Alternately, you can reheat in the microwave.

NUTRITIONAL INFORMATION PER SERVING: *Calories 166, Protein (g) 9, Carbohydrate (g) 27, Fat (g) 1, Calories from Fat (%) 8, Saturated Fat (g) 0, Dietary Fiber (g) 9, Cholesterol (mg) 0, Sodium (mg) 990, Diabetic Exchanges: 1 very lean meat, 1.5 starch, 1 vegetable*

Black-Eyed Pea Soup

Usher in the New Year with this quick soup that's perfect on a cold day.

MAKES ABOUT 7 CUPS

1   cup chopped celery

1   green bell pepper, seeded and chopped

1   cup chopped onion

1   (10-ounce) can chopped tomatoes and green chilies

2   (15.5-ounce) cans black-eye peas

2   cups beef broth or vegetable broth

In a large non-stick pot, coated with non-stick cooking spray, sauté the celery, green pepper, and onion until tender, about 5 to 7 minutes. Add the chopped tomatoes and green chilies, black-eye peas, and beef broth. Bring to a boil, reduce heat, and cook for about 20 minutes.

To Prepare and Eat Now: Eat when ready.

To Freeze: Cool to room temperature, then transfer to freezer containers, label, and freeze. Recommended freezing time: up to 3 months.

To Prepare After Freezing: Remove from freezer to defrost. Reheat in a non-stick pot over a low heat. Alternately, you can reheat in the microwave.

NUTRITIONAL INFORMATION PER SERVING: *Calories 125, Protein (g) 7, Carbohydrate (g) 23, Fat (g) 0, Calories from Fat (%) 0, Saturated Fat (g) 0, Dietary Fiber (g) 5, Cholesterol (mg) 0, Sodium (mg) 830, Diabetic Exchanges: 0.5 very lean meat, 1.5 starch, 1 vegetable*

Butternut Bisque with Ravioli

Bisque may be described as thick, rich soup and this full-bodied velvety soup topped with ravioli is one to remember. The ravioli may be omitted for an equally good Butternut Bisque.

MAKES 8 TO 10 CUPS

1   tablespoon butter

1   cup chopped onion

4   pounds butternut squash, peeled, pulp and seeds removed and cut into cubes

4   cups chicken broth or vegetable broth

    Pinch cinnamon

    Pinch nutmeg

4   ounces reduced-fat cream cheese

1   cup fat-free half and half or buttermilk

    Salt and pepper to taste

8   ounces cheese-filled ravioli

In a large non-stick pot, melt the butter and sauté the onion until tender. Add the squash, chicken broth, cinnamon, and nutmeg. Bring to a boil, lower heat, and simmer for about 15 minutes or until squash is tender.

In batches, pour soup with cream cheese into food processor or blender and puree until smooth. Season with salt and pepper.

To Prepare and Eat Now: Cook ravioli according to package directions, then add to the soup. Eat when ready.

To Freeze: Cool soup to room temperature, transfer to freezer containers, label, and freeze. Recommended freezing time: up to 3 months.

To Prepare After Freezing: Remove from freezer to defrost. Reheat in a non-stick pot over a low heat. Alternately, you can reheat in the microwave. Prepare ravioli according to package directions and add to heated bisque.

NUTRITIONAL INFORMATION PER SERVING: *Calories 209, Protein (g) 8, Carbohydrate (g) 32, Fat (g) 7, Calories from Fat (%) 28, Saturated Fat (g) 4, Dietary Fiber (g) 4, Cholesterol (mg) 26, Sodium (mg) 323, Diabetic Exchanges: 0.5 lean meat, 2 starch, 0.5 fat*

Cauliflower and Roasted Pepper Soup

When my husband and daughter asked for seconds, I knew this nutritious, tasty soup passed the test.

MAKES 6 CUPS

1	tablespoon olive oil
1	cup chopped onion
4½	cups vegetable or chicken broth, divided
1	head cauliflower, trimmed and cut into florets
¼	cup all-purpose flour
1½	cups shredded Monterey Jack cheese
⅓	cup jarred roasted pepper, chopped
	Salt and pepper to taste
	Hot sauce, as desired
	Chopped green onions (scallions)

In a large non-stick pot, heat oil and sauté onion for about 3 to 5 minutes or until tender. Add 4 cups broth and cauliflower, bringing to a boil, over medium heat. Reduce heat and cook for 10 minutes or until cauliflower is tender.

In a small bowl, whisk the remaining ½ cup chicken broth and flour. Add to the pot and cook, stirring constantly, until soup comes to a boil and thickens. Transfer soup in batches to a food processor or blender and pulse until almost pureed. Return to the pot and add the cheese and roasted pepper, stirring until the cheese is melted. Season with salt, pepper, and hot sauce.

To Prepare and Eat Now: Eat when ready with chopped green onions.

To Freeze: Cool to room temperature, then transfer to freezer containers, label, and freeze. Recommended freezing time: up to 4 months.

To Prepare After Freezing: Remove from freezer to defrost. Reheat in a non-stick pot over a low heat. Alternately, you can reheat in the microwave.

NUTRITIONAL INFORMATION PER SERVING: *Calories 169, Protein (g) 13, Carbohydrate (g) 13, Fat (g) 8, Calories from Fat (%) 41, Saturated Fat (g) 3, Dietary Fiber (g) 4, Cholesterol (mg) 15, Sodium (mg) 512, Diabetic Exchanges: 1 lean meat, 0.5 starch, 1.5 vegetable, 1 fat*

Creamy Cauliflower Soup 🥕

This outstanding creamy cauliflower soup has a buttery flavor from the Brie and resembles a potato soup. After rave reviews, I realized no one even realized the soup was made with cauliflower, making it a great way to sneak in veggies. To lower the fat content, you can use less Brie or leave it our altogether.

MAKES 10 CUPS

1   tablespoon olive oil

1   large head cauliflower, cut into small florets

1   onion, chopped

3   tablespoons all-purpose flour

4   cups vegetable or chicken broth

1   cup skim milk

½   teaspoon dried thyme leaves

6   ounces Brie cheese, rind removed

     Salt and pepper to taste

     Hot sauce

     Green onion stems or chives, optional

In a large non-stick pot, coated with non-stick cooking spray, heat the olive oil over medium heat. Add the cauliflower and onion, cooking for several minutes. Gradually add the flour and then stir in the chicken broth. Add the milk and cook for 5 to 7 minutes or until thickened and bubbly. Stir in the thyme and Brie, and season with salt and pepper, cooking only until the Brie is melted. Transfer to a food processor in batches and return to pot or puree using an emersion blender.

To Prepare and Eat Now: Eat when ready with chopped green onions.

To Freeze: Cool to room temperature, then transfer to freezer containers, label, and freeze. Recommended freezing time: up to 4 months.

To Prepare After Freezing: Remove from freezer to defrost. Reheat in a non-stick pot over a low heat. Alternately, you can reheat in the microwave. Serve with chopped green onions.

NUTRITIONAL INFORMATION PER SERVING: *Calories 120, Protein (g) 7, Carbohydrate (g) 9, Fat (g) 6, Calories from Fat (%) 46, Saturated Fat (g) 3, Dietary Fiber (g) 3, Cholesterol (mg) 18, Sodium (mg) 298, Diabetic Exchanges: 0.5 lean meat, 2 vegetable, 1 fat*

Cheddar Cheese Potato Soup

This potato soup with a touch of cheese makes a simple supper solution in no time at all. The cheese may be omitted for a traditional potato soup.

MAKES 6 CUPS

1	cup chopped onion
2	tablespoons all-purpose flour
2	cups skim milk
2½	cups canned chicken broth or vegetable broth
4	cups peeled and diced baking potatoes (about 2 large potatoes)
1	teaspoon dry mustard
1	cup shredded, reduced-fat sharp Cheddar cheese
	Salt and pepper to taste
	Chopped green onions (scallions)

In a large non-stick pot, coated with non-stick cooking spray, sauté the onion over medium heat for about 3 to 5 minutes, or until tender. Add the flour, stirring, for one minute. Gradually add the milk and broth, stirring to avoid lumps. Add the potatoes. Bring to a boil, stirring, reduce heat and cook for about 20 minutes or until potatoes or tender, stirring occasionally. Add the mustard and cheese, stirring and mashing the potatoes slightly until the cheese is melted. Season with salt and pepper.

To Prepare and Eat Now:
Eat when ready with chopped green onions.

To Freeze: Cool to room temperature, then transfer to freezer containers, label, and freeze. Recommended freezing time: up to 4 months.

To Prepare After Freezing:
Remove from freezer to defrost. Reheat in a non-stick pot over a low heat. Alternately, you can reheat in the microwave. Serve with chopped green onions.

NUTRITIONAL INFORMATION PER SERVING: *Calories 189, Protein (g) 12, Carbohydrate (g) 27, Fat (g) 4, Calories from Fat (%) 18, Saturated Fat (g) 2, Dietary Fiber (g) 3, Cholesterol (mg) 12, Sodium (mg) 323, Diabetic Exchanges: 1 lean meat, 1.5 starch, 1 vegetable*

Chicken Vermicelli page 184

Caramelized Onion Cheesecake **page 27**

Empanadas **page 32**

Meaty Biscuit Cups   page 34

Mini Muffin Rancheros **page 66**

Artichoke Cheese Toast **page 74**

Chicken Lentil Chili   **page 79**

Roasted Vegetable Minestrone   **page 128**

Beef Tenderloin Pizza with Horseradish Cream **page 150**

Cornbread and Rice Dressing **page 147**

Stuffed Potatoes Primavera **page 161**

Spinach and Corn Casserole **page 141**

Fiesta Enchiladas **page 158**

Chunky Chicken Divan   page 185

Potato Mushroom Soup

A popular potato soup gets intense with rich mushrooms and a touch of wine.

MAKES 6 CUPS

2	large potatoes, peeled and cut into ¼-inch cubes (4 cups)
3	cups vegetable broth
1	tablespoon butter
1	pound sliced baby portabella mushrooms
¼	pound shitake mushroom caps, sliced
⅓	cup finely chopped onions
½	cup skim milk
2	tablespoons Madeira or Marsala wine
	Salt and pepper to taste

In a large non-stick pot, combine the potatoes and broth. Bring to a boil, reduce heat, cover, and cook until potatoes are tender, around 15 minutes. Transfer mixture to a food processor and process until smooth. Return to pot.

Meanwhile, melt the butter in a non-stick skillet and sauté the mushrooms and onions until very tender, about 10 minutes. Stir this mixture into the potato mixture, add milk, stirring over medium heat until thoroughly heated. Add wine and season with salt and pepper.

To Prepare and Eat Now: Eat when ready.

To Freeze: Cool to room temperature, then transfer to freezer containers, label, and freeze. Recommended freezing time: up to 4 months.

To Prepare After Freezing: Remove from freezer to defrost. Reheat in a non-stick pot over a low heat. Alternately, you can reheat in the microwave.

NUTRITIONAL INFORMATION PER SERVING: *Calories 127, Protein (g) 5, Carbohydrate (g) 26, Fat (g) 1, Calories from Fat (%) 4, Saturated Fat (g) 0, Dietary Fiber (g) 4, Cholesterol (mg) 0, Sodium (mg) 489, Diabetic Exchanges: 1.5 starch, 1 vegetable*

Simply Spinach Soup

This light creamed spinach soup is heavenly served with toasted almonds and Parmesan cheese as toppers. Elegant enough for guests, we thoroughly enjoyed it for lunch and dinner one evening. Bagged spinach makes this a quick recipe.

MAKES 6 CUPS

Chilies, Stews, and Soups

2	tablespoons butter
1	cup chopped onion
½	cup finely chopped carrot
⅓	cup all-purpose flour
¼	teaspoon ground nutmeg
4	cups fat-free chicken or vegetable broth
1	cup skim milk
6	cups fresh baby spinach
1	(12-ounce) can evaporated fat-free milk
	Salt and pepper to taste
½	cup sliced almonds, toasted, optional
2	tablespoons grated Parmesan cheese

In a large non-stick pot, melt the butter and sauté the onion and carrot until tender, about 7 to 10 minutes. Add flour and nutmeg, stirring, and gradually add broth mixing until smooth. Add milk and bring to a boil over medium heat, stirring constantly until smooth and thickened, about 10 minutes. Add spinach and cook until it begins to wilt. Stir in evaporated milk and season with salt and pepper.

To Prepare and Eat Now: Eat when ready with toasted almonds and sprinkle with Parmesan cheese.

To Freeze: Cool to room temperature, then transfer to freezer containers, label, and freeze. Recommended freezing time: up to 4 months.

To Prepare After Freezing: Remove from freezer to defrost. Reheat in a non-stick pot over a low heat. Alternately, you can reheat in the microwave.

NUTRITIONAL INFORMATION PER SERVING: *Calories 158, Protein (g) 10, Carbohydrate (g) 19, Fat (g) 5, Calories from Fat (%) 27, Saturated Fat (g) 1, Dietary Fiber (g) 2, Cholesterol (mg) 5, Sodium (mg) 441, Diabetic Exchanges: 0.5 starch, 0.5 skim milk, 1 vegetable*

Southwestern Chicken Soup

Use leftover chicken or a rotisserie chicken to make this speedy chicken soup with a southwestern flair.

MAKES 6 SERVINGS

1 medium red onion, chopped

½ teaspoon minced garlic

2 (14.25 ounce) cans chicken broth or vegetable broth

1 (15.5 ounce) can great Northern beans, rinsed, and drained

1 (4-ounce) can chopped green chilies

2 teaspoons dried oregano leaves

1 teaspoon ground cumin

3 cups chopped cooked chicken

1 cup frozen corn

In a large non-stick pot coated with non-stick cooking spray, sauté the onion and garlic until tender, about 5 minutes. Add the chicken broth, beans, chilies, oregano, and cumin. Bring to a boil; reduce heat. Cover and simmer for 15 minutes. Add the chicken and corn. Cover and cook for 10 minutes more or until heated through.

To Prepare and Eat Now: Eat when ready.

To Freeze: Cool to room temperature, then transfer to freezer containers, label, and freeze. Recommended freezing time: up to 3 months.

To Prepare After Freezing: Remove from freezer to defrost. Reheat in a non-stick pot over a low heat. Alternately, you can reheat in the microwave.

NUTRITIONAL INFORMATION PER SERVING: *Calories 230, Protein (g) 28, Carbohydrate (g) 21, Fat (g) 3, Calories from Fat (%) 13, Saturated Fat (g) 1, Dietary Fiber (g) 7, Cholesterol (mg) 60, Sodium (mg) 566, Diabetic Exchanges: 3.5 very lean meat, 1 starch, 1 vegetable*

Chicken Tortilla Soup

No time to cook? Try this short cut version of one of our favorites. Pick up a rotisserie chicken for a time saver.

MAKES 6 SERVINGS

1½   pounds boneless, skinless chicken breasts, cut into 2-inch slices

1   onion, chopped

1   teaspoon minced garlic

6   cups canned fat-free chicken broth

1   (16-ounce) jar salsa

1   teaspoon chili powder

1   teaspoon ground cumin

2   tablespoons lime juice

1   (16-ounce bag) frozen corn

In a large non-stick pot coated with non-stick cooking spray, cook the chicken over medium heat, stirring constantly, until lightly browned, about 5 minutes. Add the onion and garlic and continue sautéing until tender, about 3 minutes. Add chicken broth, salsa, chili powder, cumin, and lime juice, bringing to a boil. Reduce heat and cook 10 minutes and add corn, cooking for a few more minutes.

Note:

To add a smoky flavor, use chipotle salsa or add 1 teaspoon chipotle chili flakes.

To Prepare and Eat Now: Eat when ready with tortilla strips, chopped avocado, and shredded reduced-fat Cheddar or Monterey Jack cheese.

To Freeze: Cool to room temperature, then transfer to freezer containers, label, and freeze. Recommended freezing time: up to 3 months.

To Prepare After Freezing: Remove from freezer to defrost. Reheat in a non-stick pot over a low heat. Alternately, you can reheat in the microwave. Serve with tortilla strips, chopped avocado, and shredded reduced-fat Cheddar or Monterey Jack cheese.

NUTRITIONAL INFORMATION PER SERVING: Calories 256, Protein (g) 32, Carbohydrate (g) 27, Fat (g) 2, Calories from Fat (%) 8, Saturated Fat (g) 1, Dietary Fiber (g) 4, Cholesterol (mg) 66, Sodium (mg) 760, Diabetic Exchanges: 3.5 very lean meat, 1.5 starch, 1 vegetable

Taco Soup

Canned vegetables and prepackaged seasoning make for a great simple supper solution. Try using reduced-sodium taco seasoning to lower sodium.

MAKES 8 CUPS

1 pound ground sirloin

2 (10-ounce) cans diced tomatoes and green chilies (mild)

1 (4-ounce) can chopped green chilies, drained

1 (15-ounce) can black beans, drained and rinsed

1 (15-ounce) can kidney beans, drained and rinsed

1 (1.25-ounce) package taco seasoning mix

Half (1-ounce) package original ranch salad dressing mix

2 cups water

2 cups frozen corn

In a large non-stick pot, over medium heat, cook the sirloin until done, about 5 minutes. Drain any excess grease. Add the tomatoes and green chilies, beans, taco seasoning mix, ranch dressing mix, water, and corn. Bring to a boil, reduce the heat, and cook for 5 to 10 minutes.

To Prepare and Eat Now: Eat when ready.

To Freeze: Cool to room temperature, then transfer to freezer containers, label, and freeze. Recommended freezing time: up to 4 months.

To Prepare After Freezing: Remove from freezer to defrost. Reheat in a non-stick pot over a low heat. Alternately, you can reheat in the microwave.

NUTRITIONAL INFORMATION PER SERVING: *Calories 269, Protein (g) 19, Carbohydrate (g) 32, Fat (g) 4, Calories from Fat (%) 14, Saturated Fat (g) 1, Dietary Fiber (g) 8, Cholesterol (mg) 30, Sodium (mg) 1102, Diabetic Exchanges: 2 very lean meat, 2 starch*

Southwestern Corn Chowder

This chowder includes nutritious sweet potatoes, corn, and southwestern seasonings, turning a classic dish into a spectacular southwestern meal.

MAKES 9 CUPS

1 onion, chopped

1 teaspoon minced garlic

1 green bell pepper, seeded and chopped

1 small red bell pepper, seeded and chopped

½ cup chopped celery

¼ cup all-purpose flour

4 cups fat-free chicken broth or vegetable broth

2 cups peeled, diced sweet potatoes

1 (1-pound) bag frozen corn

1½ teaspoons ground cumin

1 cup fat-free half and half

Salt and pepper to taste

Shredded, reduced-fat Cheddar cheese, optional

Chopped fresh cilantro, optional

In a large non-stick pot coated with non-stick cooking spray, sauté the onion, garlic, green and red pepper, and celery over medium heat until tender, about 6 minutes. Stir in flour, stirring for 1 minute. Gradually add chicken broth, stirring to combine. Add sweet potato, corn, and cumin, bringing to a boil. Reduce heat and cook about 20 minutes or until the potatoes are tender. Stir in half and half and serve. Season with salt and pepper.

To Prepare and Eat Now: Eat when ready with Cheddar cheese and cilantro.

To Freeze: Cool to room temperature, then transfer to freezer containers, label, and freeze. Recommended freezing time: up to 4 months.

To Prepare After Freezing: Remove from freezer to defrost. Reheat in a non-stick pot over a low heat. Alternately, you can reheat in the microwave. Serve with Cheddar cheese and cilantro.

NUTRITIONAL INFORMATION PER SERVING: *Calories 127, Protein (g) 6, Carbohydrate (g) 28, Fat (g) 1, Calories from Fat (%) 4, Saturated Fat (g) 0, Dietary Fiber (g) 4, Cholesterol (mg) 0, Sodium (mg) 225, Diabetic Exchanges: 2 starch*

Corn and Crab Chowder

Kids and adults savor every spoonful of this delicious chowder. For variations, add a pound of crabmeat.

MAKES 8 CUPS

1   tablespoon olive oil

1   tablespoon butter

4   cups peeled and diced baking potatoes (about 2 potatoes)

1   onion, chopped

1   red or green bell pepper, seeded and chopped

¼   cup all-purpose flour

½   teaspoon poultry seasoning

2   cups vegetable broth or chicken broth

3   cups skim milk

1   bay leaf

1   (16-ounce) package frozen corn

    Salt and pepper to taste

    Chopped green onions (scallions), optional

In a large non-stick pot, heat olive oil and butter over medium heat and cook potatoes, onion, and green pepper for 8 to 10 minutes, stirring until tender. Sprinkle with flour and poultry seasoning and cook for 1 minute. Gradually add broth, mixing well. Add milk and bay leaf. Bring mixture to a boil and add corn. Return to a boil, lower heat and cook for 5 to 10 minutes or until thick. Season with salt and pepper.

Note:

Old Bay Seasoning or turmeric may be used instead of poultry seasoning.

To Prepare and Eat Now: Eat when ready, garnished with green onions.

To Freeze: Cool to room temperature, then transfer to freezer containers, label, and freeze. Recommended freezing time: up to 4 months.

To Prepare After Freezing: Remove from freezer to defrost. Reheat in a non-stick pot over a low heat. Alternately, you can reheat in the microwave. Garnish with green onions before serving.

NUTRITIONAL INFORMATION PER SERVING: *Calories 201, Protein (g) 7, Carbohydrate (g) 37, Fat (g) 4, Calories from Fat (%) 16, Saturated Fat (g) 1, Dietary Fiber (g) 4, Cholesterol (mg) 2, Sodium (mg) 299, Diabetic Exchanges: 2 starch, 0.5 skim milk*

Corn and Wild Rice Soup

This thick hearty soup with wild rice and corn packs great taste and texture.

MAKES 8 SERVINGS

1 (6-ounce) package long grain and wild rice mix

2 pounds frozen corn, thawed

2 (14.5-ounce) cans vegetable or chicken broth, divided

3 tablespoons all-purpose flour

1 onion, chopped

½ cup finely diced, peeled carrots

1½ cups skim milk

Salt and pepper to taste

Prepare the wild rice according to the package directions, omitting any oil and salt; set aside.

Meanwhile, combine the corn, 1 can chicken broth, and flour in a food processor. Process until the mixture is puréed or the corn is thickened and creamy; set aside.

In a large non-stick pot coated with non-stick cooking spray, sauté the onion and carrots, cooking until the vegetables are tender, about 5 minutes. Add the corn mixture, wild rice, and the remaining can of chicken broth. Cook for 10 minutes or until very well heated. Add the milk and continue cooking until hot. Season with salt and pepper.

To Prepare and Eat Now: Eat when ready.

To Freeze: Cool to room temperature, then transfer to freezer containers, label, and freeze. Recommended freezing time: up to 3 months.

To Prepare After Freezing: Remove from freezer to defrost. Reheat in a non-stick pot over a low heat. Alternately, you can reheat in the microwave.

NUTRITIONAL INFORMATION PER SERVING: *Calories 232, Protein (g) 9, Carbohydrate (g) 51, Fat (g) 1, Calories from Fat (%) 5, Saturated Fat (g) 0, Dietary Fiber (g) 5, Cholesterol (mg) 1, Sodium (mg) 509, Diabetic Exchanges: 3 starch, 1 vegetable*

Sweet Potato Pear Soup

Take advantage of fall ingredients with this fabulous sweet potato based soup with a touch of ginger and orange and the nice crunch of pears. Apples may be substituted for the pears.

MAKES 8 CUPS

4   cups peeled and cubed sweet potatoes (yams)

2   cups peeled and cubed baking potatoes

4   cups chicken broth or vegetable broth

½   cup chopped onion

½   cup orange juice

     Salt and pepper to taste

2   tablespoons butter

2   Bartlett pears, peeled and chopped

½   teaspoon ground ginger

1   tablespoon orange liqueur, optional

½   cup buttermilk or fat-free half and half

In a large non-stick pot, combine both potatoes, chicken broth, and onion. Bring to a boil, reduce heat, and cook until potatoes are done, about 8 to 10 minutes. Transfer the mixture in batches to a food processor or blender and process until smooth. Return to the pot and add orange juice and season with salt and pepper.

To Prepare and Eat Now: In a non-stick skillet, melt the butter and sauté the pears for 5 minutes or until tender. Add the ginger. Add the pears to the puréed mixture and stir in the orange liqueur and buttermilk. Cook on low heat until thoroughly heated.

To Freeze: Cool soup to room temperature, then transfer to freezer containers, label, and freeze. Recommended freezing time: up to 3 months.

To Prepare After Freezing: Remove from freezer to defrost. Once defrosted, transfer to a non-stick pot. In a small non-stick skillet, melt the butter and sauté the pears for 5 minutes or until tender. Add the ginger. Add the pears to the puréed mixture and stir in the orange liqueur and buttermilk. Cook on low heat until thoroughly heated.

NUTRITIONAL INFORMATION PER SERVING: *Calories 161, Protein (g) 4, Carbohydrate (g) 30, Fat (g) 3, Calories from Fat (%) 18, Saturated Fat (g) 2, Dietary Fiber (g) 5, Cholesterol (mg) 8, Sodium (mg) 270, Diabetic Exchanges: 1.5 starch, 0.5 fruit, 0.5 fat*

Pear Gouda Soup 🥕

This pear soup with a touch of Gouda works great served warm in small cups for lunch or brunch. Top with toasted walnuts or even crisp chopped bacon for an added touch. Sprinkle with cracked pepper!

MAKES 2½ CUPS

2	ripe pears, cored, peeled and cut into chunks
1½	cups vegetable broth
½	teaspoon ground ginger
⅛	teaspoon nutmeg
1	tablespoon butter
1	tablespoon all-purpose flour
1	cup skim milk
4	ounces Gouda cheese (approx ¾ cup), cut into small pieces
1	cup apple juice
	Salt and pepper to taste

In a large non-stick saucepan, combine the pears, broth, ginger, and nutmeg. Bring to a boil over a medium heat, reduce heat, and simmer until pears are tender, about 10 minutes; set aside.

In a small non-stick saucepan, over low heat, melt the butter and stir in the flour. Gradually whisk in the milk, cooking over a medium heat, until mixture comes to a boil and thickens, stirring constantly. Add the cheese, stirring until the cheese is melted.

In a food processor, purée the pear mixture until smooth. Return mixture to the large saucepan and add the milk mixture. Add the apple juice, season with salt and pepper, and cook until thoroughly heated.

To Prepare and Eat Now: Eat when ready.

To Freeze: Cool to room temperature, then transfer to freezer containers, label, and freeze. Recommended freezing time: up to 4 months.

To Prepare After Freezing: Remove from freezer to defrost. Reheat in a non-stick pot over a low heat. Alternately, you can reheat in the microwave.

NUTRITIONAL INFORMATION PER SERVING: *Calories 190, Protein (g) 8, Carbohydrate (g) 21, Fat (g) 9, Calories from Fat (%) 40, Saturated Fat (g) 5, Dietary Fiber (g) 2, Cholesterol (mg) 33, Sodium (mg) 507, Diabetic Exchanges: 1 medium-fat meat, 1.5 fruit, 1 fat*

Split Pea and Pasta Soup

This soup tastes like an old family recipe, but has the updated ease of using canned soup as a base. My orthopedic doctor, Larry, insisted I taste this soup, and then I insisted he give me the recipe!

MAKES 5 TO 6 CUPS

2   slices center cut bacon, cut into small pieces, optional

½   cup chopped celery

½   cup chopped onion

2   (11.5-ounce) cans condensed split pea soup or any canned split pea soup

2   cups reduced-sodium chicken broth

1   cup water

1   cup cooked spaghetti, broken into 3 inch pieces

In a non-stick pot, cook the bacon for 3 minutes, stirring. Add the celery and onion sautéing until tender, about 5 minutes. Add the soup, broth, and water. Cook until well heated and bubbly over medium heat. Add cooked pasta.

To Prepare and Eat Now: Eat when ready. Sprinkle with grated Parmesan, if desired.

To Freeze: Cool to room temperature, then transfer to freezer containers, label, and freeze. Recommended freezing time: up to 3 months.

To Prepare After Freezing: Remove from freezer to defrost. Reheat in a non-stick pot over a low heat. Alternately, you can reheat in the microwave.

NUTRITIONAL INFORMATION PER SERVING: *Calories 228, Protein (g) 12, Carbohydrate (g) 38, Fat (g) 3, Calories from Fat (%) 13, Saturated Fat (g) 2, Dietary Fiber (g) 5, Cholesterol (mg) 4, Sodium (mg) 847, Diabetic Exchanges: 1 very lean meat, 2.5 starch*

Red Lentil Soup

Don't let lentils intimidate you, as this appealing soup is easily thrown together in about 30 minutes.

MAKES 8 CUPS

1   tablespoon olive oil

1   onion, chopped

1   tablespoon minced garlic

1   cup finely chopped carrots (about 2 carrots)

½   cup chopped celery

1   cup chopped tomatoes or canned tomatoes

1   teaspoon ground cumin

2   teaspoons grated fresh ginger

5   cups chicken or vegetable broth

1   cup dried red lentils

    Dash cayenne

    Salt to taste

2   tablespoons chopped fresh parsley

    Grated Parmesan cheese, optional

In a large non-stick pot, heat the olive oil and sauté the onion, garlic, carrots, and celery for 5 to 7 minutes or until tender. Add tomatoes, cumin, and ginger, sautéing for 2 minutes. Add the broth and lentils, continuing to cook about 20 minutes or until the lentils are tender. Transfer half of the mixture to a food processor and process until smooth. Return to pot and season with cayenne, salt, and parsley. Add more broth or water if it's too thick.

Note:

Lentils are a great source of fiber.

To Prepare and Eat Now: Eat when ready with grated Parmesan cheese.

To Freeze: Cool to room temperature, then transfer to freezer containers, label, and freeze. Recommended freezing time: up to 3 to 5 months.

To Prepare After Freezing: Remove from freezer to defrost. Reheat in a non-stick pot over a low heat. Alternately, you can reheat in the microwave. Serve with grated Parmesan cheese, if desired.

NUTRITIONAL INFORMATION PER SERVING: *Calories 133, Protein (g) 9, Carbohydrate (g) 20, Fat (g) 3, Calories from Fat (%) 17, Saturated Fat (g) 0, Dietary Fiber (g) 5, Cholesterol (mg) 0, Sodium (mg) 264, Diabetic Exchanges: 0.5 lean meat, 1 starch, 1 vegetable*

Tomato Basil Soup 🥕

Although simple to prepare, fresh basil is a must in this soup! Adjust the amount of basil according to your preference.

MAKES 4 CUPS

1	tablespoon olive oil
⅓	cup finely chopped onion
1	teaspoon minced garlic
1	(28-ounce) can chopped tomatoes, with juice
2	cups fat-free chicken or vegetable broth
1	cup loosely packed, chopped fresh basil
	Salt and pepper to taste
½	cup skim milk

In a large non-stick pot, heat the olive oil and sauté the onion and garlic over medium heat until tender, about 5 minutes. Add the tomatoes with their juice and the chicken broth. Bring to a boil, reduce the heat and cook until the soup is slightly thickened, about 20 minutes. Stir in the basil and season with salt and pepper. Transfer to a food processor and blend until very smooth. Return to pot and stir in milk.

To Prepare and Eat Now: Eat when ready.

To Freeze: Cool to room temperature, then transfer to freezer containers, label, and freeze. Recommended freezing time: up to 3 months.

To Prepare After Freezing: Remove from freezer to defrost. Reheat in a non-stick pot over a low heat. Alternately, you can reheat in the microwave.

NUTRITIONAL INFORMATION PER SERVING: *Calories 91, Protein (g) 4, Carbohydrate (g) 12, Fat (g) 4, Calories from Fat (%) 33, Saturated Fat (g) 1, Dietary Fiber (g) 1, Cholesterol (mg) 1, Sodium (mg) 749, Diabetic Exchanges: 2 vegetables, 1 fat*

Marvelous Minestrone with Tortellini

This is a great soup to make when veggies aren't in season. This meatless wonder is packed with an abundance of veggies in a light tomato broth with tortellini for a finishing touch. Sometimes, I toss in a can of white beans and sprinkle the top with Parmesan cheese before serving.

MAKES 10 CUPS

1   onion, chopped

1   teaspoon minced garlic

2   (14.5 ounce) cans diced tomatoes with Italian seasoning

1   cup coarsely chopped carrots

2   (14-ounce) cans vegetable broth

1   cup water

1   (9-ounce) package refrigerated tortellini

½   pound mushrooms, thinly sliced

2   cups zucchini, halved lengthwise and thinly sliced

1½   cups fresh baby spinach leaves

      Salt and pepper to taste

NUTRITIONAL INFORMATION PER SERVING: *Calories 129, Protein (g) 6, Carbohydrate (g) 22, Fat (g) 2, Calories from Fat (%) 16, Saturated Fat (g) 1, Dietary Fiber (g) 3, Cholesterol (mg) 11, Sodium (mg) 669, Diabetic Exchanges: 1 starch, 1.5 vegetable*

In a large non-stick pot coated with non-stick cooking spray, sauté the onion and garlic for several minutes. Add diced tomatoes, carrots, broth, and water. Bring to a boil, reduce heat and cover, simmering for 15 minutes or until carrots are tender. Transfer 1½ cups of mixture to a food processor and purée. Return the purée to the pot and add the tortellini, mushrooms, and zucchini. Bring to a boil, reduce heat and cover, cooking for 5 to 7 minutes or until vegetables are tender. Add the spinach and season with salt and pepper.

Note:

Add the tortellini and spinach after freezing when reheating for the best result.

To Prepare and Eat Now: Eat when ready.

To Freeze: Cool to room temperature, then transfer to freezer containers, label, and freeze. Recommended freezing time: up to 3 months.

To Prepare After Freezing: Remove from freezer to defrost. Reheat in a non-stick pot over a low heat. Alternately, you can reheat in the microwave.

Vegetable Soup

Every time I make this soup, I prepare it differently, depending on the vegetables I have on hand. Start with lean beef and use this recipe as a guide, adding your preferred veggies.

MAKES 8 TO 10 SERVINGS

2   pounds lean beef, cut into 2-inch cubes

1   onion, chopped

2   (14-ounce) cans beef broth

2   bay leaves

1   (46-ounce) can cocktail vegetable juice (low sodium if desired)

2   cups water

3   small red potatoes, peeled and cut in small cubes

1   sweet potato, peeled and cut into cubes

2   zucchini squash, cut into ½-inch slices

½   pound fresh green beans, ends pinched

2   cups broccoli florets

1   cup frozen corn

3   carrots, peeled and sliced

⅓   cup barley

    Salt and pepper to taste

In a large non-stick pot coated with non-stick cooking spray, cook the beef over medium heat, stirring often, until browned. Add onion, broth, and bay leaves. Bring to a boil, lower heat and simmer, covered, 30 to 40 minutes or until meat is almost tender. Add the vegetable juice, water, potatoes, squash, green beans, broccoli, corn, carrots, and barley. Return to a boil, lower heat, and cook, covered for 30 to 45 minutes or until veggies are tender and barley is done. Season with salt and pepper.

Note:

If you're preparing this to freeze, undercook the vegetables so they will cook when reheated.

To Prepare and Eat Now: Eat when ready.

To Freeze: Cool to room temperature, then transfer to freezer containers, label, and freeze. Recommended freezing time: up to 2 to 3 months.

To Prepare After Freezing: Remove from freezer to defrost. Reheat in a non-stick pot over a low heat. Alternately, you can reheat in the microwave.

NUTRITIONAL INFORMATION PER SERVING: *Calories 259, Protein (g) 23, Carbohydrate (g) 26, Fat (g) 7, Calories from Fat (%) 24, Saturated Fat (g) 2, Dietary Fiber (g) 6, Cholesterol (mg) 56, Sodium (mg) 751, Diabetic Exchanges: 2.5 lean meat, 1 starch, 2 vegetable*

Roasted Vegetable Minestrone

Roasted veggies add so much flavor to this outstanding earthy, rich, Italian vegetable soup.

MAKES 12 CUPS

1   medium zucchini, cut in chunks

2   medium yellow squash, cut in chunks

1   medium eggplant, peeled and cut into chunks (about 1 ¼ pounds)

5   Roma tomatoes cut into chunks

1   red onion, cut into chunks

6   garlic cloves, peeled

4   carrots, peeled and sliced

2   tablespoons olive oil

    Salt and pepper to taste

2   ounces prosciutto, diced

1   teaspoon dried oregano leaves

1   teaspoon dried basil leaves

    Dash red pepper flakes

2   bay leaves

1   (14.5-ounce) can whole tomatoes in juice, broken up

9   cups chicken broth

1   (16-ounce) can cannelloni beans or white beans, rinsed and drained

⅔ cup short tubular pasta

    Grated Parmesan cheese, optional

NUTRITIONAL INFORMATION PER SERVING: *Calories 142, Protein (g) 7, Carbohydrate (g) 21, Fat (g) 4, Calories from Fat (%) 23, Saturated Fat (g) 1, Dietary Fiber (g) 6, Cholesterol (mg) 4, Sodium (mg) 531, Diabetic Exchanges: 0.5 starch, 3 vegetable, 1 fat*

Preheat the oven to 400°F.

On a baking sheet covered with foil, place the zucchini, squash, eggplant, tomatoes, red onion, garlic, and carrots. Toss the vegetables with the olive oil and salt and pepper. Roast for 45 minutes to 1 hour, stirring the vegetables after 30 minutes. Remove from the oven; set aside.

In a large non-stick pot coated with non-stick cooking spray, cook the prosciutto, oregano, basil, and red pepper flakes over medium heat for 1 minute, stirring. Add the bay leaves, tomatoes, broth and white beans. Bring mixture to a boil and add the pasta. Lower heat and simmer for 15 minutes or until the pasta is done. Add vegetables, remove bay leaves, and check seasoning.

To Prepare and Eat Now: Eat when ready with Parmesan cheese. If the soup is too thick, add more chicken broth or water.

To Freeze: Cool to room temperature, then transfer to freezer containers, label, and freeze. Recommended freezing time: up to 3 months.

To Prepare After Freezing: Remove from freezer to defrost. Reheat in a non-stick pot over a low heat. Alternately, you can reheat in the microwave. Serve with Parmesan cheese. If the soup is too thick, add more chicken broth or water.

Southwestern Vegetable Soup

This tomato-based vegetable soup is an easy vegetarian soup with southwestern seasonings.

MAKES 6 SERVINGS

1   cup chopped onion

1   teaspoon minced garlic

2   cups sliced, peeled carrots

1   pound red potatoes, peeled and cut into small chunks

2   (14.5-ounce) cans vegetable broth

1   (15-ounce) can no-salt-added tomato sauce

1½ cups mild salsa

2   teaspoons dried oregano leaves

2   teaspoons ground cumin

1   (10-ounce) package frozen corn

½   cup sliced green onions (scallions), for garnish

½   cup shredded, reduced-fat Monterey Jack cheese, for garnish

In a large non-stick pot coated with non-stick cooking spray, sauté the onion and garlic until tender over medium heat, about 3 to 5 minutes. Add the carrots, potatoes, vegetable broth, tomato sauce, salsa, oregano, cumin, and corn. Bring the mixture to a boil, lower the heat, and simmer for 20 minutes, or until the carrots and potatoes are tender.

To Prepare and Eat Now: Garnish with green onions and cheese and eat when ready.

To Freeze: Cool to room temperature, then transfer to freezer containers, label, and freeze. Recommended freezing time: up to 4 months.

To Prepare After Freezing: Remove from freezer to defrost. Reheat in a non-stick pot over a low heat. Alternately, you can reheat in the microwave. Serve with green onions and Monterey Jack.

NUTRITIONAL INFORMATION PER SERVING: *Calories 187, Protein (g) 8, Carbohydrate (g) 34, Fat (g) 2, Calories from Fat (%) 12, Saturated Fat (g) 1, Dietary Fiber (g) 7, Cholesterol (mg) 5, Sodium (mg) 989, Diabetic Exchanges: 0.5 lean meat, 1 starch, 4 vegetable*

Tuscan Bean Soup

Packed with flavor, veggies, and barley, this sensational soup is perfect for a cold night.

MAKES 10 SERVINGS

1	tablespoon olive oil
1	onion, chopped
1	green bell pepper, seeded and chopped
2	teaspoons minced garlic
2	tablespoons all-purpose flour
1	teaspoon dried rosemary leaves
¼	teaspoon dried thyme leaves
1	bay leaf
2	tablespoons tomato paste
8	cups fat-free chicken broth or vegetable broth
½	cup medium pearl barley
1	large baking potato, peeled and cut into ½-inch chunks
1	cup sliced carrots
2	(15-ounce) cans cannelloni or Great Northern beans, rinsed and drained
2	cups packed fresh baby spinach leaves
	Salt and pepper to taste

In a large non-stick pot, heat olive oil and sauté the onion, green pepper, and garlic over medium heat until tender, about 7 minutes. Sprinkle with flour, stirring for one minute. Add rosemary, thyme, bay leaf, tomato paste, and chicken broth, stirring and heating to a boil. Add barley, reduce heat, cover, and simmer for 15 minutes. Add the potato and carrot and continue cooking for 20 minutes. Add beans and spinach and continue cooking for 10 minutes until well heated. If the soup gets too thick, add more broth. Season with salt and pepper and remove bay leaf.

To Prepare and Eat Now: Eat when ready.

To Freeze: Cool to room temperature, then transfer to freezer containers, label, and freeze. Recommended freezing time: up to 3 months.

To Prepare After Freezing: Remove from freezer to defrost. Reheat in a non-stick pot over a low heat. Alternately, you can reheat in the microwave.

NUTRITIONAL INFORMATION PER SERVING: *Calories 174, Protein (g) 8, Carbohydrate (g) 31, Fat (g) 2, Calories from Fat (%) 11, Saturated Fat (g) 0, Dietary Fiber (g) 7, Cholesterol (mg) 0, Sodium (mg) 497, Diabetic Exchanges: 0.5 very lean meat, 2 starch*

Quick Bean Veggie Soup

Veggies, beans, corn, and a touch of ham are the main ingredients for this simple tasty soup.

MAKES 10 CUPS

1   cup chopped green onions (scallions)

4   ounces lean ham, chopped

2   cups sliced zucchini (about 2 zucchini)

2   cups frozen corn

1   (4-ounce) can chopped green chilies, drained

2   (15-ounce) cans white navy beans, rinsed and drained

5   cups chicken broth or vegetable broth

In a large non-stick pot coated with non-stick cooking spray, cook the green onions and ham over medium heat about 4 minutes, stirring. Add the zucchini, corn, green chilies, beans, and chicken broth. Bring to a boil, reduce heat, and simmer for 10 minutes.

Note:

Canned vegetables generally provide as much dietary fiber and nutrients as their cooked fresh and frozen counterparts.

To Prepare and Eat Now: Eat when ready.

To Freeze: Cool to room temperature, then transfer to freezer containers, label, and freeze. Recommended freezing time: up to 3 months.

To Prepare After Freezing: Remove from freezer to defrost. Reheat in a non-stick pot over a low heat. Alternately, you can reheat in the microwave.

NUTRITIONAL INFORMATION PER SERVING: *Calories 163, Protein (g) 11, Carbohydrate (g) 28, Fat (g) 1, Calories from Fat (%) 8, Saturated Fat (g) 0, Dietary Fiber (g) 7, Cholesterol (mg) 6, Sodium (mg) 730, Diabetic Exchanges: 1 very lean meat, 2 starch*

Seafood Gumbo

Browned flour is used for the roux, giving this gumbo a toasty flavor without the usual fat. Use available seafood or what you prefer in the gumbo. I happen to like using crab fingers, crab, and shrimp, but fish and oysters may also be added.

MAKES 12 SERVINGS

¾   cup all-purpose flour

1   tablespoon minced garlic

2   onions, chopped

2   green bell peppers, seeded and chopped

½   cup chopped celery

5   cups water

4   cups fat-free chicken broth

1   (10-ounce) can diced tomatoes and green chilies

2   bay leaves

¼   teaspoon cayenne

2   whole cloves, optional

2   pounds small to medium shrimp, peeled

1   pint claw crabmeat

     Salt and pepper to taste

½   cup chopped green onions (scallions)

NUTRITIONAL INFORMATION PER SERVING: *Calories 141, Protein (g) 18, Carbohydrate (g) 11, Fat (g) 2, Calories from Fat (%) 14, Saturated Fat (g) 0, Dietary Fiber (g) 2, Cholesterol (mg) 132, Sodium (mg) 429, Diabetic Exchanges: 2.5 very lean meat, 0.5 starch, 1 vegetable*

Preheat oven to 400°F.

Place flour on a non-stick baking sheet and bake for 20 to 30 minutes, stirring every 7 minutes, or until flour is brown (color of pecan shells). This also works well in a toaster oven.

Meanwhile, coat a large non-stick pot with non-stick cooking spray and sauté garlic, onion, peppers, and celery until tender. Gradually add browned flour, stirring. Gradually add water, broth, tomatoes, bay leaves, cayenne, and cloves. Bring to boil; lower heat and cook for 20 minutes. Add shrimp, return to boil, and cook for 5 to 7 minutes or until shrimp is done. Add the crabmeat. Add green onions, and season with salt and pepper. Discard bay leaves and cloves before serving.

To Prepare and Eat Now: Eat when ready over rice.

To Freeze: Cool to room temperature, then transfer to freezer containers, label, and freeze. Recommended freezing time: up to 2 months.

To Prepare After Freezing: Remove from freezer to defrost. Reheat in a non-stick pot over a low heat. Alternately, you can reheat in the microwave.

Shrimp, Crab, and Corn Soup

This easy to make soup will wow your family and friends. Sometimes, I substitute a pound of shrimp for the claw crabmeat for an equally great version.

MAKES 14 SERVINGS

1	onion chopped
1	green bell pepper, seeded and chopped
1	teaspoon minced garlic
2	tablespoons all-purpose flour
2	(10.75-ounce) cans cream style corn
1	(10-ounce) can diced tomatoes and green chilies
2	cups chicken broth or vegetable broth
1	cup skim milk
1	(8-ounce) package reduced-fat cream cheese, softened
2	pounds medium shrimp, peeled
1½	cups frozen corn
1	cup claw crabmeat, picked for shells
¼	cup chopped fresh parsley
1	bunch green onions (scallions), sliced

In a heavy, large, non-stick pot coated with non-stick cooking spray, sauté onion, and green pepper until tender, about 5 minutes. Add garlic. Sprinkle with flour, stirring for one minute. Gradually add cream style corn, tomatoes and chilies, broth, and milk, heating for several minutes. Add cream cheese and stir until melted. Add the shrimp and corn, bring to a boil, reduce heat, and cook until shrimp are done, about 5 to 7 minutes. Stir in parsley and green onions, cooking until well heated.

To Prepare and Eat Now: Eat when ready.

To Freeze: Cool to room temperature, then transfer to freezer containers, label, and freeze. Recommended freezing time: up to 2 months.

To Prepare After Freezing: Remove from freezer to defrost. Reheat in a non-stick pot over a low heat. Alternately, you can reheat in the microwave.

NUTRITIONAL INFORMATION PER SERVING: Calories 178, Protein (g) 16, Carbohydrate (g) 17, Fat (g) 5, Calories from Fat (%) 26, Saturated Fat (g) 3, Dietary Fiber (g) 3, Cholesterol (mg) 117, Sodium (mg) 483, Diabetic Exchanges: 2 lean meat, 1 starch

Sides and More

Freezing, Thawing, and Preparing Sides and More

❄ **Casseroles:** Recommended freezing for 3 months.

❄ **Pizza:** Prepare as usual, but do not bake. Recommended freezing for 1 month.

❄ **Sauces:** Tomato sauces freeze well. Mayonnaise-based sauces don't freeze well because they separate.

❄ **Sweet Potatoes:** Bake sweet potatoes, wrap, label, and freeze. Recommended freezing time: 3 months.

❄ **Tomatoes:** For extra tomatoes, purée and de-seed raw tomatoes in a juicer or a food mill so you'll be able to make sauce all year long. After puréeing, chill in the refrigerator to ensure that it will freeze evenly and then store in a resealable bag in the freezer.

❄ **Veggies:** Frozen vegetables may be cooked directly from the freezer but cooking times should be only one-half to two thirds as long as fresh. Don't overcook. Cooked, creamed vegetables lose flavor rapidly and are not recommended for freezer storage.

Baked Beans

Canned beans make this a great version of savory sweet beans.

1   onion, chopped

1   green pepper, seeded and chopped

½   cup light brown sugar

½   cup tomato sauce

1   tablespoon molasses

2   tablespoons Worcestershire sauce

2   (15-ounce) cans red kidney beans, rinsed and drained

2   (19-ounce) cans small white beans, rinsed and drained

Salt and pepper to taste

In large non-stick skillet coated with non-stick cooking spray, sauté the onion and green pepper until tender, about 5 to 7 minutes. Combine with brown sugar, tomato sauce, molasses, Worcestershire sauce, kidney beans, white beans, and salt and pepper; pour into a 2 or 3-quart baking dish.

To Prepare and Eat Now: Preheat the oven to 350°F. Bake for 40 to 50 minutes until bubbly.

To Freeze: Cool to room temperature, then transfer to freezer containers, label, and freeze. Recommended freezing time: up to 3 to 4 months.

To Prepare After Freezing: Remove from freezer to defrost. Reheat in a non-stick pot over a low heat. Alternately, you can reheat in the microwave.

NUTRITIONAL INFORMATION PER SERVING: *Calories 217, Protein (g) 12, Carbohydrate (g) 46, Fat (g) 1, Calories from Fat (%) 4, Saturated Fat (g) 0, Dietary Fiber (g) 10, Cholesterol (mg) 0, Sodium (mg) 670, Diabetic Exchanges: 1 very lean meat, 3 starch*

Southwestern Rice

This wonderfully creamy rice goes southwestern with green chilies and cheese.

MAKES 8 TO 10 SERVINGS

Sides and More

1   onion, chopped

5   cups cooked rice

2   cups nonfat plain yogurt

1   cup reduced-fat cottage cheese

1   cup shredded, reduced-fat sharp Cheddar cheese

2   (4-ounce) cans diced green chilies, drained

    Salt and pepper to taste

In a non-stick skillet coated with non-stick cooking spray, sauté onion until tender. Combine with rice, yogurt, cottage cheese, cheese, green chilies, and salt and pepper. Place into a 2-quart casserole dish coated with non-stick cooking spray.

To Prepare and Eat Now: Preheat the oven to 350°F. Bake for 20 minutes or until well heated.

To Freeze: Do not bake before freezing. Cool to room temperature, then transfer to freezer containers, label, and freeze. Recommended freezing time: up to 2 to 3 months.

To Prepare After Freezing: Remove from freezer to defrost. Preheat the oven to 350°F. Bake for 25 to 35 minutes or until heated through.

NUTRITIONAL INFORMATION PER SERVING: *Calories 188, Protein (g) 11, Carbohydrate (g) 29, Fat (g) 3, Calories from Fat (%) 13, Saturated Fat (g) 2, Dietary Fiber (g) 1, Cholesterol (mg) 8, Sodium (mg) 286, Diabetic Exchanges: 1 lean meat, 2 starch*

Green Bean Casserole

This traditional green bean casserole is topped with sautéed golden onions and bread crumbs for an updated appeal.

MAKES 6 SERVINGS

½   teaspoon canola oil

1   large onion, thinly sliced

1   small onion, finely chopped

½   pound sliced mushrooms

½   teaspoon minced garlic

¼   cup all-purpose flour

2   cups skim milk

    Pinch ground nutmeg

¼   cup fat-free sour cream

2   (9-ounce) packages frozen green beans

½   cup fresh breadcrumbs or Italian breadcrumbs

    Salt and pepper to taste

In a large non-stick skillet, heat oil over low heat. Add sliced onion and cook, stirring occasionally, for 20 to 30 minutes, or until very tender and golden; set aside.

In another large non-stick pot coated with non-stick cooking spray, sauté the chopped onion, mushrooms, and garlic and cook, stirring, for 3 to 5 minutes, or until tender. Sprinkle flour over the vegetables and cook, stirring, for 1 minute. Slowly pour in milk, whisking constantly. Add nutmeg. Bring to a boil, reduce heat to low and cook, stirring until thickened. Remove from heat. Whisk in sour cream. Season with salt and pepper. Add green beans, mixing well. Transfer to a 2-quart baking dish coated with non-stick cooking spray. In a small bowl, toss together the reserved onions and breadcrumbs and spread over the beans.

To Prepare and Eat Now: Preheat the oven to 425°F. Bake for 15 to 20 minutes, or until bubbling.

To Freeze: Do not bake before freezing. Cool to room temperature, wrap, label, and freeze. Recommended freezing time: up to 3 to 4 months.

To Prepare After Freezing: Remove from freezer to defrost. Preheat the oven to 425°F. Bake for 20 to 30 minutes, or until bubbling.

NUTRITIONAL INFORMATION PER SERVING: *Calories 126, Protein (g) 7, Carbohydrate (g) 23, Fat (g) 1, Calories from Fat (%) 5, Saturated Fat (g) 0, Dietary Fiber (g) 4, Cholesterol (mg) 3, Sodium (mg) 169, Diabetic Exchanges: 0.5 starch, 0.5 skim milk, 2 vegetable*

Spinach Casserole

This all around spinach casserole is a pleaser with any meal. If you'd like, add artichoke hearts for a Spinach and Artichoke Casserole.

MAKES 8 TO 10 SERVINGS

4   (10-ounce) packages frozen chopped spinach, thawed

1   tablespoon butter

1   onion, chopped

½   pound sliced mushrooms (use baby portabella, if available)

2   tablespoons all-purpose flour

1   cup skim milk

½   cup spinach liquid, reserved from cooking spinach

4   ounces reduced-fat pasteurized, processed cheese spread

    Salt and pepper to taste

Cook the spinach according to package directions. Drain well, reserving ½ cup spinach liquid; set aside. In a large non-stick skillet, heat the butter and sauté the onion and mushrooms until tender. Add the flour, stirring, and gradually stir in the milk and spinach liquid, cooking over medium heat until thick and bubbly. Add the cheese, stirring until melted. Season with salt and pepper.

To Prepare and Eat Now: Serve.

To Freeze: Cool to room temperature, transfer to freezer container, label and freeze. Recommended freezing time: up to 2 to 3 months.

To Prepare After Freezing: Remove from freezer to defrost. In a non-stick pot, heat spinach over low heat or heat, covered, in an oven preheated to 350°F. for 20 minutes or until heated through.

NUTRITIONAL INFORMATION PER SERVING: *Calories 99, Protein (g) 8, Carbohydrate (g) 11, Fat (g) 4, Calories from Fat (%) 29, Saturated Fat (g) 2, Dietary Fiber (g) 4, Cholesterol (mg) 10, Sodium (mg) 181, Diabetic Exchanges: 0.5 lean meat, 2 vegetable, 0.5 fat*

Spinach and Corn Casserole

Cream style corn and spinach produce this delicious and colorful combination. This recipe doubles well.

MAKES 4 SERVINGS

1   (10-ounce) package frozen chopped spinach

½   cup chopped onion

1   (15-ounce) can cream style corn

¼   cup bread crumbs

1   tablespoon grated Parmesan cheese

1   tablespoon butter, melted

Cook the spinach according to package directions, drain very well.

In a small non-stick skillet coated with non-stick cooking spray, sauté the onion until tender. Combine the onion, corn, and spinach, mixing well. Transfer to a 1-quart baking dish coated with non-stick cooking spray.

In a small bowl, combine the bread crumbs, Parmesan cheese, and butter. Sprinkle over the vegetable mixture.

To Prepare and Eat Now: Preheat the oven to 350°F. Bake, covered, for 15 to 20 minutes or until thoroughly heated. Uncover for 5 minutes to brown.

To Freeze: Cool to room temperature, wrap, label, and freeze. Recommended freezing time: up to 2 to 3 months.

To Prepare After Freezing: Remove from freezer to defrost. Preheat the oven to 350°F. Bake, covered, for 20 to 25 minutes, then uncover for 5 minutes to brown.

NUTRITIONAL INFORMATION PER SERVING: *Calories 164, Protein (g) 6, Carbohydrate (g) 27, Fat (g) 5, Calories from Fat (%) 25, Saturated Fat (g) 2, Dietary Fiber (g) 4, Cholesterol (mg) 9, Sodium (mg) 448, Diabetic Exchanges: 1.5 starch, 1 vegetable, 1 fat*

Sides and More

Triple Corn Pudding

This combination of corn, cream style corn, and corn muffin mix creates a wonderful and moist baked corn casserole.

MAKES 8 SERVINGS

2 tablespoons butter, melted

¾ cup fat-free sour cream

1 egg

½ cup chopped onion

2 cups frozen corn, thawed

1 (15-ounce) can cream style corn

1 (8.5-ounce) box corn muffin mix

Preheat the oven to 350°F. Coat a 9-inch square baking dish with non-stick cooking spray.

In a large bowl, mix together the butter, sour cream, and egg until blended. Stir in the onion, corn, cream style corn, and muffin mix, mixing well. Pour into prepared baking dish and bake for 45 minutes to 1 hour or until mixture is set and light brown on top.

To Prepare and Eat Now: Serve when ready.

To Freeze: Cool to room temperature, wrap, label, and freeze. Recommended freezing time: up to 2 to 3 months.

To Prepare After Freezing: Remove from freezer to defrost. Preheat the oven to 350°F. Bake, covered, for about 30 minutes or until cheese is melted and well heated.

NUTRITIONAL INFORMATION PER SERVING: *Calories 269, Protein (g) 7, Carbohydrate (g) 44, Fat (g) 8, Calories from Fat (%) 27, Saturated Fat (g) 4, Dietary Fiber (g) 3, Cholesterol (mg) 50, Sodium (mg) 418, Diabetic Exchanges: 3 starch, 1 fat*

Macaroni and Cheese

Sometimes, I make my version of everyone's favorite comfort food to clean out all my cheeses from the fridge—from Mozzarella, American, or whatever I have on hand. I think the combination of cheeses is what makes this Macaroni and Cheese so fantastic! Any pasta may be used.

MAKES 8 SERVINGS

1 (1-pound) package penne pasta

½ cup finely chopped onion

1 teaspoon minced garlic

¼ cup all-purpose flour

2 cups skim milk

Salt and pepper to taste

Dash cayenne

1 cup shredded, reduced-fat Cheddar cheese

1 cup shredded Swiss cheese

¼ cup grated Asiago or Parmesan cheese

Prepare the pasta according to package directions; drain and set aside.

In a medium non-stick pot coated with non-stick cooking spray, sauté the onion and garlic for 5 minutes until very tender. Stir in the flour and gradually add the milk, stirring constantly. Cook over a medium heat, until bubbly and thickened. Remove from heat and add salt and pepper, cayenne, Cheddar and Swiss cheeses. Combine with the pasta. Transfer macaroni mixture to a 2-quart baking dish coated with non-stick cooking spray and sprinkle with Asiago cheese.

To Prepare and Eat Now: Preheat the oven to 350°F. Bake for 15 to 20 minutes or until cheese is melted and well heated.

To Freeze: Do not bake before freezing. Cool to room temperature, wrap, label, and freeze. Recommended freezing time: up to 3 months.

To Prepare After Freezing: Remove from freezer to defrost. Preheat the oven to 350°F. Bake for 20 to 30 minutes or until cheese is melted and well heated

NUTRITIONAL INFORMATION PER SERVING: *Calories 360, Protein (g) 18, Carbohydrate (g) 50, Fat (g) 9, Calories from Fat (%) 22, Saturated Fat (g) 5, Dietary Fiber (g) 2, Cholesterol (mg) 25, Sodium (mg) 191, Diabetic Exchanges: 2 lean meat, 3.5 starch*

Italian Macaroni and Cheese

Marinara sauce, cheese, and pasta make this a quick variation to everyone's favorite comfort food.

MAKES 6 TO 8 SERVINGS

1   pound ziti pasta

1   (26-ounce) jar marinara pasta sauce

1   cup nonfat sour cream

    Salt and pepper to taste

4   ounces sliced provolone cheese, cut into pieces

1   cup shredded, part-skim Mozzarella cheese

Cook pasta according to package directions; drain. Coat a 2-quart oblong baking dish with non-stick cooking spray.

In a large bowl, combine the pasta, marinara sauce, sour cream, and season with salt and pepper. Spread half the pasta mixture in the prepared dish. Lay half the provolone slices over the pasta and sprinkle with all the Mozzarella cheese. Cover with remaining pasta mixture and remaining provolone.

To Prepare and Eat Now: Preheat the oven to 350°F. Bake for 25 to 20 minutes or until bubbly.

To Freeze: Do not bake before freezing. Cool to room temperature, wrap, label, and freeze. Recommended freezing time: up to 3 months.

To Prepare After Freezing: Remove from freezer to defrost. Preheat the oven to 350°F. Bake for 30 to 40 minutes or until bubbly.

NUTRITIONAL INFORMATION PER SERVING: *Calories 379, Protein (g) 18, Carbohydrate (g) 56, Fat (g) 9, Calories from Fat (%) 22, Saturated Fat (g) 4, Dietary Fiber (g) 3, Cholesterol (mg) 24, Sodium (mg) 616, Diabetic Exchanges: 1.5 lean meat, 3 starch, 2 vegetable*

Noodle Pudding (Kugel) 🥕

This traditional cream cheese noodle pudding, known as kugel, has a sweet rich flavor and makes a nice side to meat dishes.

MAKES 12 TO 16 SERVINGS

1 (8-ounce) package wide noodles

3 tablespoons butter, melted

½ cup sugar

1 cup reduced-fat cottage cheese

4 ounces reduced-fat cream cheese

1 cup nonfat plain yogurt

1 egg

2 egg whites

½ teaspoon vanilla extract

Coat a non-stick 9 x 9 x 2-inch baking pan with non-stick cooking spray.

Boil noodles according to directions on package, omitting oil. Rinse, drain, and combine with butter, tossing evenly. Place noodles in prepared pan.

In food processor or mixer, combine sugar, cottage cheese, cream cheese, yogurt, egg, egg whites, and vanilla, beating until smooth. Combine with noodles, mixing well.

To Prepare and Eat Now: Preheat the oven to 350°F. Bake, covered, for 45 minutes for 1 hour or until thoroughly heated. Uncover for the last five minutes.

To Freeze: This can be frozen either before or after baking. Cool to room temperature, wrap, label, and freeze. Recommended freezing time: up to 3 months.

To Prepare After Freezing: Remove from freezer to defrost. Preheat the oven to 350°F. If it has not been baked prior to freezing, bake, covered, for 45 minutes for 1 hour or until thoroughly heated. Uncover for the last five minutes. If baked before freezing, reheat in a preheated 350°F. oven for 30 minutes or until thoroughly heated.

NUTRITIONAL INFORMATION PER SERVING: *Calories 140, Protein (g) 6, Carbohydrate (g) 18, Fat (g) 5, Calories from Fat (%) 30, Saturated Fat (g) 3, Dietary Fiber (g) 0, Cholesterol (mg) 39, Sodium (mg) 129, Diabetic Exchanges: 0.5 very lean meat, 1 starch, 1 fat*

Smothered Okra

This simple southern recipe is prepared effortlessly. If using fresh okra, slice off the ends and cut into pieces. However, I usually use frozen, already cut okra.

MAKES 6 SERVINGS

Sides and More

1   onion, chopped

⅓   cup diced, reduced-fat smoked sausage

½   teaspoon minced garlic

2   pounds frozen cut okra

1   (10-ounce) can diced tomatoes and green chilies

In a large non-stick pot coated with non-stick cooking spray, sauté the onion and sausage over medium heat until done, about 5 to 7 minutes. Add the garlic, okra, and tomatoes, cooking over a medium heat, covered, until done or until the okra is tender, about 20 minutes.

To Prepare and Eat Now: Eat when ready.

To Freeze: Cool to room temperature, then transfer to freezer containers, label, and freeze. Recommended freezing time: up to 2 months.

To Prepare After Freezing: Defrost or place directly from the freezer into a non-stick pot, and cook over a low heat until thoroughly heated. Alternately, you can reheat in the microwave.

NUTRITIONAL INFORMATION PER SERVING: *Calories 72, Protein (g) 4, Carbohydrate (g) 15, Fat (g) 1, Calories from Fat (%) 7, Saturated Fat (g) 0, Dietary Fiber (g) 4, Cholesterol (mg) 3, Sodium (mg) 256, Diabetic Exchanges: 3 vegetable*

Cornbread and Rice Dressing

Cornbread and wild rice combined with sautéed seasoning make this the ultimate dressing.

MAKES 12 TO 16 SERVINGS

2   (6-ounce) packages long grain and wild rice mix

1   (8.5-ounce) box cornbread mix

1   cup chopped celery

2   green bell peppers, seeded and chopped

1   onion, chopped

1   bunch green onions (scallions), chopped

1   tablespoon poultry seasoning

    Salt and pepper to taste

1   (16-ounce) can vegetable or chicken broth

Cook the wild rice according to package directions, omitting the butter and salt.

Prepare the cornbread according to package directions. Crumble the cornbread.

In a large non-stick skillet coated with non-stick cooking spray, sauté the celery, green peppers, and onion until tender. Pour into a large bowl and combine with the wild rice, cornbread, green onions, poultry seasoning, and salt and pepper. Mix in the broth. Transfer to a baking dish.

To Prepare and Eat Now: Preheat the oven to 350°F. Bake, covered, for about 45 minutes or until thoroughly heated.

To Freeze: Do not bake before freezing. Cool to room temperature, wrap, label, and freeze. Recommended freezing time: up to 2 months.

To Prepare After Freezing: Remove from freezer to defrost. Preheat the oven to 350°F. Bake, covered, for about 50 to 55 minutes or until thoroughly heated.

NUTRITIONAL INFORMATION PER SERVING: *Calories 205, Protein (g) 5, Carbohydrate (g) 41, Fat (g) 2, Calories from Fat (%) 10, Saturated Fat (g) 0, Dietary Fiber (g) 2, Cholesterol (mg) 2, Sodium (mg) 654, Diabetic Exchanges: 2.5 starch, 1 vegetable*

Old-Fashioned Cornbread Dressing 🥕

Cross dressing off your holiday menu and make ahead and freeze.

MAKES 8 TO 10 SERVINGS

2	(8.5-ounce) boxes corn muffin mix
4	eggs, divided
⅔	cup skim milk
8	slices white bread, toasted and crusts removed
1	cup chopped onion
1	cup chopped celery
2	egg whites, slightly beaten
2	cups canned vegetable or chicken broth
1	teaspoon poultry seasoning
	Pinch sugar
	Salt and pepper to taste
1	bunch green onions (scallions), chopped

Prepare the corn muffin mix with 2 eggs and milk and bake in a 13 x 9 x 2-inch pan coated with non-stick cooking spray according to package directions. Crumble and set aside.

Crumble the white bread.

In a small non-stick skillet coated with non-stick cooking spray, sauté the onion and celery over medium heat for 5 to 7 minutes or until tender.

In a large bowl, combine the crumbled corn bread and white bread, sautéed vegetables, 2 eggs, egg whites, chicken broth, poultry seasoning, sugar, and salt and pepper, mixing well. Transfer to a 2-quart baking dish coated with non-stick cooking spray.

To Prepare and Eat Now: Preheat the oven to 350°F. and bake for about 45 minutes or until heated through.

To Freeze: Do not cook before freezing. Cool to room temperature, wrap, label, and freeze. Recommended freezing time: up to 2 months.

To Prepare After Freezing: Remove from freezer to defrost. Preheat the oven to 350°F. Sprinkle dressing with green onions and bake for about 45 minutes or until heated through.

NUTRITIONAL INFORMATION PER SERVING: *Calories 307, Protein (g) 9, Carbohydrate (g) 47, Fat (g) 9, Calories from Fat (%) 25, Saturated Fat (g) 2, Dietary Fiber (g) 5, Cholesterol (mg) 86, Sodium (mg) 792, Diabetic Exchanges: 3 starch, 1 fat*

Eggplant Casserole

Eggplant fans will enjoy this quick version of Eggplant Parmesan baked in a casserole. I have substituted American cheese for Mozzarella (although Mozzarella may be used).

MAKES 4 SERVINGS

1½   pounds eggplant, peeled and cut into ½-inch cubes

1   cup chopped onion

1   cup chopped green bell pepper

3   slices reduced-fat American cheese, cut into strips

1   (8-ounce) can tomato sauce

½   cup Italian breadcrumbs

In a large non-stick skillet coated with non-stick cooking spray, sauté the eggplant, onion, and green pepper until tender, about 12 to 15 minutes. Place the eggplant mixture in the bottom of a 1½-quart baking dish coated with non-stick cooking spray. Place cheese strips on top of the eggplant. Pour the tomato sauce on top and sprinkle with the breadcrumbs.

To Prepare and Eat Now: Preheat the oven to 350°F. Bake for 30 to 40 minutes or until the casserole is bubbly.

To Freeze: Do not bake before freezing. Cool to room temperature, wrap, label, and freeze. Recommended freezing time: up to 2 to 3 months.

To Prepare After Freezing: Remove from freezer to defrost. Preheat the oven to 350°F. Bake for 35 to 45 minutes or until the casserole is bubbly.

NUTRITIONAL INFORMATION PER SERVING: *Calories 179, Protein (g) 8, Carbohydrate (g) 29, Fat (g) 4, Calories from Fat (%) 19, Saturated Fat (g) 2, Dietary Fiber (g) 8, Cholesterol (mg) 23, Sodium (mg) 805, Diabetic Exchanges: 1 starch, 3 vegetable, 0.5 fat*

Beef Tenderloin Pizza with Horseradish Cream

A bite of this pizza makes you feel like you are dining at a fancy steak restaurant, enjoying a filet with a heavenly horseradish sauce. For alternate toppings, try smoked salmon and capers.

MAKES 8 SERVINGS

4	ounces reduced-fat cream cheese
1	cup nonfat sour cream
1 to 2	tablespoons prepared horseradish sauce, depending on taste
1/3	cup chopped red onion
2	teaspoons lemon juice
	Dash hot sauce
	Salt and pepper to taste
1	12-inch Boboli or pizza crust
1	cup shredded, part-skim Mozzarella cheese
8	ounces cooked, medium-rare beef tenderloin, sliced
1	tablespoon chopped chives

NUTRITIONAL INFORMATION PER SERVING: *Calories 206, Protein (g) 14, Carbohydrate (g) 20, Fat (g) 7, Calories from Fat (%) 31, Saturated Fat (g) 4, Dietary Fiber (g) 1, Cholesterol (mg) 31, Sodium (mg) 330, Diabetic Exchanges: 1.5 lean meat, 1.5 starch, 0.5 fat*

In a mixing bowl, combine the cream cheese, sour cream, and horseradish. Stir in the red onion, lemon juice, hot sauce, and season with salt and pepper. Spread evenly on top of the pizza crust. Sprinkle with Mozzarella cheese.

Note:

The meat has to be placed on the pizza after the pizza is baked or the meat will be overdone.

To Prepare and Eat Now: Preheat the oven to 425°F. Bake for 10 to 12 minutes or until bubbly. Top with tenderloin and sprinkle with chives. Serve immediately.

To Freeze: Do not cook before freezing. After topping with cheese, wrap, label, and freeze. Recommended freezing time: up to 6 weeks.

To Prepare After Freezing: Preheat the oven to 425°F. Place frozen pizza into the oven and bake for 12 to 15 minutes or until bubbly. Top with tenderloin and sprinkle with chives. Serve immediately.

White Spinach Pizza

A white sauce topped with spinach, herbs, and cheeses makes a wonderful variation from classic pizza. Leave off the spinach for a cheese pizza or add whatever toppings you like.

MAKES 8 SERVINGS

1 (10-ounce) package frozen chopped spinach

1 cup skim milk

3 tablespoons all-purpose flour

Salt and pepper to taste.

½ teaspoon minced garlic

1 (12-inch) thin pizza crust

½ teaspoon dried basil leaves

½ teaspoon dried oregano leaves

¼ cup crumbled feta cheese

½ cup shredded, part-skim Mozzarella cheese

Cook the spinach according to the package directions, and drain well.

In a small non-stick pot, combine the milk and flour over medium heat, stirring until thickened. Season with salt and pepper and add garlic. Spread this sauce over crust. Top with spinach. Sprinkle with basil, oregano, feta, and Mozzarella cheese.

To Prepare and Eat Now: Preheat the oven to 425°F. Bake for 10 minutes or until crust is golden brown and cheese is melted.

To Freeze: Do not bake before freezing. Wrap, label, and freeze. Recommended freezing time: up to 6 weeks.

To Prepare After Freezing: Preheat the oven to 425°F. Place frozen pizza into the oven and bake for 10 to 15 minutes or until cheese is melted and bubbly.

NUTRITIONAL INFORMATION PER SERVING: *Calories 156, Protein (g) 9, Carbohydrate (g) 21, Fat (g) 4, Calories from Fat (%) 25, Saturated Fat (g) 2, Dietary Fiber (g) 2, Cholesterol (mg) 9, Sodium (mg) 322, Diabetic Exchanges: 0.5 lean meat, 1.5 starch*

Cheese Stuffed Manicotti

This wonderful red sauce smothers the cheesy manicotti, making this a great vegetarian standby for a luncheon or dinner.

MAKES 12

Sides and More

1	cup chopped onion
½	cup chopped green bell pepper
½	cup shredded carrots
½	pound mushrooms, sliced
½	cup sliced celery
1	teaspoon minced garlic
1	(14.5-ounce) can chopped tomatoes, with their juice
1	(10.75-ounce) can tomato purée
½	cup water
1	teaspoon dried oregano leaves
1	teaspoon dried basil leaves
½	teaspoon sugar
	Salt and pepper to taste
12	manicotti shells
	Cheese Filling (recipe follows)

In a medium non-stick saucepan, combine onion, green pepper, carrots, mushrooms, celery, and garlic, cooking until the vegetables are tender, about 7 minutes. Stir in the tomatoes, tomato purée, water, oregano, basil, sugar, and salt and pepper. Bring to a boil. Reduce heat, cover and simmer for 15 minutes, stirring occasionally.

Meanwhile, cook the manicotti shells according to the package directions omitting any oil and salt. Drain well. Fill each manicotti shell with about ⅓ cup of the Cheese Filling (see recipe). Arrange the filled shells in a 3-quart rectangular baking dish coated with non-stick cooking spray. Pour the sauce over the filled shells.

To Prepare and Eat Now: Preheat the oven to 350°F. Bake for 35 to 40 minutes or until heated through.

To Freeze: Do not bake before freezing. Cool to room temperature, wrap, label, and freeze. Recommended freezing time: up to 3 months.

To Prepare After Freezing: Remove from freezer to defrost. Preheat the oven to 350°F. Bake for 40 to 45 minutes or until heated through.

NUTRITIONAL INFORMATION PER SERVING: *Calories 163, Protein (g) 10, Carbohydrate (g) 22, Fat (g) 4, Calories from Fat (%) 24, Saturated Fat (g) 3, Dietary Fiber (g) 2, Cholesterol (mg) 20, Sodium (mg) 226, Diabetic Exchanges: 1 lean meat, 1 starch, 1.5 vegetable*

It's a Fact!

Canned tomatoes can contain anywhere from two to ten times more available lycopene as the same amount of fresh tomatoes.

Cheese Filling

2	large egg whites, beaten
1	(15-ounce) container part-skim ricotta cheese
1	cup shredded, part-skim Mozzarella cheese
2	tablespoons chopped parsley
½	teaspoon dried basil leaves
½	teaspoon dried oregano leaves
	Salt and pepper to taste

In a mixing bowl, combine the egg whites, ricotta, Mozzarella, parsley, basil, oregano, and salt and pepper.

Spinach Manicotti 🥕

These manicotti shells stuffed with a spinach-cheese filling and topped with a light fresh tomato sauce, make a magnificent meatless entrée.

MAKES 8 SERVINGS

1   (8-ounce) package manicotti shells

1   (10-ounce) package frozen chopped spinach

1   (16-ounce) container reduced-fat ricotta cheese

1   egg white, beaten

    Salt and pepper to taste

    Dash of ground nutmeg

½   cup shredded, part-skim Mozzarella cheese

1   teaspoon olive oil

1   cup chopped tomatoes

½   teaspoon minced garlic

1   onion, chopped

Cook the manicotti shells according to package directions, omitting oil and salt. Drain and set aside.

Meanwhile, cook the spinach according to package directions; drain well, squeezing out excess liquid.

In a bowl, combine the spinach with the ricotta, egg white, salt and pepper, nutmeg, and Mozzarella. Stuff the cooked shells with the spinach-cheese mixture and place in a 2-quart oblong baking dish coated with non-stick cooking spray.

To Prepare and Eat Now: Preheat the oven to 350°F. In a non-stick pan coated with non-stick cooking spray, heat the oil over medium heat and sauté the tomato, garlic, and onion until tender. Pour over the manicotti. Bake, covered, for 30 to 35 minutes.

To Freeze: Do not bake before freezing. Wrap, label, and freeze. Recommended freezing time: up to 3 months.

To Prepare After Freezing: Remove from freezer to defrost. Preheat the oven to 350°F. In a small non-stick pan coated with non-stick cooking spray, heat the oil over medium heat and sauté the tomato, garlic, and onion until tender, about five minutes. Pour over the manicotti. Bake, covered for 35 to 45 minutes.

NUTRITIONAL INFORMATION PER SERVING: *Calories 208, Protein (g) 12, Carbohydrate (g) 28, Fat (g) 5, Calories from Fat (%) 21, Saturated Fat (g) 2, Dietary Fiber (g) 2, Cholesterol (mg) 18, Sodium (mg) 131, Diabetic Exchanges: 1 lean meat, 1.5 starch, 1 vegetable*

Spinach Lasagna

Spinach, red sauce, and ricotta make a great meatless lasagna.

MAKES 8 SERVINGS

1   cup chopped onion

½   pound mushrooms, sliced

1   teaspoon minced garlic

1   (15-ounce) can tomato sauce

1   (14.5-ounce) can Italian-style tomatoes, drained and chopped

    Salt and pepper to taste

1   teaspoon dried basil leaves

1   teaspoon dried oregano leaves

1   bay leaf

1   (8-ounce) package lasagna noodles

2   (10-ounce) packages frozen chopped spinach, thawed and drained

1   (15-ounce) container reduced-fat ricotta cheese

1   large egg white, slightly beaten

1 ¼ cups shredded, reduced-fat Monterey Jack cheese

NUTRITIONAL INFORMATION PER SERVING: *Calories 294, Protein (g) 20, Carbohydrate (g) 36, Fat (g) 9, Calories from Fat (%) 26, Saturated Fat (g) 5, Dietary Fiber (g) 4, Cholesterol (mg) 35, Sodium (mg) 681, Diabetic Exchanges: 2 lean meat, 1.5 starch, 3 vegetable, 0.5 fat*

In a large non-stick saucepan over medium heat, sauté the onion, mushrooms, and garlic until tender, about 5 minutes. Add the tomato sauce, tomatoes, salt and pepper, basil, oregano, and bay leaf. Bring to a boil. Cover, reduce heat, and simmer 5 minutes, stirring occasionally. Remove the bay leaf, and set aside.

Cook the lasagna noodles according to the package directions, omitting any oil and salt. Drain well; set aside. Combine the spinach, ricotta, and egg white, mixing well; set aside.

Coat a 13 x 9 x 2-inch baking pan with non-stick cooking spray. Spread one-third of the tomato mixture on the bottom of the pan. Layer half of the lasagna noodles and then half of the spinach mixture. Repeat the layers.

To Prepare and Eat Now: Preheat the oven to 350°F. Bake, covered, for 40 minutes; uncover and bake for 10 minutes.

To Freeze: Do not bake before freezing. Cool to room temperature, wrap, label, and freeze. Recommended freezing time: up to 3 months.

To Prepare After Freezing: Remove from freezer to defrost. Preheat the oven to 350°F. Bake, covered, for 45 minutes; uncover and bake for 10 minutes.

Wonderful Won Ton Ravioli 🥕

Little won ton triangles filled with a mild corn cheese mixture transform into stuffed ravioli served with a light tomato sauce.

MAKES 16 SERVINGS

Sides and More

2   tablespoons finely chopped onion

1   cup frozen corn

2   tablespoons diced green chilies

½   teaspoon ground cumin

1   cup shredded, reduced-fat Monterey Jack cheese

    Salt and pepper to taste

48 won ton wrappers

    Tomato Sauce (recipe follows)

In a non-stick skillet coated with non-stick cooking spray, sauté the onion over low heat, stirring, until softened. Add the corn, stirring, for 2 minutes. Remove from the heat and stir in the chilies and cumin. Stir in the Monterey Jack and season with salt and pepper. Set aside to cool.

Place won ton wrapper on a lightly floured surface, mound 1 tablespoon of the filling in the center of the wrapper, and fold over to make a triangle. Pat the edges with water and press down around the filling to force out the air, sealing the edges well. Repeat with remaining wrappers and filling.

To Prepare and Eat Now:
Bring a pot of salted water to a gentle boil and add the ravioli in batches. Cook about 2 to 3 minutes or until tender. They will rise to the surface when they're done. (Do not let the water boil vigorously once the ravioli have been added). With a slotted spoon, transfer the cooked ravioli to a single layer on pan lined with paper towel. Serve with Tomato Sauce.

To Freeze: After stuffing raviolis, freeze them on a baking sheet in the freezer. Once they're frozen, transfer them to freezer zip-top bags. Extra cooked raviolis with Tomato Sauce may be frozen also. Recommended freezing time: up to 2 to 3 months.

To Prepare After Freezing:
Bring a pot of salted water to a gentle boil and add the frozen ravioli in batches. Cook about 2 to 3 minutes or until tender. They will rise to the surface when they're done. (Do not let the water boil vigorously once the ravioli have been added). With a slotted spoon, transfer the cooked ravioli to a single layer on pan lined with paper towel. Prepare the Tomato Sauce and serve over the ravioli.

It's a Fact!

Tomatoes are a great source of Vitamins A and C and potassium.

Tomato Sauce

1   tablespoon butter

½   teaspoon minced garlic

1   (28-ounce) can chopped tomatoes, drained

1   teaspoon lime juice

Salt and pepper to taste

In a non-stick skillet, melt the butter and cook the garlic, stirring for 1 minute. Add the tomatoes, and bring to a boil, stirring, for 10 minutes, or until it is thick. Stir in the lime juice, and season with salt and pepper. Serve with ravioli.

NUTRITIONAL INFORMATION PER SERVING: *Calories 118, Protein (g) 5, Carbohydrate (g) 19, Fat (g) 2, Calories from Fat (%) 19, Saturated Fat (g) 1, Dietary Fiber (g) 2, Cholesterol (mg) 8, Sodium (mg) 135, Diabetic Exchanges: 1.5 starch*

Fiesta Enchiladas 🥕

These simple ingredients of spinach, corn, Mozzarella, and ricotta create an exciting filling for these vegetarian enchiladas.

MAKES 6 SERVINGS

1½ cups shredded, part-skim Mozzarella cheese, divided

1 (10-ounce) package frozen chopped spinach, thawed and squeezed dry

1¼ cups frozen corn, thawed

1 cup chopped onion

½ teaspoon minced garlic

Salt and pepper to taste

1 (15-ounce) container reduced-fat ricotta cheese

1 egg white

12 (8-inch) flour or flavored tortillas

1 (16-ounce) jar salsa

In a large bowl, mix 1 cup of the Mozzarella and the spinach, corn, onion, garlic, salt and pepper, ricotta, and egg white. Place ⅓ cup of the mixture evenly down the center of each tortilla. Roll the tortillas and arrange them, seam side down, in a 3-quart casserole oblong dish coated with non-stick cooking spray. Pour the salsa over the filled tortillas and sprinkle with the remaining Mozzarella.

To Prepare and Eat Now: Preheat the oven to 375°F. Bake, covered, for 40 to 50 minutes or until the tortillas are heated through and the cheese is melted.

To Freeze: Do not bake before freezing. Cool to room temperature, wrap, label, and freeze. Recommended freezing time: up to 2 to 3 months.

To Prepare After Freezing: Remove from freezer to defrost. Preheat the oven to 375°F. Bake, covered, 50 minutes to 1 hour, or until the tortillas are heated through and the cheese is melted.

NUTRITIONAL INFORMATION PER SERVING: *Calories 240, Protein (g) 12, Carbohydrate (g) 37, Fat (g) 5, Calories from Fat (%) 17, Saturated Fat (g) 2, Dietary Fiber (g) 4, Cholesterol (mg) 18, Sodium (mg) 627, Diabetic Exchanges: 1 lean meat, 2 starch, 1.5 vegetable*

Easy Potato Casserole 🥕

Throw these few ingredients together for one of those "wow" potato casseroles when there's no time to cook.

MAKES 10 TO 12 SERVINGS

1   (32-ounce) bag frozen hash brown potatoes

1   (12-ounce) container low-fat cottage cheese

1   cup buttermilk

1   tablespoon cornstarch

1   bunch green onions (scallions), chopped

    Salt and pepper to taste

1½ cups shredded, part-skim Mozzarella cheese

    Paprika

Coat a 3-quart casserole dish with non-stick cooking spray.

In a large bowl, combine the hash brown potatoes, cottage cheese, buttermilk, cornstarch, green onions, salt and pepper, and cheese, mixing well. Transfer to the prepared dish. Sprinkle with paprika.

To Prepare and Eat Now: Preheat the oven to 350°F. and bake for 1 hour and 15 minutes or until bubbly.

To Freeze: Do not cook before freezing. Wrap, label, and freeze. Recommended freezing time: up to 2 to 3 months.

To Prepare After Freezing: Remove from freezer to defrost. Preheat the oven to 350°F. Bake, covered, for about 1 hour 30 minutes to 1 hour 40 minutes or until the casserole is bubbly. You can also bake this directly from the freezer. Just place the casserole in a cold oven and bake at 350°F., covered, for about 1 hour 45 minutes or until bubbly.

NUTRITIONAL INFORMATION PER SERVING: Calories 132, Protein (g) 9, Carbohydrate (g) 17, Fat (g) 3, Calories from Fat (%) 19, Saturated Fat (g) 2, Dietary Fiber (g) 2, Cholesterol (mg) 11, Sodium (mg) 244, Diabetic Exchanges: 1 lean meat, 1 starch

Sides and More

Mashed Potatoes

This epitome of comfort food freezes well and reheats easily in the microwave. Add garlic, cheese, or any seasoning to this basic recipe for a variation.

MAKES 8 SERVINGS

Sides and More

3   pounds baking potatoes, peeled and cut into chunks

2   tablespoons butter

1   cup skim milk

Salt and pepper to taste

Place the potatoes in a large pot and cover with water. Bring to a boil, reduce heat, and simmer, covered for 25 minutes or until tender. Drain, and return the potatoes to the pot and mash with a potato masher. Add the butter and gradually stir in the milk until creamy. Season with salt and pepper.

Note:
Scoop mashed potato single servings onto a cookie sheet and freeze. Transfer frozen mashed potato balls to a freezer zip-top bag to pull out as needed.

To Prepare and Eat Now:
Serve when ready.

To Freeze: Cool to room temperature, then transfer to freezer container, label, and freeze. Recommended freezing time: up to 1 to 2 months.

To Prepare After Freezing:
Remove from freezer to defrost. Reheat in a non-stick pot over a low heat. Add more milk if mixture is too thick. Alternately, you can reheat in the microwave.

NUTRITIONAL INFORMATION PER SERVING: *Calories 162, Protein (g) 4, Carbohydrate (g) 31, Fat (g) 3, Calories from Fat (%) 16, Saturated Fat (g) 2, Dietary Fiber (g) 3, Cholesterol (mg) 8, Sodium (mg) 39, Diabetic Exchanges: 2 starch, 1/2 fat*

Stuffed Potatoes Primavera 🥕

These loaded potatoes are a great way to enjoy veggies. Use whatever veggies you like. To serve these as whole potatoes, cut a thin slice off the top of each potato lengthwise and you've got a great main dish!

MAKES 12

6	medium baking potatoes
2	tablespoons butter
½	cup skim milk
	Salt and pepper to taste
½	cup chopped green onions (scallions)
1 ½	cups shredded, part-skim Mozzarella cheese
2	cups small broccoli florets
2	cups coarsely chopped yellow squash
1	cup chopped green bell pepper
1	cup chopped onion
1	cup chopped tomatoes
¼	cup balsamic vinegar
1	teaspoon dried basil leaves

Preheat the oven to 400°F.

Wash and scrub the potatoes. Bake for 1 hour or until soft when squeezed. Cut each baked potato in half lengthwise. Scoop out the inside, leaving a thin shell. In a large bowl, mash the potato flesh with the butter and milk, mixing until creamy. Season with salt and pepper. Stir in the green onions and Mozzarella.

Meanwhile, in a large non-stick skillet coated with non-stick cooking spray, sauté the broccoli, squash, green peppers, onions, tomatoes, vinegar, and basil over medium heat for 7 to 10 minutes or until the vegetables are tender. Carefully fold the vegetables into the potato mixture. Stuff the potato shells with the mixture.

To Prepare and Eat Now: Preheat the oven to 350°F. Bake potatoes on a baking sheet for 15 to 20 minutes or until well heated.

To Freeze: Do not bake before freezing. Cool to room temperature, wrap individually, label, and freeze in freezer zip-top bags. Recommended freezing time: up to 1 to 2 months.

To Prepare After Freezing: Remove from freezer to defrost. Preheat the oven to 350°F. Bake potatoes on a baking sheet for 20 to 25 minutes or until well heated.

NUTRITIONAL INFORMATION PER SERVING: *Calories 138, Protein (g) 6, Carbohydrate (g) 20, Fat (g) 4, Calories from Fat (%) 28, Saturated Fat (g) 3, Dietary Fiber (g) 2, Cholesterol (mg) 14, Sodium (mg) 117, Diabetic Exchanges: 0.5 lean meat, 1 starch, 1 vegetable, 0.5 fat*

Stuffed Southwestern Potatoes

Potatoes turn southwestern stuffed with green chilies, corn, and cheese.

MAKES 6 SERVINGS

3   medium baking potatoes

2   tablespoons butter

2   tablespoons skim milk

½   cup fat-free sour cream or nonfat plain yogurt

1   (4-ounce) can diced green chilies

1½ cups frozen corn, thawed

⅓   cup chopped green onions (scallions)

1   cup shredded, reduced-fat Cheddar cheese or Monterey Jack cheese

    Paprika

Preheat the oven to 400°F.

Wash potatoes well and dry thoroughly. With a fork, prick the potato skins over the entire surface. Place potatoes directly on the oven rack, and bake for approximately 1 hour or until soft when squeezed. Let the potatoes cool so you can handle them, then cut each potato in half lengthwise and scoop out the inside, leaving a thin shell.

In a mixing bowl, mash potatoes with butter, skim milk, and sour cream, mixing well. Stir in green chilies, corn, green onions, and cheese, combining well. Spoon mixture into shells. Sprinkle with paprika.

To Prepare and Eat Now: Eat when ready.

To Freeze: Do not bake before freezing. Cool to room temperature, wrap individually, label, and freeze. Recommended freezing time: up to 1 to 2 months

To Prepare After Freezing: Remove from freezer to defrost. Preheat the oven to 350°F. Bake for approximately 15 minutes or until the cheese is melted and the potatoes are hot.

NUTRITIONAL INFORMATION PER SERVING: Calories 213, Protein (g) 10, Carbohydrate (g) 28, Fat (g) 8, Calories from Fat (%) 31, Saturated Fat (g) 5, Dietary Fiber (g) 3, Cholesterol (mg) 24, Sodium (mg) 243, Diabetic Exchanges: 1 very lean meat, 2 starch, 1 fat

Sides and More

Stuffed Sweet Potatoes 🥕

These sinfully yummy stuffed sweet potatoes with a crumbly topping are great to pull out of the freezer.

MAKES 4 TO 6 SERVINGS

3 pounds small to medium sweet potatoes (yams), unpeeled

½ cup light brown sugar, divided

½ teaspoon ground cinnamon, divided

¼ cup golden raisins

3 tablespoons butter, divided

¼ cup skim milk

2 teaspoons vanilla extract, divided

¼ cup all-purpose flour

⅓ cup chopped pecans

Preheat the oven to 400°F.

Place potatoes on a baking sheet and cook for 1 hour or until tender. Cut a thin slice off the top of each potato. Carefully scoop pulp into a bowl, leaving ¼-inch thick shells. Mash pulp; add ¼ cup light brown sugar, ¼ teaspoon cinnamon, raisins, 1 tablespoon of the butter, milk, and 1 teaspoon of vanilla, mixing until smooth. Spoon mixture evenly into potato shells.

Melt remaining 2 tablespoons butter and combine with the flour, remaining brown sugar, pecans, remaining vanilla, and remaining cinnamon. Crumble evenly over potatoes.

To Prepare and Eat Now: Preheat the oven to 350°F. Bake for 15 to 20 minutes or until topping is browned and potatoes are thoroughly heated.

To Freeze: Do not bake before freezing. Wrap individually and freeze in zip-top bags. Recommended freezing time: up to 4 months.

To Prepare After Freezing: Remove from freezer to defrost. Preheat the oven to 350°F. Bake for 20 to 25 minutes or until topping is browned and potato thoroughly heated.

NUTRITIONAL INFORMATION PER SERVING: *Calories 457, Protein (g) 5, Carbohydrate (g) 85, Fat (g) 11, Calories from Fat (%) 21, Saturated Fat (g) 4, Dietary Fiber (g) 8, Cholesterol (mg) 15, Sodium (mg) 131, Diabetic Exchanges: 4 starch, 1/2 fruit, 1 other carbohydrate, 1.5 fat*

Sweet Potato Casserole with Crumbly Praline Topping

Fresh sweet potatoes are hard to pass by during the fall season but canned sweet potatoes work equally well. Every bite of the velvety sweet potatoes topped with a brown sugar crumbly topping is an indulgence too good to save for only holidays.

MAKES 8 TO 10 SERVINGS

3   cups cooked, mashed, sweet potatoes (yams)

½   cup sugar

1   egg

1   egg white

1   (5-ounce) can evaporated skimmed milk

1   teaspoon vanilla extract

      Praline Topping (recipe follows)

In a mixing bowl, blend together the potatoes, sugar, egg, egg white, milk and vanilla until smooth. Place in a 2-quart casserole dish coated with non-stick cooking spray and cover with Praline Topping (see recipe).

Praline Topping

1   cup light brown sugar

⅔   cup all-purpose flour

½   teaspoon ground cinnamon

6   tablespoons butter, melted

1   teaspoon vanilla extract

½   cup chopped pecans, optional

In a bowl, mix together the brown sugar, flour, and cinnamon. Stir in the butter, vanilla, and pecans until crumbly.

To Prepare and Eat Now: Preheat oven to 350°F. Bake for 45 minutes or until well heated and the crumbly topping is lightly browned.

To Freeze: Do not bake before freezing. Cool to room temperature, then transfer to freezer container, label, and freeze. Recommended freezing time: up to 1 to 2 months.

To Prepare After Freezing: Remove from freezer to defrost. Preheat oven to 350°F. Bake for 45 minutes or until well heated and the crumbly topping is lightly browned.

NUTRITIONAL INFORMATION PER SERVING:
Calories 310, Protein (g) 4, Carbohydrate (g) 57, Fat (g) 8, Calories from Fat (%) 22, Saturated Fat (g) 5, Dietary Fiber (g) 3, Cholesterol (mg) 40, Sodium (mg) 113, Diabetic Exchanges: 4 starch, 1 fat

Ultimate Red Pasta Sauce

This rich, basic red sauce boasting of flavor is a great start. Toss in veggies to cook in the sauce for a veggie pasta sauce. Serve over pasta. The sauce even tastes better after freezing.

MAKES 6 SERVINGS

1   medium onion, chopped

½   cup chopped celery

½   cup finely chopped carrots

1   teaspoon minced garlic

1   (28-ounce) can puréed tomatoes

1   (6-ounce) can tomato paste

½   cup water or vegetable or chicken broth

1   tablespoon dried oregano leaves

1   bay leaf

1   teaspoon dried basil leaves

2   tablespoons chopped parsley

    Pinch of sugar

    Salt and pepper to taste

In a large non-stick pan coated with non-stick cooking spray, sauté the onion, celery, carrots, and garlic over medium-high heat for 5 minutes. Add the tomatoes, tomato paste, water, oregano, bay leaf, basil, parsley, sugar, and salt and pepper. Cook over a medium heat for another 15 minutes. Remove bay leaf before serving.

To Prepare and Eat Now: Serve over pasta.

To Freeze: Cool to room temperature and transfer to a freezer container, label, and freeze. Recommended freezing time: up to 3 months.

To Prepare After Freezing: Remove from freezer to defrost or reheat frozen in a non-stick pot over a low heat, stirring until well heated.

NUTRITIONAL INFORMATION PER SERVING: *Calories 94, Protein (g) 4, Carbohydrate (g) 19, Fat (g) 0, Calories from Fat (%) 0, Saturated Fat (g) 0, Dietary Fiber (g) 4, Cholesterol (mg) 0, Sodium (mg) 118, Diabetic Exchanges: 4 vegetable*

Poultry

Barbecue Chicken Pizza

This is one of our favorite pizzas, so I created an at-home version. With a bought crust and leftover or rotisserie chicken, this scrumptious pizza is easy to make.

MAKES 8 SERVINGS

1   pound skinless, boneless chicken breasts, cut into small pieces

    Salt and pepper to taste

¾   cup plus 2 tablespoons barbecue sauce, divided

1   (10-ounce) can prepared pizza crust or Boboli crust

1   cup shredded Gouda cheese

1   cup shredded, part-skim Mozzarella cheese

1   small red onion, thinly sliced

2   green onions (scallions), chopped

In large non-stick skillet coated with non-stick cooking spray, season the chicken with salt and pepper and stir-fry over medium heat until done. Remove to a bowl and toss with 2 tablespoons barbecue sauce.

Coat a non-stick pizza pan with non-stick cooking spray and unroll dough and place in pan; starting at center, press out with hands. Spread pizza crust with remaining ¾ cup sauce. Sprinkle evenly with Gouda, Mozzarella, red onion slices, chicken, and green onions.

To Prepare and Eat Now: Preheat the oven to 425°F. Bake for 8 to 10 minutes or until light golden brown.

To Freeze: Do not bake before freezing. Wrap, label, and freeze. Recommended freezing time: up to 6 weeks.

To Prepare After Freezing: Preheat the oven to 425°F. Bake for 10 to 12 minutes or until light golden brown.

NUTRITIONAL INFORMATION PER SERVING: *Calories 303, Protein (g) 24, Carbohydrate (g) 29, Fat (g) 9, Calories from Fat (%) 27, Saturated Fat (g) 5, Dietary Fiber (g) 1, Cholesterol (mg) 58, Sodium (mg) 612, Diabetic Exchanges: 3 lean meat, 2 starch*

Poultry

Stuffed Chicken Breasts with Feta, Spinach, and Ham

No need to buy frozen stuffed chicken breasts when you can make your own. Chicken breasts stuffed with this fantastic mixture of feta, spinach, and ham gives you a splendid and quick dinner to pull out of the freezer.

MAKES 8 SERVINGS

8   skinless, boneless chicken breasts

    Salt and pepper to taste

3   ounces reduced-fat cream cheese

½   cup reduced-fat feta cheese

½   cup baby spinach leaves

8   thin slices ham

With a knife, make a split along one side of the chicken breast to form a pocket. Season chicken breasts with salt and pepper.

In a small bowl, mix together the cream cheese and feta with a fork. Stuff each chicken breast with the cheese mixture, spinach, and ham.

To Prepare and Eat Now: Preheat the oven to 350°F. Place the chicken breasts on a baking dish coated with non-stick cooking spray, cover with foil, and bake for 40 to 45 minutes until done.

To Freeze: Do not bake before freezing. After chicken breasts are filled, wrap individually, label, and freeze. Recommended freezing time: up to 4 to 6 months.

To Prepare After Freezing: Preheat the oven to 350°F. Place frozen chicken breasts in a baking dish coated with non-stick cooking spray, and bake, covered with foil, for one hour or until tender. You can also defrost the chicken breasts and bake them, covered, for 45 to 50 minutes or until tender.

NUTRITIONAL INFORMATION PER SERVING: *Calories 197, Protein (g) 34, Carbohydrate (g) 1, Fat (g) 5, Calories from Fat (%) 26, Saturated Fat (g) 3, Dietary Fiber (g) 0, Cholesterol (mg) 90, Sodium (mg) 463, Diabetic Exchanges: 4.5 lean meat*

Poultry

Stuffed Chicken Breasts with Enchilada Sauce

Chicken breasts filled with green chilies and cheese with a southwestern crust baked in enchilada sauce and corn is hot to trot!

MAKES 6 TO 8 SERVINGS

2   pounds boneless, skinless chicken breasts, flattened

1   (4-ounce) can green chilies, drained

2   tablespoons minced garlic

4   ounces reduced-fat Monterey Jack cheese, cut into slices

1½ cups breadcrumbs or seasoned breadcrumbs

1   tablespoon chili powder

1   teaspoon ground cumin

    Salt and pepper to taste

1   cup fat-free sour cream

2   cups canned enchilada sauce

1   cup frozen corn, thawed

    Chopped green onions (scallions)

Spread each piece of chicken with the green chilies and garlic. Top each breast with a slice of cheese and roll up. Secure with a toothpick if needed. Combine breadcrumbs, chili powder, cumin, and salt and pepper in a bowl. Dip each chicken roll in sour cream and roll in crumb mixture. Chill before baking, time permitted.

To Prepare and Eat Now: Place breasts, seam side down, in a baking dish. Preheat the oven to 400°F. Mix enchilada sauce with corn and pour over the chicken. Bake for 45 minutes or until chicken is done. Sprinkle with green onions before serving.

To Freeze: Wrap individually or together in baking dish, label, and freeze. Recommended freezing time: up to 3 months.

To Prepare After Freezing: Remove from freezer to defrost. Preheat the oven to 400°F. Place breasts, seam side down, in a baking dish. Mix enchilada sauce with corn and pour over the chicken. Cook for 45 minutes to 1 hour or until chicken is done. Sprinkle with green onions before serving.

NUTRITIONAL INFORMATION PER SERVING: *Calories 327, Protein (g) 36 , Carbohydrate (g) 31, Fat (g) 6 , Calories from Fat (%) 16, Saturated Fat (g) 2 , Dietary Fiber (g) 3, Cholesterol (mg) 78, Sodium (mg) 684, Diabetic Exchanges: 4 very lean meat, 2 starch*

Chicken and Artichokes

Chicken strips and artichokes baked in this wonderful paprika sauce is great served with vermicelli.

MAKES 6 TO 8 SERVINGS

2 pounds skinless, boneless chicken breasts, cut into large strips

1 tablespoon paprika

Salt and pepper to taste

1 (14-ounce) can quartered artichoke hearts, drained

¼ cup all-purpose flour

1 (14.5-ounce) can fat-free chicken broth

½ cup dry sherry

1 teaspoon dried rosemary leaves

Chopped green onions (scallions), optional

Preheat the oven to 350°F.

Lay the chicken breasts in a 3-quart oblong baking dish coated with non-stick cooking spray. Season with paprika and salt and pepper. Place the artichokes around the chicken.

Place the flour in a non-stick saucepan and gradually stir in the chicken broth. Cook over medium heat until thickened, about 3 to 5 minutes. Add the sherry and rosemary and continue cooking for 1 minute. Pour over the chicken breasts. Bake, covered, for 1 hour or until chicken is done.

To Prepare and Eat Now: Sprinkle with green onions. Eat when ready.

To Freeze: Cool to room temperature. Wrap, label, and freeze. Recommended freezing time: up to 3 months.

To Prepare After Freezing: Remove from freezer to defrost. Preheat the oven to 350°F. and bake, covered, for about 20 minutes or until well heated. Sprinkle with chopped green onions, if desired, before serving.

NUTRITIONAL INFORMATION PER SERVING: *Calories 167, Protein (g) 28, Carbohydrate (g) 6, Fat (g) 2, Calories from Fat (%) 9, Saturated Fat (g) 0, Dietary Fiber (g) 1, Cholesterol (mg) 66, Sodium (mg) 245, Diabetic Exchanges: 3 very lean meat, 1 vegetable*

Chicken and Broccoli

This one meal dish of chicken and broccoli in a quick sauce is really good over pasta or rice.

MAKES 4 SERVINGS

Poultry

4	cups broccoli florets
1	red bell pepper, seeded and cut into chunks
1	onion, chopped
1	pound boneless, skinless chicken breasts, cut into strips
1	(10.75-ounce) can reduced-fat cream of broccoli soup
½	cup water
1	teaspoon dried basil leaves
½	cup shredded, reduced-fat Cheddar cheese

In a large non-stick skillet coated with non-stick cooking spray, stir-fry the broccoli, red pepper, and onion until crisp-tender, about 4 minutes. Remove the vegetables from the skillet; set aside.

Coat the pan again with non-stick cooking spray and add the chicken. Stir-fry until no longer pink, about 6 minutes. Add the cream of broccoli soup, water, and basil. Mix well. Stir in the pepper mixture. Bring to a boil; reduce heat, and cook for 10 minutes. Add the cheese, stirring until the cheese is melted.

To Prepare and Eat Now: Eat when ready.

To Freeze: Cool to room temperature, then wrap, label, and freeze. Recommended freezing time: up to 3 months.

To Prepare After Freezing: Remove from freezer to defrost. Reheat in a non-stick skillet over a low heat.

NUTRITIONAL INFORMATION PER SERVING: *Calories 456, Protein (g) 42, Carbohydrate (g) 59, Fat (g) 6, Calories from Fat (%) 11, Saturated Fat (g) 3, Dietary Fiber (g) 6, Cholesterol (mg) 76, Sodium (mg) 627, Diabetic Exchanges: 4 very lean meat, 3.5 starch, 2 vegetable*

Chicken and Dumplings

Here is an easy version of this comforting and satisfying, one-dish meal people pleaser. You might want to make extra dumplings, as my family always wants more.

MAKES 6 TO 8 SERVINGS

2   pounds skinless, boneless chicken breasts, cut into 1-inch pieces

1   cup chopped onion

1   cup thinly sliced celery

¼   cup all-purpose flour

10   cups chicken broth

2   cups sliced carrots

1   teaspoon dried thyme leaves

    Dumplings (recipe follows)

In a large non-stick pot coated with non-stick cooking spray over medium heat, stir chicken and onion about 5 minutes or until chicken is browned. Add celery, and sauté several minutes longer. Sprinkle chicken mixture with flour and gradually stir in broth, carrots, and thyme. Bring to a boil, cover and reduce heat, stirring occasionally, until chicken is tender, about 20 minutes. Prepare the Dumplings (see recipe) and drop dough by tablespoonfuls into soup. Cover and cook over medium-low heat 15 minutes or until dumplings are done.

Note:
You can also make dumplings by mixing 1⅔ cups biscuit baking mix and ⅔ cup milk. Drop into soup.

Dumplings

2   cups all-purpose flour

1   tablespoon baking powder

¾   cup buttermilk

    Salt and pepper to taste

In a bowl, mix together the flour and baking powder. Stir in buttermilk and season with salt and pepper.

To Prepare and Eat Now: Eat when ready.

To Freeze: Cool to room temperature, then transfer to a freezer container, label, and freeze. Recommended freezing time: up to 3 months.

To Prepare After Freezing: Remove from freezer to defrost. Re-heat over low heat in a non-stick pan.

NUTRITIONAL INFORMATION PER SERVING: *Calories 307, Protein (g) 34, Carbohydrate (g) 35, Fat (g) 2, Calories from Fat (%) 7, Saturated Fat (g) 1, Dietary Fiber (g) 4, Cholesterol (mg) 67, Sodium (mg) 766, Diabetic Exchanges: 3.5 very lean meat, 2 starch, 1 vegetable*

Poultry

Chicken Cherries Jubilee

Chicken baked in sweet and spicy sauce produces extremely tender chicken. Wild rice goes great with this dish.

MAKES 12 SERVINGS

Poultry

3   pounds skinless, boneless chicken breasts and thighs

Salt and pepper to taste

1   cup water

1   (12-ounce) bottle chili sauce

½   cup light brown sugar

1   cup sherry

1   (16-ounce) can pitted dark cherries, drained

Preheat the oven to 325°F.

Place the chicken in a 3-quart oblong baking dish.

In a small pot or the microwave, combine water, chili sauce, brown sugar, sherry, and cherries until brown sugar is dissolved. Pour the sauce over chicken. Bake, covered, for 1½ hours or until chicken is tender.

To Prepare and Eat Now: Eat when ready.

To Freeze: Cool to room temperature, then wrap, label, and freeze. Recommended freezing time: up to 3 months.

To Prepare After Freezing: Remove from freezer to defrost. Preheat the oven to 350°F. and bake for 25 to 30 minutes, covered, or until thoroughly heated

NUTRITIONAL INFORMATION PER SERVING: *Calories 222, Protein (g) 26, Carbohydrate (g) 22, Fat (g) 1, Calories from Fat (%) 6, Saturated Fat (g) 0, Dietary Fiber (g) 0, Cholesterol (mg) 66, Sodium (mg) 465, Diabetic Exchanges: 3 very lean meat, 0.5 fruit, 1 other carbohydrate*

Chicken Cacciatore

Chicken broth and white wine create a lighter version of this classic recipe, and a better one too.

MAKES 6 TO 8 SERVINGS

2	pounds skinless, boneless chicken breasts, cut in half
1/3 to 1/2	cup all-purpose flour
2	tablespoons olive oil
1	onion, chopped
1	green bell pepper, seeded and chopped
1/2	pound sliced mushrooms
1	teaspoon minced garlic
2	ounces chopped prosciutto, optional
1	(28-ounce) can chopped tomatoes and juice
1	cup white wine
1	cup chicken broth
1	teaspoon dried basil leaves
1	teaspoon dried oregano leaves
1	bay leaf
	Salt and pepper to taste

Dredge chicken breasts in the flour to coat well.

In a large non-stick pot, heat the olive oil and cook the chicken on medium heat until chicken is brown on all sides, about 5 to 7 minutes. Transfer chicken to a platter.

In the same non-stick pot, add the onion, green pepper, mushrooms, garlic, and prosciutto, and sauté over medium heat until tender, about 5 minutes. Add the tomatoes, wine, chicken broth, basil, oregano, and bay leaf. Return the chicken to the skillet. Bring to a boil, reduce heat, and simmer, covered, for about 35 to 45 minutes or until chicken is tender. Season with salt and pepper.

To Prepare and Eat Now: Serve with pasta and grated Parmesan cheese.

To Freeze: Cool to room temperature, then wrap, label, and freeze. Recommended freezing time: up to 3 months.

To Prepare After Freezing: Remove from freezer to defrost. Reheat in a non-stick pot over low heat until thoroughly heated.

NUTRITIONAL INFORMATION PER SERVING: *Calories 230, Protein (g) 29, Carbohydrate (g) 12, Fat (g) 5, Calories from Fat (%) 20, Saturated Fat (g) 1, Dietary Fiber (g) 1, Cholesterol (mg) 66, Sodium (mg) 397, Diabetic Exchanges: 3 lean meat, 2.5 vegetable*

Poultry

Chicken Eleganté

Chicken with mushrooms, peppers, and pimientos in a white sauce is truly elegant, and provides a light option for guests or any night of the week.

MAKES 4 TO 6 SERVINGS

2	tablespoons butter

⅓	cup chopped mushrooms

1	green bell pepper, seeded and chopped

4	green onions (scallions), chopped

⅓	cup all-purpose flour

2	cups chicken broth

1	cup fat-free evaporated milk

2	cups cooked, diced chicken

¼	teaspoon chopped pimiento

	Salt and pepper to taste

In a large non-stick skillet, melt the butter and sauté the mushrooms, green pepper, and green onions until tender. Blend in ⅓ cup flour, stirring until combined. Gradually add the broth and milk, stirring. Bring to a boil, stirring constantly, and boil for one minute. Reduce the heat and add the chicken and pimiento, stirring until thoroughly heated.

To Prepare and Eat Now: Serve over toast points, pasta, or rice.

To Freeze: Cool to room temperature, transfer to freezer container, label, and freeze. Recommended freezing time: up to 3 months.

To Prepare After Freezing: Remove from freezer to defrost. Reheat over low heat in non-stick pan until well heated.

NUTRITIONAL INFORMATION PER SERVING: *Calories 191, Protein (g) 20, Carbohydrate (g) 14, Fat (g) 6, Calories from Fat (%) 28, Saturated Fat (g) 3, Dietary Fiber (g) 2, Cholesterol (mg) 51, Sodium (mg) 244, Diabetic Exchanges: 2 lean meat, 0.5 starch, 0.5 skim milk*

Chicken Florentine

This colorful lightly lemon-flavored chicken, spinach, noodle, and water chestnut casserole is a great crowd pleaser.

MAKES 8 TO 10 SERVINGS

1 (10-ounce) package frozen chopped spinach

¼ cup all-purpose flour

1 cup skim milk

1 cup canned fat-free chicken broth

8 ounces wide noodles

2 cups fat-free sour cream

⅓ cup lemon juice

1 (8-ounce) can mushroom stems and pieces, drained

1 (8-ounce) can sliced water chestnuts, drained

1 (2-ounce) jar diced pimientos, drained

1 onion, chopped

¼ teaspoon cayenne pepper

1 teaspoon paprika

Salt and pepper to taste

5 cups cooked, cubed chicken breasts

1 cup shredded, reduced-fat Cheddar cheese

NUTRITIONAL INFORMATION PER SERVING: *Calories 336, Protein (g) 35, Carbohydrate (g) 34, Fat (g) 6, Calories from Fat (%) 16, Saturated Fat (g) 3, Dietary Fiber (g) 3, Cholesterol (mg) 97, Sodium (mg) 325, Diabetic Exchanges: 4 lean meat, 2 starch, 1 vegetable*

Cook the spinach according to package directions, omitting any salt.

In a large non-stick pot, blend the flour, milk, and chicken broth. Cook over low heat, stirring continuously, until bubbly and thickened, about 7 minutes.

Meanwhile, prepare the noodles according to package directions, omitting any oil and salt. Drain the noodles and add to the sauce along with the cooked spinach, sour cream, lemon juice, mushrooms, water chestnuts, pimiento, onion, cayenne, paprika, and salt and pepper to the thickened broth.

In a 3-quart oblong baking dish coated with non-stick cooking spray, alternate layers of the noodle mixture and chicken. Top with the cheese.

To Prepare and Eat Now: Bake at 350°F. for 30 minutes or until bubbly.

To Freeze: Do not bake before freezing. Cool to room temperature, wrap, label, and freeze. Recommended freezing time: up to 2 to 3 months.

To Prepare After Freezing: Remove from freezer to defrost. Bake at 350°F. for 40 to 45 minutes or until bubbly.

Herb Chicken

This simple spectacular dish features herbs and wine creating a sauce to remember.

MAKES 4 SERVINGS

4	boneless, skinless chicken breasts
	Salt and pepper to taste
1	tablespoon all-purpose flour
2	tablespoons butter
2	green onions (scallions), chopped
2	tablespoons finely chopped fresh parsley
¾	cup white wine
½	teaspoon dried rosemary leaves
½	teaspoon dried thyme leaves

Season the chicken with salt and pepper and dust with flour.

In a large non-stick skillet, melt the butter and brown the chicken on both sides, about 5 to 7 minutes each side. If serving immediately, make sure chicken is done. Remove the chicken to a baking dish.

In a small bowl, mix the green onions, parsley, wine, rosemary, and thyme leaves. Pour into the skillet and stir with bits remaining in pan. Cook over medium heat until bubbly. Pour over the chicken.

To Prepare and Eat Now: Make sure to fully cook the chicken in the browning stage, follow recipe, and serve.

To Freeze: Cool to room temperature, wrap, label and freeze in oven-proof casserole dish. Recommended freezing time: up to 2 months.

To Prepare After Freezing: Remove from freezer to defrost. Bake at 325°F. for 30 to 40 minutes or until chicken is done.

NUTRITIONAL INFORMATION PER SERVING: *Calories 224, Protein (g) 28, Carbohydrate (g) 3, Fat (g) 7, Calories from Fat (%) 30, Saturated Fat (g) 4, Dietary Fiber (g) 1, Cholesterol (mg) 83, Sodium (mg) 123, Diabetic Exchanges: 3.5 lean meat*

Poultry

Greek Chicken

Chicken cooked in a light herby tomato sauce sprinkled with feta is a sure hit. Serve with pasta.

MAKES 6 TO 8 SERVINGS

2   pounds boneless, skinless chicken breasts, cut into strips

1   green bell pepper, seeded and chopped

1   cup chopped green onions (scallions)

1   tablespoon dried basil leaves

½   teaspoon dried oregano leaves

½   teaspoon dried thyme leaves

1   (28-ounce) can diced tomatoes with juice

1   teaspoon light brown sugar

⅓   cup crumbled feta cheese

In a large non-stick skillet coated with non-stick cooking spray, sauté the chicken and green pepper over medium heat, about 5 to 7 minutes or until peppers are softened. Stir in green onions, basil, oregano, thyme, tomatoes, and brown sugar. Simmer about 15 minutes or until the chicken is tender and the sauce thickens slightly.

To Prepare and Eat Now: Before serving, stir in the feta and serve chicken and sauce over pasta.

To Freeze: Cool to room temperature, wrap, label, and freeze. Recommended freezing time: up to 2 months.

To Prepare After Freezing: Remove from freezer to defrost. Reheat in a non-stick skillet over low heat until well heated. Stir in the feta and serve over pasta.

NUTRITIONAL INFORMATION PER SERVING: *Calories 170, Protein (g) 28, Carbohydrate (g) 7, Fat (g) 3, Calories from Fat (%) 15, Saturated Fat (g) 1, Dietary Fiber (g) 1, Cholesterol (mg) 71, Sodium (mg) 420, Diabetic Exchanges: 3.5 very lean meat, 1.5 vegetable*

Chicken Oregano

A robust oregano-seasoned red sauce served with pasta is a perfect scenario.

MAKES 4 TO 6 SERVINGS

1½ pounds skinless, boneless chicken breasts

1 onion, chopped

½ teaspoon minced garlic

Salt and pepper to taste

1 tablespoon dried oregano leaves

1 (16-ounce) can whole tomatoes, crushed, with their juices

½ pound mushrooms, sliced

¼ cup dry red wine, optional

In a large non-stick skillet coated with non-stick cooking spray, brown the chicken on both sides over medium heat, about 5 minutes in all, cooking in batches if necessary. Add the onion and garlic and cook 5 minutes more, or until the vegetables are tender. Sprinkle with salt and pepper and oregano. Add the tomatoes, mushrooms, and wine. Cover and cook over low heat about 25 to 30 minutes, or until the chicken is tender. If the sauce gets too thick, add a little water.

To Prepare and Eat Now: Serve with angel hair pasta.

To Freeze: Cool to room temperature, wrap, label, and freeze. Recommended freezing time: up to 3 months.

To Prepare After Freezing: Remove from freezer to defrost. Reheat in non-stick skillet over low heat until thoroughly heated. Serve with pasta.

NUTRITIONAL INFORMATION PER SERVING: *Calories 171, Protein (g) 29, Carbohydrate (g) 9, Fat (g) 2, Calories from Fat (%) 9, Saturated Fat (g) 0, Dietary Fiber (g) 2, Cholesterol (mg) 66, Sodium (mg) 194, Diabetic Exchanges: 3 very lean meat, 2 vegetable*

Poultry

Chicken Caesar Casserole

Attention all Caesar salad fans! Toss Caesar dressing, pasta, and leftover cooked or rotisserie chicken together for this quick all age pleasing recipe.

MAKES 6 TO 8 SERVINGS

2   pounds skinless, boneless seasoned chicken breasts, cooked and cut into chunks

½   cup chopped red bell pepper

½   cup chopped green onions (scallions)

⅓   cup light Creamy Caesar dressing

½   cup chicken broth

1½ cups shredded, part-skim Mozzarella cheese

1   (12-ounce) package tubular pasta, cooked according to package directions, drained

¼   cup Caesar or Italian croutons, crushed, optional

In a 2-quart baking dish coated with non-stick cooking spray, combine the chicken, red pepper, green onions, Caesar dressing, chicken broth, Mozzarella cheese, and pasta.

To Prepare and Eat Now: Preheat the oven to 350°F. Top with crushed croutons. Bake for 20 to 25 minutes or until bubbly.

To Freeze: Do not bake before freezing. Cool to room temperature, wrap, label, and freeze. Recommended freezing time: up to 3 months.

To Prepare After Freezing: Preheat the oven to 350°F. Top with crushed croutons. Bake for 30 to 35 minutes or until bubbly.

NUTRITIONAL INFORMATION PER SERVING: *Calories 349, Protein (g) 32, Carbohydrate (g) 39, Fat (g) 6, Calories from Fat (%) 16, Saturated Fat (g) 3, Dietary Fiber (g) 2, Cholesterol (mg) 52, Sodium (mg) 723, Diabetic Exchanges: 4 very lean meat, 1.5 starch*

Chicken Pot Pie

Chicken, veggies, and sweet potatoes in a white sauce are topped with easy refrigerated crescent rolls, creating the ultimate comfort food. Rotisserie chicken may be used.

MAKES 6 SERVINGS

½ cup chopped celery

1 cup chopped onion

1 cup chopped carrots

1 cup diced, peeled sweet potatoes (yams)

⅓ cup all-purpose flour

1½ cups chicken broth

½ cup skim milk

2 cups diced, cooked skinless chicken breasts

½ cup frozen peas

1 (8-ounce) can refrigerated reduced-fat crescent rolls, use only 6 triangles

In a non-stick skillet coated with non-stick cooking spray, sauté the celery, onion, carrots, and sweet potatoes over medium heat, until tender, about 7 to 10 minutes. Add the flour, stirring, and gradually stir in the chicken broth and milk, bringing to a boil. Reduce the heat and stir until thickened. Add the chicken and peas.

Transfer mixture to a 9 x 9 x 2-inch baking pan coated with non-stick cooking spray. Lay the crescent roll triangles on top, sealing the sides.

To Prepare and Eat Now: Preheat the oven to 375°F. Bake for 10 to 15 minutes or until top is lightly browned.

To Freeze: Do not bake before freezing. Cool to room temperature, wrap, label, and freeze. The crescent roll crust may be added before or after freezing. Recommended freezing time: up to 3 months.

To Prepare After Freezing: Remove from freezer to defrost. Preheat the oven to 375°F. Cover with crescent roll crust to seal, if did not do before freezing. Bake for 20 minutes or until heated inside and crust is lightly browned. Cover top lightly with foil if crust starts to get too brown.

NUTRITIONAL INFORMATION PER SERVING: *Calories 298, Protein (g) 21, Carbohydrate (g) 34, Fat (g) 8, Calories from Fat (%) 25, Saturated Fat (g) 2, Dietary Fiber (g) 3, Cholesterol (mg) 40, Sodium (mg) 500, Diabetic Exchanges: 2 lean meat, 2 starch, 1 vegetable*

Chicken Fettuccine

Rotisserie chicken may be used for this dynamic chicken and pasta casserole.

MAKES 10 SERVINGS

2 pounds boneless, skinless chicken breasts

Salt and pepper to taste

1 (1-pound) package fettuccine

2 tablespoons butter

1 cup chopped green pepper

1 cup chopped onion

1 teaspoon minced garlic

½ pound sliced baby Portabella mushrooms

2 tablespoons all-purpose flour

1 (12-ounce) can evaporated fat-free milk

1 cup skim milk

1 tablespoon grainy mustard

1 tablespoon Worcestershire sauce

½ cup grated Parmesan cheese, divided

1 bunch green onions (scallions), chopped, divided

¼ cup chopped parsley, divided

NUTRITIONAL INFORMATION PER SERVING: *Calories 371, Protein (g) 33, Carbohydrate (g) 46, Fat (g) 6, Calories from Fat (%) 14, Saturated Fat (g) 3, Dietary Fiber (g) 3, Cholesterol (mg) 64, Sodium (mg) 238, Diabetic Exchanges: 3 very lean meat, 2.5 starch, 0.5 skim milk*

Season the chicken breasts with salt and pepper and cook over medium heat in a non-stick skillet coated with non-stick cooking spray for 6 to 8 minutes on each side. Slice and set aside. Meanwhile, prepare pasta according to package directions omitting any oil. Drain and set aside.

In a large non-stick pot, melt the butter and sauté the green pepper, onion, garlic, and mushrooms over medium heat until tender. Stir in flour and cook for 30 seconds. Gradually add evaporated milk, skim milk, mustard, and Worcestershire sauce and bring to a boil. Reduce heat and stir until thick. Stir in cheese, green onions, and parsley (reserving 2 tablespoons of each for garnish), and cook over a low heat.

Transfer mixture to a 3-quart oblong casserole dish coated with non-stick cooking spray and sprinkle with reserved cheese, green onions, and parsley.

To Prepare and Eat Now: Preheat the oven to 350°F. and bake, covered, for about 30 minutes or until well heated. Uncover for last 5 minutes.

To Freeze: Do not bake before freezing. Cool to room temperature, wrap, label, and freeze. Recommended freezing time: up to 3 months.

To Prepare After Freezing: Remove from freezer to defrost. Preheat the oven to 350°F. and bake, covered, for about 30 to 40 minutes or until well heated. Uncover for last 5 minutes.

Poultry

Chicken Vermicelli

When you want delicious, homemade comfort food, here is the recipe. Use leftover chicken, purchase rotisserie chicken, or sauté chicken in a skillet for the cooked chicken. I usually prepare one casserole for dinner and freeze the other since this recipe feeds a lot of people. It's also great to make to take to someone's home.

MAKES 16 SERVINGS

Poultry

1   (16-ounce) package vermicelli, broken into 3- to 4-inch pieces

1   green bell pepper, seeded and chopped

1   onion, chopped

    Salt and pepper to taste

1   tablespoon minced garlic

2   tablespoons all-purpose flour

1   (10-ounce) can diced tomatoes and green chilies

2   cups skim milk

1   tablespoons Worcestershire sauce

½   cup chopped, jarred, roasted red peppers

1   cup frozen green peas

4   cups cubed, cooked, bone-less, skinless chicken breasts

1½ cups shredded, reduced-fat sharp Cheddar cheese

Cook the vermicelli according to package directions; set aside.

In a large non-stick pot coated with non-stick cooking spray, sauté the green pepper, onion, and garlic about 5 to 7 minutes or until tender. Stir in the flour. Add the tomatoes, milk, and Worcestershire sauce, stirring until mixture comes to a boil and thickens. Lower the heat and add the red peppers and peas, mixing well. Add the vermicelli, chicken, and cheese, stirring to mix well and heat through. Transfer to a 3-quart baking dish coated with non-stick cooking spray.

To Prepare and Eat Now: Preheat the oven to 350°F. Bake for 20 minutes or until bubbly.

To Freeze: Do not bake before freezing. Cool to room temperature, wrap, label, and freeze. Recommended freezing time: up to 3 months.

To Prepare After Freezing: Remove from freezer to defrost. Preheat the oven to 350°F. Bake for 30 to 40 minutes or until bubbly.

NUTRITIONAL INFORMATION PER SERVING: *Calories 250, Protein (g) 25, Carbohydrate (g) 29, Fat (g) 3, Calories from Fat (%) 12, Saturated Fat (g) 2, Dietary Fiber (g) 3, Cholesterol (mg) 47, Sodium (mg) 323, Diabetic Exchanges: 3 very lean meat, 1.5 starch, 1.5 vegetable*

Chicken Chunky Divan

This old classic is still a family pleaser with the two favorites of chicken and broccoli in one dish. For a speedy version, use leftover cooked chicken or a rotisserie chicken.

MAKES 4 TO 6 SERVINGS

2   pounds skinless, boneless chicken breasts

    Salt and pepper to taste

2   (10-ounce) packages frozen chopped broccoli

¼   cup all-purpose flour

1½ cups skim milk

1   cup shredded, reduced-fat Monterey Jack cheese

1   (2-ounce) jar chopped pimientos, drained

    Paprika

Season the chicken with salt and pepper and cook in a non-stick skillet coated with non-stick cooking spray over medium heat for 10 minutes or until done and lightly browned. Cut chicken into chunks; set aside.

Meanwhile, cook the broccoli according to package directions, omitting any salt. Drain and place along the bottom of a 2-quart oblong baking dish coated with non-stick cooking spray. Sprinkle with salt and pepper. Cover the broccoli with the cooked chicken.

Combine the flour and milk in a non-stick saucepan, and cook over medium heat, stirring, until thickened. Add the cheese, stirring until the cheese is melted. Remove from the heat, add the pimientos, and season with salt and pepper. Pour the sauce evenly over the chicken and sprinkle with paprika.

To Prepare and Eat Now: Preheat the oven to 350°F. Bake for about 20 to 30 minutes or until the mixture is bubbly and heated through.

To Freeze: Do not bake before freezing. Cool to room temperature, wrap, label, and freeze. Recommended freezing time: up to 2 months.

To Prepare After Freezing: Remove from freezer to defrost. Preheat the oven to 350°F. Bake about 30 minutes or until the mixture is bubbly and heated through.

NUTRITIONAL INFORMATION PER SERVING: *Calories 287, Protein (g) 46, Carbohydrate (g) 12, Fat (g) 6, Calories from Fat (%) 18, Saturated Fat (g) 3, Dietary Fiber (g) 3, Cholesterol (mg) 99, Sodium (mg) 267, Diabetic Exchanges: 6 very lean meat, 0.5 starch, 1 vegetable*

Salsa Chicken

Tossing chicken strips with salsa, tomatoes, and green chilies, and corn flavors and tenderizes the chicken in this terrific dish. Sprinkle with cheese and you have a winner.

MAKES 8 SERVINGS

2   pounds boneless, skinless chicken breasts, cut into strips

        Pepper to taste

1   cup mild salsa

1   tablespoon minced garlic

1   (10-ounce) can diced tomatoes and green chilies

1   (11-ounce) can shoe peg corn, drained

1½   cups shredded, reduced-fat Monterey Jack cheese

½   cup chopped green onions (scallions)

Preheat the oven to 350°F.

Place the chicken in a 2-quart oblong casserole dish coated with non-stick cooking spray and sprinkle with pepper. Add the salsa, garlic, tomatoes and green chilies, and corn to the chicken, mixing well. Bake, covered, for 1 hour or until chicken is tender.

To Prepare and Eat Now: Uncover and sprinkle with cheese and green onions. Continue baking for 5 minutes or until the cheese is melted.

To Freeze: Cool to room temperature, wrap, label, and freeze. Recommended freezing time: up to 2 to 3 months.

To Prepare After Freezing: Remove from freezer to defrost. Preheat the oven to 350°F. Bake, covered, for about 30 to 35 minutes or until well heated. Uncover and sprinkle with cheese and green onions. Continue baking for 5 minutes or until the cheese is melted. Alternately, you can reheat in the microwave.

NUTRITIONAL INFORMATION PER SERVING: Calories 246, Protein (g) 34, Carbohydrate (g) 12, Fat (g) 6, Calories from Fat (%) 21, Saturated Fat (g) 3, Dietary Fiber (g) 1, Cholesterol (mg) 77, Sodium (mg) 580, Diabetic Exchanges: 4 lean meat, 0.5 starch, 1 vegetable

Poultry

Chicken Salsa Lasagna

Chicken and salsa give lasagna flavor and fun with no fuss. Leave out the chicken for a great vegetarian option.

MAKES 8 TO 10 SERVINGS

3   cups cooked, coarsely chopped, skinless, boneless chicken breasts

1   (10-ounce) can diced tomatoes and green chilies

1   (16-ounce) jar thick and chunky salsa

1   (8-ounce) can tomato sauce

1   tablespoon dried oregano leaves

    Black pepper to taste

1   (16-ounce) container fat-free cottage cheese

2   large egg whites

1   (8-ounce) package no-boil lasagna noodles

1   (8-ounce) package shredded, part-skim Mozzarella cheese

1   (15-ounce) can black beans, drained and rinsed

Preheat the oven to 350°F.

Coat a 2-quart oblong baking dish with non-stick cooking spray.

Combine the chicken, tomatoes and green chilies, salsa, tomato sauce, oregano, and pepper in a large bowl; set aside.

In a food processor, blend the cottage cheese and egg whites until smooth.

Spread a heaping cup of the chicken-tomato mixture in the bottom of the baking dish. Top with four lasagna noodles. Top with half the cottage cheese mixture, half the Mozzarella, half the black beans, and four more lasagna noodles. Continue layering and top with the remaining chicken-tomato mixture. Cover tightly with foil; place additional foil underneath the pan (it may bubble over). Bake for 60 to 75 minutes or until the pasta is tender.

Note:

If you're not using no-boil-noodles, do not bake before freezing.

To Prepare and Eat Now: Serve when ready.

To Freeze: Cool to room temperature, wrap, label, and freeze. Recommended freezing time: up to 3 months.

To Prepare After Freezing: Remove from freezer to defrost. Preheat the oven to 350°F. Bake, covered for 30 minutes or until well heated and bubbly. Alternately, you can reheat in the microwave if cut into pieces.

NUTRITIONAL INFORMATION PER SERVING: *Calories 307, Protein (g) 30, Carbohydrate (g) 31, Fat (g) 6, Calories from Fat (%) 18, Saturated Fat (g) 3, Dietary Fiber (g) 4, Cholesterol (mg) 52, Sodium (mg) 891, Diabetic Exchanges: 3.5 very lean meat, 1.5 starch, 1.5 vegetable*

Quick Chicken Lasagna

Take the easy but delicious way out of preparing lasagna with commercial pasta sauce, rotisserie chicken, and no-boil noodles to create my friend Karen's masterpiece—perfect for the person who doesn't have time to cook but wants to impress.

MAKES 8 SERVINGS

1   rotisserie chicken, skin removed and chicken coarsely chopped (3 cups)

2   (26-ounce) jars pasta sauce

1   (8-ounce) package no-boil lasagna noodles

2   cups shredded, part-skim Mozzarella cheese

2   (10-ounce) packages frozen chopped spinach, thawed and drained

1   (4-ounce) package crumbled goat cheese, optional

Preheat the oven to 350°F.

In a bowl, combine the chicken and pasta sauce.

In an oblong dish coated with non-stick cooking spray, spread a thin layer of chicken sauce. Top with a layer of noodles, chicken sauce, Mozzarella, half the spinach, and goat cheese. Repeat layering with noodles, chicken sauce, Mozzarella, remaining spinach, and goat cheese. Bake, covered, for 50 minutes or until bubbly. Uncover and bake 5 minutes longer.

Note:

If you're not using no-boil-noodles, do not bake before freezing.

To Prepare and Eat Now:
Serve when ready.

To Freeze: Cool to room temperature, wrap, label, and freeze. Recommended freezing time: up to 3 months.

To Prepare After Freezing:
Remove from freezer to defrost. Preheat the oven to 350°F. and bake, covered, for 25 to 30 minutes or until bubbly. Uncover and bake 5 minutes longer. Alternately, you can reheat in the microwave if cut into pieces.

NUTRITIONAL INFORMATION PER SERVING: *Calories 393, Protein (g) 29, Carbohydrate (g) 40, Fat (g) 13, Calories from Fat (%) 29, Saturated Fat (g) 5, Dietary Fiber (g) 6, Cholesterol (mg) 57, Sodium (mg) 1026, Diabetic Exchanges: 2.5 lean meat, 2 starch, 2 vegetable, 1 fat*

Chicken Artichoke and Spinach Ravioli Lasagna

Ravioli stands in for lasagna noodles layered with a white sauce and an artichoke, chicken, and spinach layer, making this dish sound impressive, but easy to prepare.

MAKES 8 SERVINGS

3   tablespoons all-purpose flour

1½   cups skim milk

     Salt and pepper to taste

     Dash nutmeg

1   (16-ounce) package cheese or spinach ravioli (reduced-fat if possible)

2   cups cubed, cooked chicken breasts

1   (14.5-ounce) artichoke hearts, drained and coarsely chopped

2   (10-ounce) packages frozen chopped spinach, defrosted and squeezed dry

1   cup shredded, part-skim Mozzarella cheese

In a medium non-stick pot, whisk flour with milk and bring to a boil over medium heat. Lower heat, and continue cooking until mixture thickens. Season with salt and pepper and add nutmeg.

Note:

Leave out the chicken for great vegetarian lasagna.

Meanwhile, cook ravioli according to package directions, drain, and set aside. In a medium bowl, combine the cooked chicken, artichoke hearts, and spinach.

In a 13 x 9 x 2-inch baking dish, spread a very thin layer of sauce, layer half the ravioli, half the chicken mixture, half the sauce, and half the cheese. Repeat layers.

To Prepare and Eat Now: Preheat the oven to 350°F. Bake for 20 to 30 minutes or until bubbly.

To Freeze: Do not bake before freezing. Cool to room temperature, wrap, label, and freeze. Recommended freezing time: up to 3 months.

To Prepare After Freezing: Remove from freezer to defrost. Preheat the oven to 350°F. Bake for 25 to 35 minutes or until bubbly.

NUTRITIONAL INFORMATION PER SERVING: *Calories 310, Protein (g) 28, Carbohydrate (g) 33, Fat (g) 8, Calories from Fat (%) 23, Saturated Fat (g) 4, Dietary Fiber (g) 4, Cholesterol (mg) 62, Sodium (mg) 498, Diabetic Exchanges: 3 lean meat, 2 starch, 1 vegetable*

Poultry

Chicken and Bean Enchiladas

The spicy red sauce smothering these enchiladas filled with chicken, pinto beans, and cheese make enticing enchiladas.

MAKES 6 TO 8 SERVINGS

1½ pounds skinless, boneless chicken breasts, cut into bite-size pieces

1 cup chopped red onion

1 green bell pepper, seeded and chopped

1 tablespoon chili powder

2 tablespoons chopped fresh cilantro

1 (16-ounce) can pinto beans, drained and rinsed

1 (14.5-ounce) can diced tomatoes and green chilies, drained

1 (8-ounce) can tomato sauce

¼ teaspoon pepper

1 cup shredded, reduced-fat Monterey Jack cheese

12 (8-inch) flour tortillas

Note:

Black beans may be substituted for the pinto beans.

Place the chicken in a large non-stick skillet coated with non-stick cooking spray and sauté over medium heat until lightly browned, about 5 to 7 minutes. Add the onion and green pepper, and sauté 3 to 5 minutes more, or until the chicken is done. Remove from the heat. Add the chili powder, cilantro, and beans; stir.

In a bowl, combine the tomatoes and green chilies, tomato sauce, and pepper; stir. Spoon ⅓ cup of the tomato mixture into an oblong baking dish coated with non-stick cooking spray. Divide the chicken mixture and cheese evenly down the center of each tortilla. Roll the tortillas tightly and place, seam side down, in the baking dish. Pour the remaining tomato mixture over the tortillas

To Prepare and Eat Now:
Preheat the oven to 350°F. Bake, covered for 30 to 40 minutes, or until thoroughly heated.

To Freeze: Do not bake before freezing. Cool to room temperature, wrap, label, and freeze. Recommended freezing time: up to 3 months.

To Prepare After Freezing:
Remove from freezer to defrost. Preheat the oven to 350°F. Bake, covered for 40 to 45 minutes, or until thoroughly heated.

NUTRITIONAL INFORMATION PER SERVING: *Calories 392, Protein (g) 34, Carbohydrate (g) 50, Fat (g) 5, Calories from Fat (%) 12, Saturated Fat (g) 2, Dietary Fiber (g) 8, Cholesterol (mg) 57, Sodium (mg) 1146, Diabetic Exchanges: 3.5 very lean meat, 3 starch, 1 vegetable*

Chicken Enchiladas

Many times I take the easy way out and buy canned enchilada sauce. However, once you make this rich, full-flavored sauce, you will be hooked. Rotisserie chicken makes it a quickie. I love the touch of olives, but my kids prefer without. The choice is yours.

MAKES 6 TO 8 SERVINGS

1 tablespoon olive oil

1 cup finely chopped onion

2 tablespoons minced garlic

1 teaspoon dried oregano leaves

1 teaspoon ground cumin

4 tablespoons chili powder

¼ teaspoon ground cinnamon

1 tablespoon cocoa

3 tablespoons all-purpose flour

4 cups chicken broth

3 cups shredded or chopped cooked, skinless chicken breasts

2 cups shredded, reduced-fat Monterey Jack cheese

1 bunch green onions (scallions), chopped

⅓ cup sliced pimiento-stuffed green olives, optional

12 (8-inch) whole wheat or flour tortillas

NUTRITIONAL INFORMATION PER SERVING: *Calories 420, Protein (g) 33, Carbohydrate (g) 46, Fat (g) 10, Calories from Fat (%) 23, Saturated Fat (g) 4, Dietary Fiber (g) 6, Cholesterol (mg) 60, Sodium (mg) 966, Diabetic Exchanges: 3.5 lean meat, 2.5 starch, 1.5 vegetable*

In a large non-stick saucepan over medium heat, heat the oil and sauté the onion until tender, about 5 to 7 minutes. Add the garlic, oregano, cumin, chili powder, cinnamon, cocoa, and flour, stirring for one minute. Gradually add the broth, stirring to mix well. Bring to a boil over medium heat, reduce heat and cook over low heat for 30 minutes. Remove from heat.

Spread one third of the sauce in a 13 x 9 x 2-inch baking dish coated with non-stick cooking spray. Combine the chicken with 1 cup of the sauce, mixing well. Divide the chicken mixture, cheese, green onions, and olives among the tortillas. Roll up and place seam-side down in the baking dish. Spoon the remaining sauce and any remaining green onions and cheese over the enchiladas.

To Prepare and Eat Now: Preheat the oven to 350°F. Bake, covered with foil, for 20 minutes. Remove foil and continue baking for 10 minutes longer.

To Freeze: Do not bake before freezing. Cool to room temperature, wrap, label, and freeze.

Recommended freezing time: up to 3 months.

To Prepare After Freezing: Remove from freezer to defrost. Preheat the oven to 350°F. Bake, covered with foil, for 30 minutes. Remove foil and continue baking for 10 minutes longer or until bubbly.

Chicken Enchilada Casserole

A family-pleasing dish to pull out on those busy nights or a great dish to take to someone as every bite melts in your mouth.

MAKES 8 SERVINGS

½ cup chopped onion

1 tablespoon minced garlic

1 (14.5-ounce) can diced tomatoes, drained

½ cup chopped green onions (scallions), divided

1 (4-ounce) can chopped green chilies, drained

3 cups cooked chicken breast, cut into bite-size pieces

⅓ cup all-purpose flour

1 (12-ounce) can evaporated fat-free milk

½ cup chicken broth

½ teaspoon chili powder

½ teaspoon ground cumin

6 (6-inch) flour tortillas, quartered

1 cup shredded, reduced-fat Monterey Jack cheese

1 cup shredded, reduced-fat Cheddar cheese

NUTRITIONAL INFORMATION PER SERVING: *Calories 306, Protein (g) 31, Carbohydrate (g) 28, Fat (g) 7, Calories from Fat (%) 22, Saturated Fat (g) 4, Dietary Fiber (g) 3, Cholesterol (mg) 61, Sodium (mg) 609, Diabetic Exchanges: 3.5 lean meat, 1 starch, 0.5 skim milk, 1 vegetable*

In a non-stick skillet coated with non-stick cooking spray, sauté onion and garlic until tender, about 3 to 5 minutes. Add tomatoes and bring to a boil. Reduce heat and cook for 10 minutes. Add ¼ cup green onions, green chilies, and chicken, stirring until mixed.

In a non-stick saucepan, place flour and gradually add milk. Heat over medium heat, whisking constantly, until mixture is thickened and bubbly. Add broth, chili powder, and cumin, stirring until thickened.

In a 2½-quart round dish, spread half the sauce. Layer tortillas, chicken mixture, sauce, and cheeses; repeat layers twice.

To Prepare and Eat Now: Preheat the oven to 350°F. Bake for 25 to 35 minutes or until heated thoroughly. Sprinkle with remaining green onions before serving.

To Freeze: Do not bake before freezing. Cool to room temperature, wrap, label, and freeze. Recommended freezing time: up to 3 months.

To Prepare After Freezing: Remove from freezer to defrost. Preheat the oven to 350°F. Bake for 30 to 40 minutes or until heated thoroughly. Sprinkle with remaining green onions before serving.

Poultry

Ham and Sweet Potato Pot Pie with Pecan Crust **page 224**

Chicken Oregano **page 180**

Shrimp Fettucine **page 261**

Mexican Lasagna   page 238

Pork Tender Wellington page 219

Different Twist Pork Stew   **page 86**

Stuffed Meaty Pizza **page 244**

Crab Cakes with Dill Sauce **page 252**

Seafood Stuffed Potatoes **page 272**

Pear Gouda Soup   **page 122**

Banana Cheesecake with Caramel Sauce and Walnuts   page 278

Lemon Ice   **page 291**
Frozen Surprise S'mores   **page 277**
Chocolate-Dipped Frozen Bananas **page 276**

Ice Cream Crispy Dessert   page 288

Pecan Caramel Pie   **page 296**

Diet Sprite Paradise Bundt Cake **page 320**

Mexican Chicken Casserole

Fresh green peppers, onion, and tomatoes with canned soup give a fresh appeal to this traditional casserole.

MAKES 6 TO 8 SERVINGS

1   green bell pepper, seeded and chopped

1   onion, chopped

2   cups chopped tomatoes

1   (10.5-ounce) can reduced-fat cream of chicken soup

1   (10.5-ounce) can reduced-fat cream of mushroom soup

⅔   cup picante sauce

1   tablespoon chili powder

10 (6-inch) flour tortillas, cut into 1-inch strips

1½ pounds cooked, skinless, chicken breasts, cut into pieces

1   cup shredded, reduced-fat Cheddar cheese

In a large non-stick pot coated with non-stick cooking spray, sauté the green pepper and onion until tender, about 3 to 5 minutes. Remove from the heat and add the tomatoes, soups, picante sauce, and chili powder, mixing well.

Line the bottom of a 3-quart casserole dish coated with non-stick cooking spray with half the tortilla strips. Top with half the chicken and half the soup mixture. Repeat the layers and sprinkle the top with Cheddar.

To Prepare and Eat Now: Preheat the oven to 350°F. Bake, uncovered, for 35 to 45 minutes, or until the casserole is bubbly.

To Freeze: Do not bake before freezing. Cool to room temperature, wrap, label, and freeze. Recommended freezing time: up to 3 months.

To Prepare After Freezing: Remove from freezer to defrost. Preheat the oven to 350°F. Bake, uncovered, for 40 to 45 minutes, or until the casserole is bubbly.

NUTRITIONAL INFORMATION PER SERVING: *Calories 357, Protein (g) 35, Carbohydrate (g) 35, Fat (g) 7, Calories from Fat (%) 19, Saturated Fat (g) 3, Dietary Fiber (g) 3, Cholesterol (mg) 84, Sodium (mg) 1074, Diabetic Exchanges: 4 very lean meat, 2 starch, 1 vegetable*

Poultry

Quick Chicken and Rice Casserole

The five ingredients in this recipe add loads of flavor with a southwestern touch all combined into a casserole. For a quick version, use rotisserie chicken.

MAKES 8 SERVINGS

2 cups cubed, cooked chicken breast

2 (4-ounce) cans diced green chilies

2 cups fat-free sour cream

Salt and pepper to taste

3 cups cooked rice

2 cups shredded, reduced-fat Monterey Jack cheese

In a large bowl, combine the chicken, green chilies, sour cream, and salt and pepper.

Coat a 2-quart baking dish with non-stick cooking spray and spread with half the rice. Spread with half the sour cream mixture over the top, sprinkle with half the Monterey Jack cheese. Repeat layering.

To Prepare and Eat Now: Preheat the oven to 350°F. and bake for 30 minutes or until heated.

To Freeze: Do not bake before freezing. Cool to room temperature, wrap, label, and freeze. Recommended freezing time: up to 2 months.

To Prepare After Freezing: Remove from freezer to defrost. Preheat the oven to 350°F. and bake for 40 to 45 minutes or until heated.

NUTRITIONAL INFORMATION PER SERVING: *Calories 281, Protein (g) 25, Carbohydrate (g) 28, Fat (g) 7, Calories from Fat (%) 22, Saturated Fat (g) 3, Dietary Fiber (g) 1, Cholesterol (mg) 55, Sodium (mg) 359, Diabetic Exchanges: 3 lean meat, 2 starch*

Poultry

Maple Dijon Glazed Turkey Breast

This succulent turkey breast is great to make ahead of time to pull out for fresh turkey sandwiches for a crowd.

MAKES 12 TO 14 SERVINGS

1	(5 to 6 pound) turkey breast
1	small orange, cut in half
1	small onion cut in half
⅓	cup pure maple syrup
½	cup chicken broth
¼	cup Dijon mustard
4	garlic cloves, cut in slivers
	Salt and pepper to taste

Preheat the oven to 325°F. Wash and dry the turkey and place in roasting pan. Stuff the orange and onion in the turkey cavity.

In a small bowl, combine the maple syrup, chicken broth, and mustard; set aside. With a knife, make slits throughout the turkey and stuff with garlic. Pour sauce all over the turkey. Season heavily with salt and pepper.

Bake for 2 to 2½ hours or until a thermometer registers 170°F. Baste with glaze throughout baking time. Cover loosely with foil if the turkey gets too brown. Remove orange and onion and discard.

Poultry

To Prepare and Eat Now:
Slice and serve.

To Freeze: Cool to room temperature, wrap, label, and freeze. Recommended freezing time: up to 1 to 2 months.

To Prepare After Freezing:
Remove from freezer to defrost, slice, and serve.

NUTRITIONAL INFORMATION PER SERVING: *Calories 175, Protein (g) 32, Carbohydrate (g) 6, Fat (g) 2, Calories from Fat (%) 9, Saturated Fat (g) 0, Dietary Fiber (g) 0, Cholesterol (mg) 91, Sodium (mg) 162, Diabetic Exchanges: 4.5 very lean meat, 0.5 other carbohydrate*

Meat

Freezing, Thawing, and Preparing Meats

Meat

❄ Creamed meat, fish, and poultry: Recommended freezing for 2 to 4 months.

❄ Trim excess fat from meat. The more saturated fat content the meat has (fish has less fat), the longer it will keep. Beef, lamb steaks, and roasts freeze up to 9 months wrapped properly. Prepare roast, trim fat and freeze in large pieces.

❄ For long time storage: freeze meat and sliced meat with gravy or sauce to keep from drying out.

❄ Meat should be thawed in the refrigerator (allow 1 day for each 5 pounds) and can take up to 48 hours, depending on the cut. Alternately, it can be defrosted in the microwave. If you're using the microwave, make sure you cook the meat immediately as meat has already started the cooking process.

❄ Only freeze meat in its supermarket wrapping for a short time (1 months). For longer storage, wrap properly or place in airtight freezer containers.

❄ Pork will last about 6 to 8 months and sausage for about 3 months. Ham and other cured meats lose color and may become rancid quicker than other meats.

❄ Meatloaf: Prepare as usual. Do not put bacon strips on top. Can be frozen baked or unbaked. Recommended freezing for 3 to 4 months.

Sirloin Strips and Asparagus

Sirloin strips, asparagus, and a rich beefy sauce make this a nice evening choice. Serve over rice, potatoes, or pasta.

MAKES 4 SERVINGS

1   pound asparagus, ends trimmed, cut into 2-inches pieces

1   onion, sliced

1   (10.75-ounce) can beef broth, divided

1   pound boneless sirloin steak, trimmed of excess fat and cut into thin strips

1   (10.75-ounce) can tomato puree

1   teaspoon dried basil leaves

¼   teaspoon pepper

Coat a large non-stick skillet with non-stick cooking spray and cook asparagus, onion, and ⅔ cup beef broth, stirring occasionally, for 5 to 7 minutes, or until the liquid has almost evaporated; remove the asparagus mixture from the skillet. Add the steak and cook for about 5 to 7 minutes, stirring, until the steak is no longer pink. Return the asparagus mixture to the skillet. Stir in the remaining broth and the tomato purée, basil, and pepper. Cook for 5 to 7 minutes longer, stirring frequently, until the meat is done.

To Prepare and Eat Now: Eat when ready.

To Freeze: Cool to room temperature, then transfer to freezer containers, label, and freeze. Recommended freezing time: up to 2 months.

To Prepare After Freezing: Remove from freezer to defrost. Reheat in a non-stick skillet over a low heat until thoroughly heated. Alternately, you can reheat in the microwave.

NUTRITIONAL INFORMATION PER SERVING: *Calories 225, Protein (g) 30, Carbohydrate (g) 15, Fat (g) 5, Calories from Fat (%) 20, Saturated Fat (g) 2, Dietary Fiber (g) 4, Cholesterol (mg) 46, Sodium (mg) 396, Diabetic Exchanges: 3 lean meat, 3 vegetable*

Meat

Swiss Steak

This is a sophisticated name for smothered round steak in tomato gravy. The meat needs cooking awhile to tenderize. Try serving with wild rice mixed with peas.

MAKES 6 SERVINGS

2	pound round steak, trimmed of excess fat
	Salt and pepper to taste
1½	cups chopped onion
1	teaspoon minced garlic
½	pound mushrooms, sliced
1	(15.5-ounce) can chopped tomatoes, with their juice
1	(8-ounce) can tomato sauce
1	(16-ounce) package baby carrots

Season the steak with salt and pepper.

In a large non-stick skillet coated with non-stick cooking spray, sauté the onion, garlic, and mushrooms over medium heat until tender, about 5 minutes.

Add the steak to the skillet and brown on both sides for about 7 minutes. Add the tomatoes, tomato sauce, and carrots. Bring to a boil; reduce the heat, and cook, covered, until the meat is very tender, about 1½ to 2 hours.

To Prepare and Eat Now: Eat when ready.

To Freeze: Cool to room temperature, then wrap, label, and freeze. Recommended freezing time: up to 2 months.

To Prepare After Freezing: Remove from freezer to defrost. Reheat in non-stick skillet over low heat until well heated.

NUTRITIONAL INFORMATION PER SERVING: *Calories 263, Protein (g) 37, Carbohydrate (g) 16, Fat (g) 5, Calories from Fat (%) 18, Saturated Fat (g) 2, Dietary Fiber (g) 2, Cholesterol (mg) 85, Sodium (mg) 478, Diabetic Exchanges: 4.5 very lean meat, 3 vegetable*

Meat

Best Beef Brisket

This is a great make-ahead recipe since all you do is season the meat, pop it in the oven, and forget about it. The sweet-spicy sauce infuses the brisket with tons of flavor. Serve for a meal or use leftover brisket (if you have some) to make the best sandwiches.

MAKES 12 TO 14 SERVINGS

1	(5 to 6 pound) trimmed beef brisket
	Salt and pepper to taste
1	onion, finely chopped
1	teaspoon ground ginger
1	tablespoon minced garlic
¼	cup grainy or Creole mustard
1	cup diet cola
½	cup ketchup
¼	cup soy sauce
¼	cup honey

Season the brisket with salt and pepper and set aside.

In a small bowl, mix together the onion, ginger, garlic, mustard, cola, ketchup, soy sauce, and honey. Spread over the brisket, cover, and refrigerate overnight.

Preheat the oven to 325°F. Place the brisket and marinade in the oven in a heavy pot. Bake, covered, for 5 to 6 hours or until the brisket is very tender.

To Prepare and Eat Now: Slice against the grain and serve.

To Freeze: Cool to room temperature, then transfer both the brisket and the sauce to a freezer container, label, and freeze. Recommended freezing time: up to 2 to 4 months.

To Prepare After Freezing: Remove from freezer to defrost. Preheat the oven to 325°F. and bake, covered, with sauce. Slice against the grain to serve.

NUTRITIONAL INFORMATION PER SERVING: *Calories 286, Protein (g) 41, Carbohydrate (g) 9, Fat (g) 9, Calories from Fat (%) 28, Saturated Fat (g) 3, Dietary Fiber (g) 0, Cholesterol (mg) 83, Sodium (mg) 507, Diabetic Exchanges: 6 lean meat, 0.5 other carbohydrate*

Meat

Barbecued Pot Roast

No need to hit the barbecue pit with this mouth-watering indoor roast cooked in this spectacular barbecue sauce. Leftovers make great sandwiches.

MAKES 8 TO 10 SERVINGS

4	pound sirloin tip roast, trimmed of fat
	Salt and pepper
	Garlic powder
1	large onion, sliced into rings
1	red bell pepper, seeded and sliced into rings
1¼	cups barbecue sauce
¼	cup molasses
1	tablespoon chili powder
1	tablespoon dry mustard
1	(1-pound) bag baby carrots

Preheat the oven to 325°F. Season the meat with salt and pepper and garlic powder.

In a roaster or large heavy pot coated with non-stick cooking spray, mix together the onions, red pepper, barbecue sauce, molasses, chili powder, and dry mustard. Place in the roaster and cover with sauce. Bake, covered, for 1 ½ hours. Add the baby carrots and continue cooking for another 1 ½ hours or until the meat is tender.

To Prepare and Eat Now: Eat when ready.

To Freeze: Cool to room temperature, then wrap, label, and freeze. Recommended freezing time: up to 2 to 4 months.

To Prepare After Freezing: Remove from freezer to defrost. Preheat the oven at 325°F. Bake, covered for 30 minutes or until meat is well heated. Alternately, you can reheat in the microwave.

NUTRITIONAL INFORMATION PER SERVING: Calories 377, Protein (g) 40, Carbohydrate (g) 26, Fat (g) 11, Calories from Fat (%) 27, Saturated Fat (g) 3, Dietary Fiber (g) 2, Cholesterol (mg) 78, Sodium (mg) 336, Diabetic Exchanges: 5.5 lean meat, 1.5 other carbohydrate, 1 vegetable

Meat

Pork Tender Wellington

This is easy elegance with fantastic flavor. Don't let phyllo dough scare you away as this simple layering process wraps the spinach-covered tenderloins, making them absolutely delicious!

MAKES 6 TO 8 SERVINGS

2   (10-ounce) packages frozen chopped spinach

½   pound sliced mushrooms

1   onion, chopped

½   teaspoon minced garlic

2   (1-pound) pork tenderloins, trimmed of fat

    Salt and pepper to taste

1   package phyllo dough

Cook spinach according to package directions, drain and squeeze dry; set aside. In a large non-stick skillet coated with non-stick cooking spray, sauté the mushrooms, onion, and garlic until tender. Add the spinach. Transfer mixture to a food processor and pulse until puréed. Season to taste.

Season each tenderloin with salt and pepper. Mold the spinach mixture around the sides and top of each tenderloin.

On waxed paper, layer ten sheets of phyllo dough, spraying each layer with non-stick cooking spray. Lay the spinach-covered tenderloin on one end of the phyllo dough and roll up, tucking the ends on each side under. Repeat procedure with the remaining phyllo dough and tenderloins. Spray each wrapped tenderloin with non-stick cooking spray.

To Prepare and Eat Now: Preheat the oven to 375°F. Place the wrapped tenderloins on a baking sheet coated with non-stick cooking spray. Bake for 45 minutes or until the phyllo is lightly brown and a meat thermometer stuck into a tenderloin reads 160°F.

To Freeze: Do not bake before freezing. Wrap the individual tenderloins, label, and freeze. Recommended freezing time: up to 2 months.

To Prepare After Freezing: Remove from freezer to defrost or place directly on a baking sheet in an oven preheated at 375°F. Bake for 45 minutes to 1 hour or until a meat thermometer stuck into a tenderloin reads 160°F.

NUTRITIONAL INFORMATION PER SERVING: Calories 346, Protein (g) 30, Carbohydrate (g) 43, Fat (g) 6, Calories from Fat (%) 16, Saturated Fat (g) 2, Dietary Fiber (g) 4, Cholesterol (mg) 63, Sodium (mg) 328, Diabetic Exchanges: 3 very lean meat, 2.5 starch, 1.5 vegetable

Meat

Marinated Pork Tenderloin

The marinade in this recipe infuses the tenderloins with great flavor.

MAKES 6 TO 8 SERVINGS

⅓ cup cider vinegar

2 tablespoons sugar

2 tablespoons ketchup

2 tablespoons molasses

1 tablespoon minced garlic

1 Serrano pepper, seeded and chopped

2 teaspoons peeled, minced fresh ginger

2 (1-pound) pork tenderloins, trimmed of excess fat

In a large freezer zip-top bag, combine the vinegar, sugar, ketchup, molasses, garlic, pepper, and ginger. Add the pork tenderloins and shake the bag so the marinade coats the tenderloin.

To Prepare and Eat Now: After letting the tenderloin marinate for several hours in the refrigerator, either grill or preheat the oven to 350°F. Place the tenderloins on a baking sheet coated with non-stick cooking spray or on a rack in a shallow roasting pan. Bake for 40 to 45 minutes or until meat thermometer inserted into the thickest portion of the tenderloin registers 160°F. Slice tenderloins and serve.

To Freeze: Freeze tenderloins in marinade in a freezer zip-top bag. Recommended freezing time: up to 2 months.

To Prepare After Freezing: Remove from freezer to defrost or place directly on the grill or in an oven pre-heated to 350°F. Place the tenderloins on a baking sheet coated with non-stick cooking spray or on a rack in a shallow roasting pan. Bake for 40 to 45 minutes or until a meat thermometer inserted into the thickest portion of the tenderloin registers 160°F. Slice tenderloins and serve.

NUTRITIONAL INFORMATION PER SERVING: *Calories 139, Protein (g) 23, Carbohydrate (g) 2, Fat (g) 4, Calories from Fat (%) 26, Saturated Fat (g) 1, Dietary Fiber (g) 0, Cholesterol (mg) 63, Sodium (mg) 56, Diabetic Exchanges: 3 lean meat*

Meat

Pepper-Glazed Pork Tenderloin

Pork tenderloins are a great source of lean meat and can easily be kept in the freezer to pull out for a quick dinner. This wonderful glaze enhances the meat with a subtly sweet and spicy flavor.

MAKES 6 TO 8 SERVINGS

2	(1-pound) pork tenderloins, trimmed of excess fat
	Pepper
¼	cup honey
1	tablespoon Dijon mustard
2	tablespoons Worcestershire sauce
¼	cup reduced-sodium soy sauce
1	teaspoon minced garlic

NUTRITIONAL INFORMATION PER SERVING: *Calories 142, Protein (g) 23, Carbohydrate (g) 3, Fat (g) 4, Calories from Fat (%) 26, Saturated Fat (g) 1, Dietary Fiber (g) 0, Cholesterol (mg) 63, Sodium (mg) 178, Diabetic Exchanges: 3 lean meat*

Season tenderloins with pepper. In a freezer zip-top bag, combine the honey, mustard, Worcestershire sauce, soy sauce, and garlic. Add the pork tenderloins and shake the bag so the marinade coats the tenderloins. Refrigerate for several hours or freeze.

To Prepare and Eat Now: After the tenderloins marinate for several hours in the refrigerator, grill or preheat the oven to 350°F placing the tenderloins on a baking sheet coated with non-stick cooking spray or on a rack in a shallow roasting pan. Bake for 40 to 45 minutes or until meat thermometer inserted into the thickest portion of the tenderloins registers 160°F. Slice tenderloins and serve.

To Freeze: Freeze tenderloins in marinade in a freezer zip-top bag. Recommended freezing time: up to 2 months.

To Prepare After Freezing: Remove from freezer to defrost. Grill or bake in a preheated oven to 350°F. Place the tenderloins on a baking sheet coated with non-stick cooking spray or on a rack in a shallow roasting pan. Bake for 40 to 45 minutes or until a meat thermometer inserted into the thickest portion of the tenderloin registers 160°F. Slice tenderloin and serve.

Meat

Pork Chops with Dark Cherry Sauce

The rich intense sauce turns pork chops into an innovative pleasing dish.

MAKES 6 SERVINGS

6	boneless center cut pork chops
	Salt and pepper to taste
1	tablespoon olive oil
½	cup beef broth
3	tablespoons bourbon
1	(17-ounce) can pitted dark sweet cherries, drained with the juice reserved
2	teaspoons cornstarch
1	teaspoon dried rosemary leaves

Season the pork chops with salt and pepper.

Heat the olive oil in a large non-stick skillet and brown the pork chops, about 5 minutes on each side. Add the broth and bourbon, reduce heat, cover, and cook for 15 to 20 minutes or until pork chops are tender.

In a small bowl, whisk the cherry juice and cornstarch. Add to the pork chops, along with the cherries and rosemary, cooking until thickened, a few minutes.

To Prepare and Eat Now: Eat when ready.

To Freeze: Cool to room temperature, then wrap, label, and freeze. Recommended freezing time: up to 2 months.

To Prepare After Freezing: Remove from freezer to defrost. Reheat in non-stick skillet over low heat until thoroughly heated. Alternately, you can reheat in the microwave.

NUTRITIONAL INFORMATION PER SERVING: Calories 263, Protein (g) 23, Carbohydrate (g) 17, Fat (g) 9, Calories from Fat (%) 30, Saturated Fat (g) 3, Dietary Fiber (g) 0, Cholesterol (mg) 63, Sodium (mg) 128, Diabetic Exchanges: 3 lean meat, 1 fruit

Meat

Oven-Baked Pork Chops

Looking for that old-fashioned dish with updated taste? These moist pork chops are layers of flavor and provide a quick dinner solution. The wire rack keeps the pork chops crispy on both sides, no soggy bottom or crumbs sticking to the foil, and clean up is a breeze.

MAKES 4 SERVINGS

4	boneless pork loin chops (about 1¼ pounds)
	Salt and pepper to taste
⅓	**cup Dijon mustard**
1	**tablespoon Worcestershire sauce**
⅔	**cup Italian breadcrumbs**

Season the pork chops with salt and pepper. In a small bowl, mix together the Dijon and Worcestershire sauce. Dip each pork chop in the mustard mixture to cover and coat heavily with breadcrumbs.

To Prepare and Eat Now: Preheat the oven to broil. Cover a baking sheet with foil and lay a baking rack on top. Lay the coated pork chops on the baking rack and broil for 5 to 7 minutes on each side or until done

To Freeze: After breading pork chops, wrap individually, label, and freeze. Recommended freezing time: up to 2 months.

To Prepare After Freezing: Remove from freezer to defrost or place on rack directly from the freezer. Preheat the oven to broil. Cover a baking sheet with foil and lay a baking rack on top. Lay the coated pork chops on the baking rack and broil for 8 to 12 minutes on each side or until done

NUTRITIONAL INFORMATION PER SERVING: *Calories 302, Protein (g) 34, Carbohydrate (g) 18, Fat (g) 10, Calories from Fat (%) 30, Saturated Fat (g) 3, Dietary Fiber (g) 2, Cholesterol (mg) 81, Sodium (mg) 797, Diabetic Exchanges: 4 lean meat, 1 starch*

Ham and Sweet Potato Pot Pie with Pecan Crust

This twist on classic pot pie has ham, sweet potatoes, and a pecan crust, creating a scrumptious comfort food that pleases with every bite.

MAKES 4 TO 6 SERVINGS

1   cup chopped onion

2   cups peeled, cubed sweet potatoes (yams)

1   cup chicken broth, divided

½   cup all-purpose flour

1   cup skim milk

2   cups cubed, cooked lean ham

⅓   cup frozen peas

1   9-inch refrigerated pie crust

⅓   cup chopped pecans

In a large non-stick pot coated with non-stick cooking spray, sauté the onion over medium heat for 5 minutes. Add sweet potatoes and ⅔ cup broth. Bring mixture to a boil and simmer over medium heat for 10 minutes or until sweet potatoes are tender. Add flour, stirring. Gradually add milk and remaining broth, stirring until well combined. Add ham and peas, and bring mixture to a boil. Remove from heat and transfer mixture to a 9 x 9 x 9-inch baking dish or ramekins coated with non-stick cooking spray. If the mixture is too thick, add more broth or milk.

Unfold the crust and sprinkle pecans on top. Fold the crust in half, and roll with a rolling pin, pressing pecans into the crust until it is big enough to cover baking dish. Lay pecan crust on top.

To Prepare and Eat Now: Preheat the oven to 350°F. Bake for 25 to 30 minutes or until the crust is brown.

To Freeze: After topping with crust, cool to room temperature, then wrap, label, and freeze. Recommended freezing time: up to 1 month.

To Prepare After Freezing: Remove from freezer to defrost. Preheat the oven to 350°F. Bake for 30 to 40 minutes or until the crust is brown and the mixture is heated through. If crust browns too quickly, cover with foil.

NUTRITIONAL INFORMATION PER SERVING: *Calories 302, Protein (g) 34, Carbohydrate (g) 18, Fat (g) 10, Calories from Fat (%) 30, Saturated Fat (g) 3, Dietary Fiber (g) 2, Cholesterol (mg) 81, Sodium (mg) 797, Diabetic Exchanges: 4 lean meat, 1 starch*

Easy Beef Enchiladas

It's hard to believe this simple recipe with basic ingredients makes such outstanding full-flavored enchiladas.

MAKES 10 TO 12 ENCHILADAS

1 ¼	pounds ground sirloin
1	onion, chopped
1	cup nonfat sour cream
1	cup frozen corn
2	cups canned mild enchilada sauce, divided
2	cups shredded, reduced-fat Mexican, Monterey Jack, or Cheddar cheese, divided
10 to 12	(6- to 8-inch) tortillas

In a large non-stick skillet, cook the meat and onion over medium heat for about 6 to 8 minutes or until meat is done. Drain any excess grease. Remove from heat and stir in the sour cream, corn, and ¼ cup enchilada sauce.

Spread about ⅓ cup enchilada sauce on the bottom of a 13 x 9 x 2-inch baking dish coated with non-stick cooking spray. Spoon about 2 tablespoons of the meat mixture and about 1 tablespoon of cheese onto each tortilla. Roll tortilla around filling and place seam side down on sauce in baking dish. Pour remaining sauce over the filled enchiladas. Sprinkle with remaining cheese.

To Prepare and Eat Now: Preheat the oven to 350°F. Bake, covered, for 20 minutes or until thoroughly heated. Remove foil and continue baking until the cheese is melted and bubbly.

To Freeze: Do not bake before freezing. Cool to room temperature, then wrap, label, and freeze. Recommended freezing time: up to 2 months.

To Prepare After Freezing: Remove from freezer to defrost. Preheat the oven to 350°F. Bake, covered, for 20 to 30 minutes or until thoroughly heated. Remove foil and continue baking until cheese is melted and bubbly.

NUTRITIONAL INFORMATION PER SERVING: *Calories 246, Protein (g) 19, Carbohydrate (g) 29, Fat (g) 6, Calories from Fat (%) 21, Saturated Fat (g) 3, Dietary Fiber (g) 2, Cholesterol (mg) 39, Sodium (mg) 615, Diabetic Exchanges: 2 lean meat, 2 starch*

Meat

Enchilada Casserole

Layers of meaty enchilada sauce, cheese, and tortillas make this easy recipe a family favorite.

MAKES 8 SERVINGS

1	pound ground sirloin
1	teaspoon minced garlic
½	cup chopped onion
	Salt and pepper to taste
1	tablespoon chili powder
1¼	cups canned enchilada sauce
1	(4-ounce) can diced green chilies, drained
10	(6-inch) flour tortillas
1½	cups shredded, reduced-fat Monterey Jack or Mexican blend cheese
1	cup nonfat sour cream

In large non-stick skillet, cook the meat with the garlic, onion, salt and pepper, and chili powder until the meat is browned, about 7 minutes. Drain any excess grease. Add the enchilada sauce and green chilies. Continue cooking over low heat for 5 to 7 minutes.

Cut the tortillas into quarters. Coat a 13 x 9 x 2-inch baking dish coated with non-stick cooking spray and cover the bottom with half the tortilla quarters, overlapping lightly. Spoon half the meat mixture over the tortillas. Sprinkle with half the cheese. Arrange the remaining tortilla quarters over the cheese, overlapping slightly and top with remaining meat. Carefully spread with the sour cream and sprinkle with the remaining cheese.

To Prepare and Eat Now: Preheat the oven to 350°F. Bake, covered, for 25 to 30 minutes or until bubbly. Uncover and bake for 5 minutes longer, or until the cheese is melted.

To Freeze: Do not bake before freezing. Cool to room temperature then wrap, label, and freeze. Recommended freezing time: up to 2 to 3 months.

To Prepare After Freezing: Remove from freezer to defrost. Preheat the oven to 350°F. Bake, covered, for 40 to 45 minutes or until bubbly. Uncover and bake for 5 minutes longer, or until the cheese is melted.

NUTRITIONAL INFORMATION PER SERVING: *Calories 286, Protein (g) 23, Carbohydrate (g) 33, Fat (g) 7, Calories from Fat (%) 21, Saturated Fat (g) 3, Dietary Fiber (g) 2, Cholesterol (mg) 46, Sodium (mg) 758, Diabetic Exchanges: 3 lean meat, 2 starch*

Meat

Beefy Green Chili Enchilada Casserole

One evening, I craved Mexican food but didn't feel like making individual enchiladas so I decided to create a casserole. For a change, I used a green chili sauce, which is a little lighter than a red sauce. The outcome was sensational, with everyone going back for more!

MAKES 8 SERVINGS

1	pound ground sirloin
1	teaspoon minced garlic
1	(10-ounce) can tomatoes and green chilies
2	tablespoons chili powder
	Salt and pepper to taste
12	(6-inch) flour tortillas, cut into quarters
1	cup frozen corn
2	cups canned green chili enchilada sauce
1	cup shredded, reduced-fat Monterey Jack cheese
1	cup shredded, reduced-fat Cheddar cheese

In a large non-stick skillet, cook the sirloin and garlic until done, drain any excess liquid. Add the tomatoes and green chilies, chili powder, and season with salt and pepper, set aside.

Coat a 13 x 9 x 2-inch baking dish with non-stick cooking spray. Cover the bottom of the baking dish with quartered tortillas. Layer with half the meat, all the corn, some of the green enchilada sauce, Monterey Jack cheese, and Cheddar. Repeat layers, reserving a small amount of cheese for the top.

To Prepare and Eat Now: Preheat the oven to 350°F. Bake for 25 to 30 minutes or until bubbly. Let sit for 5 minutes and serve.

To Freeze: Do not bake before freezing. Cool to room temperature, then wrap, label, and freeze. Recommended freezing time: up to 2 to 3 months.

To Prepare After Freezing: Remove from freezer to defrost. Preheat the oven to 350°F. Bake for 30 to 35 minutes or until bubbly. Let sit for 5 minutes and serve.

NUTRITIONAL INFORMATION PER SERVING: *Calories 327, Protein (g) 24, Carbohydrate (g) 39, Fat (g) 8, Calories from Fat (%) 23, Saturated Fat (g) 4, Dietary Fiber (g) 3, Cholesterol (mg) 45, Sodium (mg) 1052, Diabetic Exchanges: 3 lean meat, 2.5 starch*

Meat

Tamale Pie

Here's a time saving way to enjoy tamales without all the effort. This meaty casserole satisfies any craving for Mexican food, with salsa and cream style corn layered with tortillas.

MAKES 10 TO 12 SERVINGS

2	pounds ground sirloin
1	onion, chopped
1	teaspoon minced garlic
1	(8-ounce) can tomato sauce
1	(16-ounce) jar salsa
1	teaspoon dried ground cumin
1	teaspoon chili powder
1	(15-ounce) can cream style corn
6	(8-inch) flour tortillas, cut into 1-inch strips
½	cup shredded, reduced-fat Cheddar cheese

In a large non-stick skillet, cook the sirloin, onion, and garlic, about 8 minutes, or until the meat is done. Drain any excess grease. Add the tomato sauce, salsa, cumin, chili powder, and corn, mixing well.

Coat a 13 x 9 x 2-inch non-stick baking pan with non-stick cooking spray and layer the meat mixture with the tortilla strips, starting with a fourth of the meat mixture and topping with a third of the tortilla strips. Continue layering, ending with the meat mixture. Sprinkle with cheese.

To Prepare and Eat Now: Preheat the oven to 350°F. Bake, covered, for 40 to 45 minutes, or until thoroughly heated.

To Freeze: Do not bake before freezing. Cool to room temperature, then wrap, label, and freeze. Recommended freezing time: up to 2 to 3 months.

To Prepare After Freezing: Remove from freezer to defrost. Preheat the oven to 350°F. Bake, covered, for 50 to 55 minutes, or until thoroughly heated

NUTRITIONAL INFORMATION PER SERVING: *Calories 209, Protein (g) 19, Carbohydrate (g) 23, Fat (g) 5, Calories from Fat (%) 21, Saturated Fat (g) 2, Dietary Fiber (g) 2, Cholesterol (mg) 42, Sodium (mg) 603, Diabetic Exchanges: 2 lean meat, 1 starch, 1.5 vegetable*

Meat

Italian Stuffed Meatloaf

Meatloaf gets flair with this moist, Italian-flavored meatloaf stuffed with cheese, spinach, and roasted red peppers.

MAKES 6 TO 8 SERVINGS

2　pounds ground sirloin

1　large egg white

1　cup tomato juice

　　Salt and pepper to taste

1　teaspoon minced garlic

1　teaspoon dried oregano leaves

1　onion, chopped

4　ounces sliced, part-skim Mozzarella or provolone cheese

½　cup frozen spinach, cooked according to directions and squeezed dry

½　cup jarred, roasted red peppers, drained and chopped

Preheat the oven to 350°F.

In large bowl, combine the sirloin, egg white, tomato juice, salt and pepper, garlic, and oregano.

In small non-stick skillet coated with non-stick cooking spray, sauté onion until tender. Add the cooked onion to the meat mixture, mixing well. Put half the meat mixture into a non-stick 9 x 5 x 3-inch loaf pan coated with non-stick cooking spray, layer with Mozzarella cheese, spinach, and red peppers and cover with remaining meat mixture. Bake meatloaf for one hour or until meat is done.

To Prepare and Eat Now: Eat when ready.

To Freeze: Cool to room temperature, then wrap, label, and freeze. Recommended freezing time: up to 2 to 3 months.

To Prepare After Freezing: Remove from freezer to defrost. Preheat the oven to 350°F. Bake for 20 to 30 minutes or until thoroughly heated. Alternately, you can reheat meatloaf slices in the microwave.

NUTRITIONAL INFORMATION PER SERVING: *Calories 188, Protein (g) 27, Carbohydrate (g) 4, Fat (g) 7, Calories from Fat (%) 34, Saturated Fat (g) 3, Dietary Fiber (g) 1, Cholesterol (mg) 69, Sodium (mg) 284, Diabetic Exchanges: 3.5 lean meat, 1 vegetable*

Meat

Jumbo Stuffed Shells

Nothing beats these stuffed shells. Stuffing shells takes some time, so plan ahead. If you're in a pinch, use commercial sauce—few will know the difference!

MAKES 6 TO 8 SERVINGS

1	(12-ounce) package jumbo shells
1½	pounds ground sirloin
2	large egg whites
¼	cup grated Parmesan cheese
¼	cup Italian bread crumbs
1	tablespoon chopped parsley
1	teaspoon dried basil leaves
½	teaspoon dried oregano leaves
	Salt and pepper to taste
	Tomato Sauce (recipe follows)
1	(8-ounce) package part-skim Mozzarella cheese, shredded

Cook pasta shells according to directions on package, omitting oil and salt; drain and set aside.

In a non-stick skillet, cook the sirloin until done; drain any excess fat. Add egg whites, Parmesan cheese, bread crumbs, parsley, basil, oregano, and season with salt and pepper. Pour half the Tomato Sauce (see recipe) in a 2-quart baking dish. Stuff shells with filling. Arrange stuffed shells in baking dish and cover with remaining sauce.

To Prepare and Eat Now: Preheat the oven to 350°F. Bake for 20 minutes. Sprinkle with Mozzarella cheese and continue baking for 10 minutes longer.

To Freeze: Do not bake before freezing. Cool to room temperature, then wrap, label, and freeze. Recommended freezing time: up to 3 months.

To Prepare After Freezing: Remove from freezer to defrost. Preheat the oven to 350°F. Bake for 25 to 30 minutes or until heated. Sprinkle with Mozzarella cheese and continue baking for 10 minutes longer.

NUTRITIONAL INFORMATION PER SERVING: *Calories 402, Protein (g) 33, Carbohydrate (g) 45, Fat (g) 10, Calories from Fat (%) 22, Saturated Fat (g) 5, Dietary Fiber (g) 3, Cholesterol (mg) 65, Sodium (mg) 667, Diabetic Exchanges: 3.5 lean meat, 2.5 starch, 1.5 vegetable*

Meat

It's a Fact!

Baked pasta dishes can be put directly from the freezer into the oven. Just remove any plastic wrap and cover with foil.

Tomato Sauce

1	medium onion, chopped
2	cloves garlic, minced
3	cups tomato juice
1	(6-ounce) can tomato paste
½	teaspoon sugar
	Salt and pepper to taste

In a non-stick skillet coated with non-stick cooking spray, sauté the onion until tender. Add garlic, tomato juice, tomato paste, sugar, and season with salt and pepper; simmer 10 minutes.

Meat

Meat and Macaroni Casserole

It's nothing fancy, but this basic meaty pasta casserole with corn and seasonings is one of those repeated standbys and a crowd pleaser.

MAKES 10 SERVINGS

2   onions, chopped

2   green bell peppers, seeded and chopped

1   red bell pepper, seeded and chopped

1   pound fresh mushrooms, sliced

1½   pounds ground sirloin

1   (16-ounce) package shell macaroni

2   (15-ounce) cans tomato sauce

1   (6-ounce) can tomato paste

1   tablespoon chili powder

2   cups frozen corn, thawed

     Salt and pepper to taste

1½   cups shredded, reduced-fat sharp Cheddar cheese.

In a large non-stick pot coated with non-stick cooking spray, sauté the onion, green pepper, red pepper, and mushrooms, about 5 minutes. Add the sirloin, cooking until done, about 7 minutes. Drain any excess grease.

Meanwhile, cook the macaroni according to the package directions omitting salt and oil. Drain. Add the pasta to the meat mixture with the tomato sauce, tomato paste, chili powder, corn, and season with salt and pepper. Place in a large casserole and top with cheese.

To Prepare and Eat Now: Preheat the oven to 325°F. Bake for 25 to 30 minutes or until thoroughly heated. Remove the foil the last 5 minutes and cook until cheese is melted.

To Freeze: Do not bake before freezing. Cool to room temperature, then wrap, label, and freeze. Recommended freezing time: up to 3 months.

To Prepare After Freezing: Remove from freezer to defrost. Preheat the oven to 325°F. Bake for 30 to 40 minutes or until thoroughly heated. Remove the foil the last 5 minutes and cook until cheese is melted.

NUTRITIONAL INFORMATION PER SERVING: *Calories 392, Protein (g) 29, Carbohydrate (g) 55, Fat (g) 7, Calories from Fat (%) 17, Saturated Fat (g) 4, Dietary Fiber (g) 4, Cholesterol (mg) 45, Sodium (mg) 699, Diabetic Exchanges: 2.5 lean meat, 3 starch, 2 vegetable*

Meat Sauce Bolognese

"Bolognese" is a thick, full-bodied meat sauce with vegetables, enhanced with wine or milk—I have used both milk and wine here to create this Italian wonder.

MAKES 8 CUPS

3	slices center cut bacon, cut into small pieces
⅔	cup chopped carrots
⅔	cup chopped celery
1	onion, chopped
2	tablespoons minced garlic
2	pounds ground sirloin
1	(6-ounce) can tomato paste
1	(14-ounce) can beef broth
1	cup red wine
1	(14.5-ounce) can whole tomatoes in juice, cut into pieces
1	teaspoon dried basil leaves
1	teaspoon dried oregano leaves
½	teaspoon dried rosemary leaves
	Dash red pepper flakes
1	cup skim milk

In a large non-stick skillet, cook the bacon for about 3 minutes or until begins to cook. Add the carrots, celery, onion, and garlic and sauté for 7 minutes or until tender. Add the sirloin, stirring until brown. Add the tomato paste, broth, wine, tomatoes, basil, oregano, rosemary, and pepper flakes. Bring to a boil and cook for 10 minutes. Add the milk and continue cooking over low heat for 20 to 30 minutes.

To Prepare and Eat Now: Serve with pasta.

To Freeze: Cool to room temperature, then transfer to freezer containers, label, and freeze. Recommended freezing time: up to 3 months.

To Prepare After Freezing: Remove from freezer to defrost. Reheat in a non-stick pot over a low heat until thoroughly heated. Alternately, reheat in the microwave. Serve with pasta.

NUTRITIONAL INFORMATION PER SERVING: *Calories 253, Protein (g) 27, Carbohydrate (g) 12, Fat (g) 9, Calories from Fat (%) 32, Saturated Fat (g) 3, Dietary Fiber (g) 1, Cholesterol (mg) 66, Sodium (mg) 575, Diabetic Exchanges: 3 lean meat, 2.5 vegetable*

Meat

Meatballs and Tomato Sauce

These incredible meatballs have a slightly different personality with a touch of nutmeg and pork. Served in a mild tomato sauce, the combination is a superb one. All ages will enjoy this simple approach to one of the classics.

MAKES 8 SERVINGS

½ cup fresh breadcrumbs (bread pulsed in food processor)

¾ cup skim milk

1 onion, chopped

1¾ pounds ground sirloin

¼ pound lean ground pork

2 egg whites

Heavy dash nutmeg

Salt and pepper to taste

¼ cup finely chopped, fresh flat-leaf parsley leaves

Tomato Sauce (recipe follows)

Preheat the broiler.

In a large bowl, soak the breadcrumbs in milk for 5 minutes. Add onion, sirloin, pork, egg whites, nutmeg, salt and pepper, and parsley, blending together. With moistened clean hands, form mixture into 2-inch balls and arrange on a baking sheet coated with non-stick cooking spray. Broil the meatballs for 5 to 7 minutes on each side; watching carefully. Add to Tomato Sauce (recipe follows).

To Prepare and Eat Now: Eat when ready.

To Freeze: You can freeze the meatballs and prepare the sauce later. To do this, place meatballs on a single tray to freeze, then transfer to a freezer zip-top bag. Or you can freeze the meatballs in the sauce. Recommended freezing time: up to 2 to 3 months.

To Prepare After Freezing: Remove from freezer to defrost. Reheat on top of the stove in a non-stick pot over low heat or until thoroughly heated. Alternately, you can reheat in the microwave.

Meat

It's a Fact!

Freeze individual portions so you can easily defrost the exact amount you need for dinner.

Tomato Sauce

1   (28- to 32-ounce) can whole plum tomatoes including juice

2   teaspoons minced garlic

1½ teaspoons dried oregano leaves

2   tablespoons finely chopped fresh, flat-leafed parsley leaves

Salt and pepper to taste

In a large colander or sieve set over a bowl, drain the tomatoes, reserving the juice. Purée the tomatoes. Add the juice and puréed tomatoes, garlic, oregano, and parsley to a non-stick pot. Season with salt and pepper. Heat until the mixture comes to a boil.

NUTRITIONAL INFORMATION PER SERVING: *Calories 198, Protein (g) 25, Carbohydrate (g) 9, Fat (g) 8, Calories from Fat (%) 33, Saturated Fat (g) 3, Dietary Fiber (g) 1, Cholesterol (mg) 63, Sodium (mg) 380, Diabetic Exchanges: 3 lean meat, 2 vegetable*

Meat Sauce

One Sunday, my daughter craved meat sauce with angel hair, so I used my pantry ingredients to create this ultimate meat sauce with cheese as a secret ingredient.

MAKES 8 SERVINGS

2	pounds ground sirloin
1	onion, chopped
1	tablespoon minced garlic
½	pound mushrooms, sliced
1	tablespoon Worcestershire sauce
1	(6-ounce) can tomato paste
2	(16-ounce) cans chopped tomatoes, with their juices
½	teaspoon sugar
1	tablespoon dried oregano leaves
1	tablespoon dried basil leaves
	Salt and pepper to taste
⅓	cup dry red wine (optional)
⅓	cup grated Parmesan cheese

In a large non-stick skillet coated with non-stick cooking spray, cook the sirloin, onion, garlic, and mushrooms over medium heat until the meat is done, about 7 minutes. Drain any excess grease. Add the Worcestershire sauce, tomato paste, tomatoes, sugar, oregano, basil, salt and pepper, and wine. Continue cooking for another 15 minutes. Stir in the Parmesan cheese.

To Prepare and Eat Now: Serve with pasta.

To Freeze: Cool to room temperature, then transfer to freezer containers, label, and freeze. Recommended freezing time: up to 3 months.

To Prepare After Freezing: Remove from freezer to defrost. Reheat in a non-stick pot over a low heat until thoroughly heated. Alternately, you can reheat in the microwave. Serve with pasta.

NUTRITIONAL INFORMATION PER SERVING: *Calories 200, Protein (g) 26, Carbohydrate (g) 12, Fat (g) 6, Calories from Fat (%) 26, Saturated Fat (g) 3, Dietary Fiber (g) 1, Cholesterol (mg) 63, Sodium (mg) 500, Diabetic Exchanges: 3 lean meat, 2.5 vegetable*

Traditional Lasagna

No-boil lasagna noodles, Italian meat sauce, and surprise ricotta filling make this classic lasagna a winner.

MAKES 8 TO 10 SERVINGS

1½   pounds ground sirloin

1   onion, chopped

½   cup finely chopped carrots

1   tablespoon minced garlic

1   tablespoon dried basil leaves

1   tablespoon dried oregano leaves

1   (6-ounce) can tomato paste

1   (14.5-ounce) can Italian style diced tomatoes and juice (pulse in food processor)

1   (15-ounce) can tomato sauce

2   bay leaves

      Salt and pepper to taste

1   (15-ounce) container light ricotta cheese

1   egg white

¼   cup chopped Italian parsley

¼   cup grated Parmesan cheese

2   cups shredded, part-skim Mozzarella cheese

1   (8-ounce) package no-boil lasagna noodles

Preheat the oven to 350°F.

In a large non-stick skillet coated with non-stick cooking spray, sauté sirloin, onion, carrots, and garlic for 5 minutes, over medium heat, until beef is done; drain any excess grease. Add the basil, oregano, tomato paste, tomatoes, tomato sauce, bay leaves and salt and pepper, cooking for 10 minutes. Remove bay leaves.

In a bowl, blend the ricotta, egg white, parsley and Parmesan.

In a 13 x 9 x 2-inch baking dish coated with non-stick cooking spray, spread a thin layer of meat sauce, then layer half the noodles, half the meat sauce, all of the ricotta mixture, and half of the Mozzarella. Repeat layers with noodles, meat and Mozzarella. Cover with foil and bake for 50 to 60 minutes or until pasta is done. Let sit 5 minutes before serving.

To Prepare and Eat Now: Eat when ready.

To Freeze: Cool to room temperature, then wrap, label, and freeze. Recommended freezing time: up to 3 months.

To Prepare After Freezing: Remove from freezer to defrost. Preheat the oven to 350°F. and bake for 20 to 25 minutes, covered, or until the lasagna is well heated.

NUTRITIONAL INFORMATION PER SERVING: *Calories 315, Protein (g) 28, Carbohydrate (g) 30, Fat (g) 9, Calories from Fat (%) 26, Saturated Fat (g) 5, Dietary Fiber (g) 2, Cholesterol (mg) 61, Sodium (mg) 645, Diabetic Exchanges: 3 lean meat, 1.5 starch, 1.5 vegetable*

Meat

Mexican Lasagna

Lasagna heads southwest with enchilada sauce and chili powder for an instant success. Try using no-boil lasagna noodles for a step saver. Just cook covered for about one hour or until noodles are tender.

MAKES 10 TO 12 SERVINGS

1¼ pounds ground sirloin

⅔ cup chopped onion

1 (14.5-ounce) can chopped tomatoes, with juice

1 (8-ounce) can tomato sauce

1 (10-ounce) can enchilada sauce

1 tablespoon dried oregano leaves

¼ teaspoon crushed red pepper flakes

2 tablespoons chili powder

1 (15-ounce) can pinto beans, rinsed and drained

1 (8-ounce) package lasagna noodles

1 cup reduced-fat ricotta cheese

1 egg white

2 tablespoons chopped green chilies

2 cups shredded, reduced-fat Monterey Jack cheese

In a large non-stick skillet, sauté the sirloin and onion until the meat is done, about 7 minutes; drain any excess grease. Add the tomatoes, tomato sauce, enchilada sauce, oregano, red pepper flakes, and chili powder. Add the beans and simmer, uncovered, 15 minutes.

Meanwhile, cook the noodles according to package directions, omitting any salt and oil.

In a small bowl, combine the ricotta cheese, egg white, and green chilies; set aside.

Spread 1 cup of the meat sauce over the bottom of a 13 x 9 x 2-inch casserole dish coated with non-stick cooking spray. Top with half the noodles, overlapping slightly. Sprinkle with half the remaining meat sauce. Spoon all of the ricotta cheese mixture over the meat mixture and spread it out lightly. Top with half the shredded cheese, the remaining noodles, and the remaining meat sauce and cheese.

To Prepare and Eat Now: Preheat the oven to 375°F. Bake, covered with foil, for 30 to 40 minutes. Uncover and bake 10 minutes or until bubbly.

To Freeze: Do not bake before freezing. Cool to room temperature, then wrap, label, and freeze. Recommended freezing time: up to 2 to 3 months.

To Prepare After Freezing: Remove from freezer to defrost. Preheat the oven to 375°F. Bake, covered with foil, for 40 to 45 minutes. Uncover and bake 10 minutes or until bubbly.

NUTRITIONAL INFORMATION PER SERVING: *Calories 302, Protein (g)24, Carbohydrate (g) 32, Fat (g) 8, Calories from Fat (%) 24, Saturated Fat (g) 4, Dietary Fiber (g) 4, Cholesterol (mg) 42, Sodium (mg) 807, Diabetic Exchanges: 2.5 lean meat, 1.5 starch, 2 vegetable*

Meat

Southwestern Lasagna

This might be one of the best lasagnas and my favorite to prepare, as there is no boiling noodles. Texture, color, flavor, and simplicity are the key.

MAKES 8 SERVINGS

1¼ pounds ground sirloin

½ cup chopped onion

1 teaspoon minced garlic

1 (14.5-ounce) can chopped tomatoes and green chilies

1 cup canned mild enchilada sauce

2 teaspoons chili powder

1½ teaspoons ground cumin

Salt and pepper to taste

1 (15-ounce) container light ricotta cheese

1 egg white

14 (6-inch) corn or flour tortillas, cut into quarters

1½ cups frozen corn

8 ounces shredded, reduced-fat Monterey Jack cheese

In a large non-stick skillet coated with non-stick cooking spray, cook the sirloin, onion, and garlic over medium heat until done, and drain any excess liquid. Add the chopped tomatoes and green chilies, enchilada sauce, chili powder, cumin, and salt and pepper, cooking for 5 minutes. Remove from heat and set aside.

Meanwhile, in a small bowl, blend the ricotta and egg white; set aside.

Coat a 13 x 9 x 2-inch baking dish with non-stick cooking spray. Cover the bottom of the baking dish with six quartered tortillas. Layer all of the corn, half the meat mixture, half the cheese, four quartered tortillas, then all of the ricotta mixture, the remaining half of the meat mixture, and the remaining four quartered tortillas and top with remaining cheese.

To Prepare and Eat Now: Preheat the oven to 350°F. Bake uncovered, for 30 minutes.

To Freeze: Do not bake before freezing. Cool to room temperature, then wrap, label, and freeze. Recommended freezing time: up to 3 months.

To Prepare After Freezing: Remove from freezer to defrost. Preheat the oven to 350°F. and bake, covered with foil, for 30 minutes. Remove the foil and continue baking for 5 to 10 minutes longer or until well heated.

NUTRITIONAL INFORMATION PER SERVING: *Calories 262, Protein (g) 24, Carbohydrate (g) 22, Fat (g) 9, Calories from Fat (%) 31, Saturated Fat (g) 5, Dietary Fiber (g) 3, Cholesterol (mg) 52, Sodium (mg) 535, Diabetic Exchanges: 3 lean meat, 1 starch, 1.5 vegetable*

Meat

Lasagna Roll Ups with Pesto Cream Sauce

These spectacular meat cheese-filled lasagna rolls baked in an easy pesto cream sauce take lasagna to new levels.

MAKES 8 SERVINGS

1   onion, chopped

1   teaspoon minced garlic

½   pound sliced mushrooms

½   cup finely chopped carrots

1   pound ground sirloin

1   cup reduced-fat ricotta cheese

1   (16-ounce) can chopped tomatoes, drained or 1 cup fresh chopped tomatoes

1   egg white

1   teaspoon dried basil leaves

1   teaspoon dried oregano leaves

      Salt and pepper to taste

1   pound lasagna noodles, cooked and drained

      Pesto Cream Sauce (recipe follows)

      Grated Parmesan cheese, optional

In a large non-stick skillet coated with non-stick cooking spray, sauté the onion, garlic, mushrooms, and carrots for 5 minutes over medium heat, until almost tender. Add the sirloin and cook until beef is done. Remove from heat and drain any excess fat. Add the ricotta, tomatoes, egg white, basil, oregano, and salt and pepper.

Meanwhile, prepare the pasta according to directions on the package; drain. Spread each lasagna noodle with about 2 tablespoons ground meat mixture. Roll up lengthwise and set in 13 x 9 x 2-inch baking pan coated with non-stick cooking spray. Pour Pesto Cream Sauce (see recipe) over lasagna.

NUTRITIONAL INFORMATION PER SERVING: *Calories 418, Protein (g) 28, Carbohydrate (g) 56, Fat (g) 11, Calories from Fat (%) 22, Saturated Fat (g) 3, Dietary Fiber (g) 4, Cholesterol (mg) 40, Sodium (mg) 233, Diabetic Exchanges: 2.5 lean meat, 3 starch, 2 vegetable*

Meat

It's a Fact!

For a shortcut, purchase pesto sauce and add the half and half to it.

Pesto Cream Sauce

2	teaspoons minced garlic
1	cup fresh basil leaves
3	tablespoons pine nuts
¼	cup grated Parmesan cheese
2	tablespoons olive oil
1½	cups fat-free half and half

In a food processor, blend together the garlic, basil leaves, and pine nuts. Add cheese and process until mixture becomes a paste. Drizzle oil in a thin stream through the processor tube. After the oil is added and mixed, gradually add the half and half through the tube.

To Prepare and Eat Now: Preheat the oven to 350°F. Bake, covered with foil, for 30 to 40 minutes. Uncover, sprinkle with Parmesan cheese, and continue baking for 5 minutes.

To Freeze: Do not bake before freezing. While you may freeze the roll ups with the pesto sauce, it is best to make the pesto sauce right before you serve it. Cool the roll ups to room temperature, then wrap, label, and freeze. Recommended freezing time: up to 3 months.

To Prepare After Freezing: Remove from freezer to defrost. Preheat the oven to 350°F. Prepare the Pesto Cream Sauce and pour over lasagna rolls in a casserole dish. Bake, covered with foil, for 30 to 40 minutes. Sprinkle with Parmesan cheese, uncover, and continue baking for 5 minutes.

Meat

Eggplant Beef Rice Dish

This excellent eggplant, meat, and rice combination served in a casserole and topped with marinara can also be used to stuff bell peppers.

MAKES 8 SERVINGS

6   cups chopped, peeled eggplant

1   onion, chopped

1   teaspoon minced garlic

½   pound ground sirloin

1   teaspoon dried oregano leaves

½   teaspoon dried basil leaves

    Salt and pepper to taste

3   cups cooked white or brown rice

2   cups marinara sauce

1   cup shredded, part-skim Mozzarella cheese

In a large non-stick skillet coated with non-stick cooking spray, sauté the eggplant, onion, garlic, and sirloin until the meat is done and the eggplant is tender, about 20 minutes. Add the oregano, basil, salt and pepper, and rice, mixing well. Transfer to a 2-quart casserole dish coated with non-stick cooking spray. Spread with the marinara sauce on top of the rice mixture and sprinkle with cheese.

To Prepare and Eat Now: Preheat the oven to 350°F. Bake for 20 to 30 minutes or until thoroughly heated.

To Freeze: Do not bake before freezing. Cool to room temperature, then wrap, label, and freeze. Recommended freezing time: up to 2 months.

To Prepare After Freezing: Remove from freezer to defrost. Preheat the oven to 350°F. Bake for 25 to 35 minutes or until thoroughly heated.

NUTRITIONAL INFORMATION PER SERVING: *Calories 205, Protein (g) 12, Carbohydrate (g) 28, Fat (g) 5, Calories from Fat (%) 22, Saturated Fat (g) 2, Dietary Fiber (g) 4, Cholesterol (mg) 24, Sodium (mg) 364, Diabetic Exchanges: 1 lean meat, 1 starch, 2.5 vegetable*

Meat

Cabbage Roll Casserole

Here is an easy version of a traditional stuffed cabbage with a sweet and sour sauce. A great New Year's Day dish and no one even realized there was cabbage in this scrumptious dish.

MAKES 6 TO 8 SERVINGS

1½	pounds ground sirloin
1	onion, chopped
1	teaspoon minced garlic
¼	teaspoon pepper
3	cups cooked rice
1	(16-ounce) bag shredded cabbage
1	(26-ounce) jar pasta sauce
¼	cup light brown sugar
1	cup shredded, part-skim Mozzarella cheese, optional

In a large non-stick skillet coated with non-stick cooking spray, cook the sirloin, onion, and garlic until the meat is done, about 8 minutes. Drain any excess liquid. Add the pepper and rice, mixing well. Spoon the meat mixture into a 3-quart oblong casserole dish coated with non-stick cooking spray. Top with the shredded cabbage.

In a bowl, mix together the pasta sauce and brown sugar. Pour over the cabbage.

To Prepare and Eat Now: Preheat the oven to 350°F. Bake, covered, for 1 hour or until the cabbage is tender. Sprinkle with cheese and uncover for the last 5 minutes.

To Freeze: Do not bake before freezing. Cool to room temperature, then wrap, label, and freeze. Recommended freezing time: up to 2 months.

To Prepare After Freezing: Remove from freezer to defrost. Preheat the oven to 350°F. Bake, covered, for about 1 hour to 1 hour 15 minutes or until cabbage is tender. Sprinkle with cheese and uncover for the last 5 minutes.

NUTRITIONAL INFORMATION PER SERVING: *Calories 278, Protein (g) 20, Carbohydrate (g) 36, Fat (g) 6, Calories from Fat (%) 19, Saturated Fat (g) 2, Dietary Fiber (g) 3, Cholesterol (mg) 45, Sodium (mg) 449, Diabetic Exchanges: 2.5 lean meat, 2 starch, 1.5 vegetable*

Meat

Stuffed Meaty Pizza

This amazing meat mixture stuffed into a bread shell and smothered with cheese makes a hearty snack or a quick dinner, needing only a salad.

MAKES 10 SERVINGS

1   loaf Italian or French bread

1½   pounds ground sirloin

1   teaspoon minced garlic

1   onion, finely chopped

⅓   cup finely chopped, peeled carrots

1   tablespoon Worcestershire sauce

½   teaspoon ground allspice

½   cup red wine

½   cup beef broth

1   (14.5-ounce) can crushed tomatoes or whole tomatoes, coarsely mashed

      Salt and pepper to taste

2   tablespoons chopped parsley

1½   cups shredded, part-skim Mozzarella cheese or smoked Gouda

2   tablespoons grated Romano cheese

2   tablespoons chopped fresh basil, optional

NUTRITIONAL INFORMATION PER SERVING: *Calories 281, Protein (g) 23, Carbohydrate (g) 28, Fat (g) 8, Calories from Fat (%) 24, Saturated Fat (g) 3, Dietary Fiber (g) 2, Cholesterol (mg) 47, Sodium (mg) 546, Diabetic Exchanges: 2.5 lean meat, 1.5 starch, 1 vegetable*

Preheat the oven to 450°F.

Split bread lengthwise and hollow out most of the inside of each bread half leaving a shell. Lightly crisp the bread in the oven for 5 minutes, watching carefully.

In a large non-stick skillet over medium heat, cook the sirloin, garlic, onion, and carrots until the meat is done and vegetables are tender. Drain any excess grease. Add the Worcestershire, allspice, wine, broth, and tomatoes, cooking for 10 minutes or until liquid is reduced. Season with salt and pepper and add parsley. Transfer meat mixture to fill the inside of the bread. Sprinkle with cheeses.

To Prepare and Eat Now: Heat broiler and broil the loaves only until the cheese is melted, about one minute. Sprinkle with basil and serve.

To Freeze: Do not bake before freezing. Cool to room temperature, then wrap, label, and freeze. Recommended freezing time: up to 2 months.

To Prepare After Freezing: Defrost or cook directly from freezer. If cooking directly from the freezer, bake at 375°F. for about 15 minutes or until heated and cheese is melted. Otherwise, heat the broiler and broil the loaves only until the cheese is melted, about one minute. Sprinkle with basil and serve.

Make Ahead Meat Patties

By adding salsa to ground meat, these patties are moist and well seasoned, perfect to pull out as needed. Try using different salsas for a variety of flavors.

MAKES 4

1	pound ground sirloin
½	cup salsa
	Salt and pepper to taste

Combine the sirloin with salsa, and season with salt and pepper. Mold into 4 patties.

To Prepare and Eat Now: Cook patties on the grill or in a non-stick skillet over medium heat until done. Serve.

To Freeze: Cool to room temperature, then wrap, label, and freeze. Recommended freezing time: up to 2 to 3 months.

To Prepare After Freezing: Defrost and cook on grill or non-stick skillet over medium heat until done.

NUTRITIONAL INFORMATION PER SERVING: *Calories 140, Protein (g) 22, Carbohydrate (g) 2, Fat (g) 5, Calories from Fat (%) 32, Saturated Fat (g) 2, Dietary Fiber (g) 0, Cholesterol (mg) 60, Sodium (mg) 180, Diabetic Exchanges: 3 lean meat*

Meat

It's a Fact!

Did you know: A half-cup serving of salsa is equal to serving of vegetables.

Veal Paprika

When you are hunting for a quick dinner, this veal dish has an incredible paprika sauce. Serve with rice to take advantage of the tasty sauce.

MAKES 6 SERVINGS

1 ½ pounds lean veal scaloppini

⅓ cup plus 1 tablespoon all-purpose flour, divided

Salt and pepper to taste

2 tablespoons olive oil

½ cup chopped onion

½ pound sliced mushrooms

1 teaspoon minced garlic

2 tablespoons paprika

2 cups chicken broth

1 cup fat-free sour cream

Dust the veal with ⅓ cup flour seasoned with salt and pepper.

In a large non-stick skillet coated with non-stick cooking spray, heat the olive oil and stir-fry the veal in batches on both sides until lightly browned, about 3 minutes. Transfer to a plate; keep warm.

In the same skillet, coated again with non-stick cooking spray, sauté the onion, mushrooms, and garlic until tender, scraping bits from the pan. Add the paprika and remaining 1 tablespoon flour, stirring for one minute. Gradually add the broth, stirring and cooking until slightly thickened with the pan juices. Stir in the sour cream and return veal to pan, heating but not boiling. Season with salt and pepper.

To Prepare and Eat Now: Eat when ready.

To Freeze: Cool to room temperature, then wrap, label, and freeze. Recommended freezing time: up to 2 months.

To Prepare After Freezing: Remove from freezer to defrost. Reheat over a low heat, slowly, so the sauce doesn't come to a boil. Alternately, reheat in the microwave.

NUTRITIONAL INFORMATION PER SERVING: *Calories 292, Protein (g) 31, Carbohydrate (g) 17, Fat (g) 10, Calories from Fat (%) 32, Saturated Fat (g) 2, Dietary Fiber (g) 2, Cholesterol (mg) 100, Sodium (mg) 236, Diabetic Exchanges: 3.5 lean meat, 1 starch*

Veal Stroganoff

Try veal for a change! This dish, with veal and mushrooms in an incredible gravy, makes a great dinner option.

MAKES 6 SERVINGS

1½ pounds lean, trimmed veal cutlets (¼-inch thick)

2 cups sliced fresh mushrooms

1 cup chopped onion

½ teaspoon minced garlic

1 cup beef broth

¼ teaspoon dry mustard

¼ teaspoon paprika

¾ cup nonfat plain yogurt

¼ cup chopped fresh parsley

Coat a large non-stick skillet with non-stick cooking spray. Add the veal, cooking over medium heat until browned, about 5 minutes. Remove from skillet and add the mushrooms, onion, and garlic to the pan and sauté until tender. Gradually add the broth, stirring, and add the mustard and paprika. Return the veal to the skillet. Cover and simmer over low heat for 20 minutes or until the veal is tender. Gradually add the yogurt, stirring over low heat only until thoroughly heated. Do not boil. Sprinkle with parsley.

To Prepare and Eat Now: Eat when ready.

To Freeze: Cool to room temperature, then wrap, label, and freeze. Recommended freezing time: up to 2 months.

To Prepare After Freezing: Remove from freezer to defrost. Reheat in a non-stick pot over a low heat. Alternately, you can reheat in the microwave.

NUTRITIONAL INFORMATION PER SERVING: *Calories 195, Protein (g) 29, Carbohydrate (g) 6, Fat (g) 6, Calories from Fat (%) 27, Saturated Fat (g) 2, Dietary Fiber (g) 1, Cholesterol (mg) 94, Sodium (mg) 248, Diabetic Exchanges: 3.5 lean meat, 1 vegetable*

Meat

Seafood

Freezing, Thawing, and Preparing Seafood

- ❄ Seafood: Always start with high quality seafood.

- ❄ A good rule of thumb: don't buy prepackaged products.

- ❄ Check for freshness by using sight, smell, and touch.

- ❄ Oxidation is especially a problem in the storage of the high-fat species of fish like salmon, trout, and whitefish.

- ❄ To best eliminate air in freezer bags, place the seafood into the bags, seal, and freeze it. After a few days, remove the frozen product from the freezer, open the package, and add a small amount of cold tap water to eliminate any air, and freeze. Use as little water as possible. It is best to not add water to the bag before freezing to keep the seafood from absorbing water until it is frozen, which can affect flavor and texture.

- ❄ Fish may be frozen in waxed paper milk cartons. To do this, place the fish in a half-gallon or quart-size carton, add water until the fish is covered to remove air, seal, and freeze. Although this method works, the seafood will absorb water during freezing, which will eventually affect its flavor and texture.

- ❄ It is best to freeze fish and seafood products rapidly. Properly packed and frozen fatty fish (salmon, trout) can be frozen for at least three months and twice that for lean fish.

- ❄ As a rule, seafood should be thawed as quickly as possible, but never in hot water or at room temperature. Cold running water remains the fastest and best means of thawing seafood. With thin packages, such as individual fillets, the thawing process should take no longer than 5 to 10 minutes. The thawing process will take longer with thicker packages.

- ❄ Seafood can also be taken directly from the freezer and cooked. But it will take longer to cook.

Seafood

Crabmeat au Gratin

This dish is simple elegance, quick to prepare for a last minute dish that's sure to impress. Make ahead of time, and refrigerate until you're ready.

MAKES 4 TO 6 SERVINGS

2   tablespoons butter

1   cup finely chopped onion

½   cup chopped green bell pepper

3   tablespoons chopped parsley

¼   cup all-purpose flour

1   (5-ounce) can fat-free evaporated milk

1¼ cups skim milk

1   egg yolk

½   cup shredded, part-skim Mozzarella cheese

    Salt and pepper to taste

    Dash cayenne

¼   cup plus 1 tablespoon chopped green onion stems (scallions)

1   pound lump crabmeat, picked for shells

½   cup shredded, reduced-fat sharp Cheddar cheese, optional

    Paprika

NUTRITIONAL INFORMATION PER SERVING: *Calories 247, Protein (g) 27, Carbohydrate (g) 14, Fat (g) 9, Calories from Fat (%) 33, Saturated Fat (g) 5, Dietary Fiber (g) 1, Cholesterol (mg) 115, Sodium (mg) 485, Diabetic Exchanges: 3 lean meat, 0.5 starch, 0.5 skim milk*

In a medium non-stick pot, melt the butter over medium heat. Add the onion, green pepper, and parsley and sauté until very tender, about 7 minutes. Add the flour and stir. Gradually add the evaporated milk and milk, stirring and cooking over medium heat until thickened and bubbly. Stir a small amount of this hot mixture into the egg yolk and return the egg mixture to the pot, cooking over medium heat for 3 to 5 minutes longer. Stir in the Mozzarella, salt and pepper, and cayenne to taste. Add the ¼ cup green onions. Carefully fold in crabmeat and transfer to a 2-quart baking dish coated with non-stick cooking spray. Sprinkle with Cheddar cheese, remaining 1 tablespoon green onions, and paprika.

To Prepare and Eat Now: Preheat the oven to 350°F. Bake for 10 to 15 minutes or until cheese is melted and bubbly.

To Freeze: Cool to room temperature, then wrap, label, and freeze. Recommended freezing time: up to 1 to 2 months.

To Prepare After Freezing: Remove from freezer to defrost. Preheat the oven to 350°F. Bake for 15 to 18 minutes or until cheese is melted and bubbly.

Crab Cakes with Dill Sauce

I think this recipe is tops with the crab cake coated in a light Parmesan breadcrumb coating. This is one recipe in which I like using fresh bread-crumbs, but Italian or plain breadcrumbs work fine too.

MAKES 8 SERVINGS

¼	cup chopped onion
¼	cup chopped green bell pepper
¼	cup sliced green onions (scallions)
2	tablespoons skim milk
1	tablespoon Dijon mustard
1	egg
	Cayenne pepper
1	cup breadcrumbs, divided
	Salt and pepper to taste
1	pound white or back fin lump crabmeat, picked for shells
¼	cup grated Parmesan cheese
	Dill Sauce (recipe follows)

In a bowl, mix together the onion, green pepper, green onions, milk, mustard, egg, cayenne, ½ cup bread-crumbs, and salt and pepper. Carefully fold in the crabmeat.

In another mixing bowl, combine the remaining breadcrumbs and Parmesan cheese. Form the mixture into eight patties and pat the crumb mixture onto both sides of the patties.

Note:

For fresh bread crumbs, just process some bread in the food processor, pulsing until you have fine crumbs.

To Prepare and Eat Now: Refrigerate for at least 1 hour before cooking. Heat a non-stick skillet with non-stick cooking spray and cook over medium heat for about 3 to 5 minutes on each side or until golden brown. Serve with Dill Sauce (see recipe).

To Freeze: Refrigerate and wrap individually and store in zip-top freezer bags. Recommended freezing time: up to 1 to 2 months.

To Prepare After Freezing: Remove from freezer to defrost or cook directly from the freezer. In a non-stick skillet coated with non-stick cooking spray, cook on medium heat for 5 minutes on each side or until cooked through and golden. If cooking frozen, cook on low heat until defrosted. Serve with Dill Sauce.

Seafood

Dill Sauce

This sauce is also great as a dip for fresh veggies. Be sure to make it right before you serve it. It doesn't freeze well.

MAKES 1 CUP

¼   cup light mayonnaise

⅓   cup buttermilk

¼   cup nonfat yogurt

1   tablespoon plus 1 teaspoon dried dill weed leaves

1   tablespoon finely chopped green onions (scallions)

2   tablespoons finely chopped onions

1   tablespoon finely chopped parsley

2   teaspoons lemon juice

     Dash cayenne

In a bowl, mix together the mayonnaise, buttermilk, yogurt, dill weed, green onion, onion, parsley, lemon juice, and cayenne.

NUTRITIONAL INFORMATION PER SERVING: *Calories 37, Protein (g) 1, Carbohydrate (g) 2, Fat (g) 3, Calories from Fat (%) 65, Saturated Fat (g) 1, Dietary Fiber (g) 0, Cholesterol (mg) 3, Sodium (mg) 76, Diabetic Exchanges: 0.5 fat*

NUTRITIONAL INFORMATION PER SERVING: *Calories 160, Protein (g) 15, Carbohydrate (g) 11, Fat (g) 6, Calories from Fat (%) 34, Saturated Fat (g) 1, Dietary Fiber (g) 1, Cholesterol (mg) 82, Sodium (mg) 368, Diabetic Exchanges: 2 lean meat, 1 starch*

Shrimp Creole

Here is a quick version of the classic shrimp dish in a light tomato sauce. Shrimp Creole is usually served over rice, but I personally enjoy it over couscous.

MAKES 6 SERVINGS

2	tablespoons canola oil
1	onion, chopped
1	teaspoon minced garlic
1	green bell pepper, seeded and chopped
3	tablespoons all-purpose flour
1	(8-ounce) can tomato sauce
1½	cups water
¼	teaspoon dried thyme leaves
2	tablespoons finely chopped parsley
2	pounds medium peeled shrimp
	Salt and pepper to taste
⅛	teaspoon cayenne
	Chopped green onions (scallions), for garnish

In a large non-stick skillet, heat the oil and sauté the onion, garlic, and green pepper until tender, about 5 to 7 minutes. Stir in the flour, stirring, for one minute. Gradually add the tomato sauce and water. Stir in the thyme, parsley, and shrimp, bring to a boil, reduce heat and cook over low heat, covered for about 10 to 15 minutes or until shrimp is done. Season with salt and pepper and add cayenne.

To Prepare and Eat Now: Sprinkle with green onions and serve.

To Freeze: Cool to room temperature, then wrap, label, and freeze. Recommended freezing time: up to 2 months.

To Prepare After Freezing: Remove from freezer to defrost. Reheat in a large skillet over a low heat until thoroughly heated. Sprinkle with green onions and serve.

NUTRITIONAL INFORMATION PER SERVING: *Calories 194, Protein (g) 26, Carbohydrate (g) 8, Fat (g) 6, Calories from Fat (%) 28, Saturated Fat (g) 1, Dietary Fiber (g) 1, Cholesterol (mg) 224, Sodium (mg) 480, Diabetic Exchanges: 3.5 lean meat, 1.5 vegetable*

Seafood

Shrimp and Rice Florentine

Yellow rice mixed with cheese, spinach, and water chestnuts create a scrumptious make-ahead dish.

MAKES 8 SERVINGS

1   (5-ounce) package yellow saffron rice

1   cup chopped onion

1   teaspoon minced garlic

1½ pounds medium shrimp, peeled

1   (10.75-ounce) can reduced-fat cream of mushroom soup

1   cup shredded, reduced-fat Monterey Jack cheese

⅓   cup dry sherry

2   cups cooked rice (long grain)

1   (8-ounce) can sliced water chestnuts, drained

1   (10-ounce) packages frozen chopped spinach, cooked and drained

2   tablespoons grated Parmesan cheese, divided

    Salt and pepper to taste

Cook the yellow rice according to package directions, omitting any oil and salt.

In a large non-stick skillet coated with non-stick cooking spray, sauté the onion, garlic, and shrimp until the shrimp is done and the onion is tender, about 6 to 8 minutes. Stir in the mushroom soup, Monterey Jack, and sherry, heating until the soup is warm. Add the yellow rice, rice, water chestnuts, spinach, Parmesan, and salt and pepper, mixing well. Pour into a 2-quart casserole coated with non-stick cooking spray.

To Prepare and Eat Now: Preheat the oven to 350°F. Bake, covered, for 30 minutes or until thoroughly heated.

To Freeze: Cool to room temperature, then wrap, label, and freeze. Recommended freezing time: up to 1 to 2 months.

To Prepare After Freezing: Remove from freezer to defrost. Preheat the oven to 350°F. Bake, covered, for 30 to 40 minutes or until thoroughly heated.

NUTRITIONAL INFORMATION PER SERVING: *Calories 286, Protein (g) 23, Carbohydrate (g) 35, Fat (g) 5, Calories from Fat (%) 16, Saturated Fat (g) 2, Dietary Fiber (g) 3, Cholesterol (mg) 136, Sodium (mg) 718, Diabetic Exchanges: 2.5 lean meat, 2 starch, 1 vegetable*

Seafood

Shrimp Casserole

Nothing beats this quick and tasty shrimp and rice casserole.

MAKES 4 TO 6 SERVINGS

1½   pounds medium shrimp, peeled

½   green bell pepper, seeded and chopped

½   cup chopped onion

1   teaspoon minced garlic

3   tablespoons all-purpose flour

1½   cups skim milk

1½   cups cooked rice

1   tablespoon lemon juice

Salt and pepper to taste

½   cup soft breadcrumbs

1   tablespoon grated Parmesan cheese

1   tablespoon chopped parsley

In a large non-stick skillet coated with non-stick cooking spray, cook the shrimp, pepper, onion, and garlic, about 5 minutes over medium heat, until the vegetables are tender and the shrimp are pink. Gradually stir in the flour and milk. Cook 5 minutes or until the mixture is thickened and bubbly, stirring constantly. Stir in cooked rice, lemon juice, and salt and pepper. Remove from the heat and pour into a 2-quart casserole dish coated with non-stick cooking spray.

In a small bowl, combine the breadcrumbs, cheese, and parsley. Sprinkle over the casserole.

To Prepare and Eat Now: Preheat the oven to 350°F. Bake for 15 minutes or until thoroughly heated.

To Freeze: Cool to room temperature, then wrap, label, and freeze. Recommended freezing time: up to 1 to 2 months.

To Prepare After Freezing: Remove from freezer to defrost. Preheat the oven to 350°F. Bake for 20 to 30 minutes or until thoroughly heated.

NUTRITIONAL INFORMATION PER SERVING: *Calories 194, Protein (g) 22, Carbohydrate (g) 21, Fat (g) 2, Calories from Fat (%) 7, Saturated Fat (g) 0, Dietary Fiber (g) 1, Cholesterol (mg) 170, Sodium (mg) 259, Diabetic Exchanges: 3 very lean meat, 1.5 starch*

Seafood

Eggplant Shrimp Casserole

Eggplant, shrimp, and rice make an ideal combination. The shrimp may be omitted here for a plain eggplant casserole.

MAKES 6 TO 8 SERVINGS

1	cup chopped onion
½	cup chopped green bell pepper
4	cups peeled and diced eggplant (about 1 pound)
1	teaspoon minced garlic
1	tablespoon olive oil
1	pound medium shrimp, peeled
3	cups cooked rice (white, wild, or brown)
1	tablespoon Worcestershire sauce
½	teaspoon dried thyme leaves
½	cup light mayonnaise
1	bunch green onions (scallions), chopped

In a non-stick skillet coated with non-stick cooking spray, sauté the onion, green pepper, eggplant, and garlic in the oil until tender, about 5 to 7 minutes. Add the shrimp, cooking until they turn pink, about 5 minutes. Add the rice, Worcestershire sauce, thyme, and mayonnaise, mixing well. Transfer to a 2-quart casserole dish coated with non-stick cooking spray. Sprinkle with green onions.

To Prepare and Eat Now: Preheat the oven to 350°F. Bake for 30 minutes or until well heated.

To Freeze: Cool to room temperature, then wrap, label, and freeze. Recommended freezing time: up to 1 to 2 months.

To Prepare After Freezing: Remove from freezer to defrost. Preheat the oven to 350°F. Bake for 30 minutes or until well heated.

NUTRITIONAL INFORMATION PER SERVING: *Calories 217, Protein (g) 11, Carbohydrate (g) 25, Fat (g) 7, Calories from Fat (%) 32, Saturated Fat (g) 1, Dietary Fiber (g) 3, Cholesterol (mg) 89, Sodium (mg) 240, Diabetic Exchanges: 1 very lean meat, 1.5 starch, 1 vegetable, 1 fat*

Seafood

Cheesy Shrimp and Rice

This incredibly quick shrimp and rice dish with a hint of cheese and salsa is a highly requested recipe.

MAKES 6 SERVINGS

1	onion, chopped
1	teaspoon minced garlic
½	cup chopped red or green bell pepper
1½	pounds medium shrimp, peeled
⅓	cup salsa
1	tablespoon Worcestershire sauce
½	cup fat-free evaporated milk
1	bunch green onions (scallions), chopped
2	tablespoons canned, diced green chilies, drained
1½	cups shredded, reduced-fat Cheddar cheese
3	cups cooked rice

In a large non-stick skillet coated with non-stick cooking spray, sauté the onion, garlic, pepper, and shrimp over medium heat for about 5 to 7 minutes. Add the salsa, Worcestershire sauce, milk, green onions, and green chilies. Stir in the cheese and rice and cook until the cheese is melted and well combined, about 5 minutes.

To Prepare and Eat Now: Eat when ready.

To Freeze: Cool to room temperature, then transfer to freezer container, label, and freeze. You can also freeze the shrimp and salsa mixture without the rice and cheese; adding when reheating. Recommended freezing time: up to 1 to 2 months.

To Prepare After Freezing: Remove from freezer to defrost. Reheat in a non-stick saucepan over a low heat or in the microwave. If you're freezing only the shrimp salsa mixture, reheat it and then add the cooked rice and cheese cooking until the cheese is melted and well combined.

NUTRITIONAL INFORMATION PER SERVING: *Calories 318, Protein (g) 30, Carbohydrate (g) 32, Fat (g) 6, Calories from Fat (%) 18, Saturated Fat (g) 4, Dietary Fiber (g) 3, Cholesterol (mg) 184, Sodium (mg) 504, Diabetic Exchanges: 3.5 lean meat, 1.5 starch, 2 vegetable*

Seafood

Shrimp Enchiladas

Ignore the long list of ingredients, this recipe is easy to just throw together.

MAKES 8 TO 10

½   cup chopped red onion

1   green bell pepper, seeded and chopped

1   jalapeño pepper, cored, seeded and minced

½   teaspoon minced garlic

3   tablespoons all-purpose flour

1   cup skim milk

½   teaspoon dried oregano leaves

½   teaspoon chili powder

½   teaspoon ground cumin

1   pound medium shrimp, peeled

1   cup shredded, reduced-fat Monterey Jack cheese, divided

⅓   cup fat-free sour cream

Salt and pepper to taste

¾   cup chopped green onions (scallions), divided

1   cup chopped tomatoes, divided

8 to 10 (8-inch) flour tortillas

NUTRITIONAL INFORMATION PER SERVING: *Calories 225, Protein (g) 16, Carbohydrate (g) 31, Fat (g) 3, Calories from Fat (%) 13, Saturated Fat (g) 1, Dietary Fiber (g) 3, Cholesterol (mg) 75, Sodium (mg) 511, Diabetic Exchanges: 2 very lean meat, 2 starch*

In a large non-stick skillet coated with non-stick cooking spray, sauté the onion, green pepper, jalapeño, and garlic until tender, about 5 to 7 minutes. Stir in the flour and gradually add the milk, stirring until well blended. Reduce the heat, stirring until slightly thickened. Add the oregano, chili powder, cumin, and shrimp, cooking over medium heat, stirring, until the shrimp are done, about 5 minutes. Stir in ½ cup cheese. Remove from heat and stir in sour cream, salt and pepper, ½ cup green onions, and ½ cup tomatoes. Divide the shrimp mixture onto the center of the tortillas and roll tightly, placing seam side down in 3-quart oblong baking dish coated with non-stick cooking spray.

To Prepare and Eat Now: Preheat the oven to 350°F. Cover the dish with foil and bake for 15 to 20 minutes. Remove foil and sprinkle with remaining cheese, green onions, and tomatoes; continue cooking for 5 to 10 minutes.

To Freeze: Cool to room temperature, then wrap, label, and freeze. Recommended freezing time: up to 2 months.

To Prepare After Freezing: Remove from freezer to defrost. Preheat the oven to 350°F. Cover dish with foil and bake for 20 to 30 minutes. Remove foil and sprinkle with remaining cheese, green onions, and tomatoes; continue cooking for 5 to 10 minutes.

Seafood

Shrimp with Creamy Roasted Red Pepper Sauce

A jar of roasted red peppers and cream cheese are all it takes to create this fantastic roasted red pepper sauce with all the flavor and no effort. Serve over rice or pasta.

MAKES 6 TO 8 SERVINGS

½ cup chopped onion

1 (12-ounce) jar roasted red peppers, drained

1 (8-ounce) package reduced-fat cream cheese, softened

1 teaspoon paprika

½ cup chicken broth

1 teaspoon minced garlic

2 pounds medium shrimp, peeled

In a large non-stick skillet coated with non-stick cooking spray, sauté the onion until tender. Meanwhile, in a food processor, process the red peppers, cream cheese, paprika, chicken broth, and garlic until smooth. Transfer to the skillet and heat over medium heat for several minutes. Add the shrimp and continue cooking, stirring, over medium heat for 5 to 7 minutes or until the shrimp are done.

To Prepare and Eat Now: Eat when ready. Serve over pasta or wild rice.

To Freeze: Cool to room temperature, then wrap, label, and freeze. Recommended freezing time: up to 2 months.

To Prepare After Freezing: Defrost and reheat in a non-stick pot coated with non-stick cooking spray over low heat until thoroughly heated. Serve with pasta or rice.

NUTRITIONAL INFORMATION PER SERVING: Calories 174, Protein (g) 21, Carbohydrate (g) 5, Fat (g) 7, Calories from Fat (%) 38, Saturated Fat (g) 4, Dietary Fiber (g) 0, Cholesterol (mg) 188, Sodium (mg) 509, Diabetic Exchanges: 3 lean meat, 1 vegetable

Seafood

Shrimp Fettuccine

Shrimp in a mild cheesy sauce tossed with fettuccine makes an easy, popular nightly meal. Any type of pasta may be used.

MAKES 8 TO 10 SERVINGS

1   (16-ounce) package fettuccine

2   pounds medium shrimp, peeled

1   large onion, chopped

1   green bell pepper, seeded and chopped

½   pound mushrooms, sliced

1   teaspoon minced garlic

¼   cup all-purpose flour

1   (12-ounce) can fat-free evaporated milk

1   (8-ounce) package shredded, reduced-fat sharp Cheddar cheese

1   bunch green onions (scallions), chopped

⅓   cup chopped parsley

Cook the fettuccine according to package directions, omitting any oil and salt. Drain and set aside.

Meanwhile, in a large non-stick pot coated with non-stick cooking spray, sauté the shrimp, onion, green pepper, mushrooms, and garlic over medium heat until tender, about 7 to 9 minutes. Stir in the flour. Gradually add the evaporated milk, cooking and stirring until bubbly and thickened. Add the cheese, green onions, and parsley stirring until the cheese is melted and shrimp is done. Toss with the pasta.

To Prepare and Eat Now: Eat when ready.

To Freeze: Cool to room temperature, then wrap, label, and freeze. Recommended freezing time: up to 3 months.

To Prepare After Freezing: Remove from freezer to defrost. Preheat the oven to 350°F. Bake, covered, for about 30 minutes or until heated through.

NUTRITIONAL INFORMATION PER SERVING: Calories 368, Protein (g) 31, Carbohydrate (g) 46, Fat (g) 6, Calories from Fat (%) 14, Saturated Fat (g) 3, Dietary Fiber (g) 3, Cholesterol (mg) 146, Sodium (mg) 350, Diabetic Exchanges: 3 lean meat, 2.5 starch, 1.5 vegetable

Seafood

Shrimp Loaf

Three simple ingredients compose a super sandwich. Cut larger slices for lunch or thin slices for pick-ups.

MAKES 10 TO 12 SERVINGS

1 (16-ounce) loaf French bread

¾ pound grilled or cooked peeled shrimp

½ cup shredded, reduced-fat Monterey Jack cheese

1 tomato, thinly sliced or ⅓ cup salsa

Slice a loaf of French bread in half lengthwise. Scoop out one side of the bread. Fill with shrimp and sprinkle with cheese. Arrange tomato slices on top. Top with the other half of bread.

To Prepare and Eat Now: Preheat the oven to 350°F. Bake, wrapped in foil, until well heated and cheese is melted, about 20 minutes. Remove from the oven and slice.

To Freeze: Wrap bread in foil, label, and freeze. Recommended freezing time: up to 1 month.

To Prepare After Freezing: Defrost or cook directly from the freezer. Preheat the oven to 350°F. Bake, wrapped in foil, until well heated and cheese is melted, about 25 to 30 minutes depending if cooking frozen or defrosted. Remove from the oven, slice, and serve.

NUTRITIONAL INFORMATION PER SERVING: Calories 147, Protein (g) 11, Carbohydrate (g) 20, Fat (g) 2, Calories from Fat (%) 14, Saturated Fat (g) 1, Dietary Fiber (g) 1, Cholesterol (mg) 58, Sodium (mg) 324, Diabetic Exchanges: 1 very lean meat, 1.5 starch

Seafood

Crawfish and Rice Casserole

Wild rice and crawfish tails make this a crowd-pleasing choice. Cooked shrimp or crab may be substituted for the crawfish.

MAKES 8 TO 10 SERVINGS

2   cups chopped onions

2   cups chopped green bell peppers

1   tablespoon minced garlic

2   pounds crawfish tails, rinsed and drained

1   (8-ounce) container light garlic and herb spreadable cheese

4   ounces light pasteurized, processed cheese spread, cubed

3   cups cooked wild rice

2   cups cooked rice (long grain)

2   bunches green onions (scallions), chopped

¼   teaspoon cayenne

In a large non-stick skillet coated with non-stick cooking spray, sauté the onions, peppers, and garlic until tender, about 5 to 7 minutes. Add the crawfish tails and both cheeses, cooking until creamy. Add the wild rice, rice, green onions, and cayenne. Transfer to a 2 to 3-quart casserole dish coated with non-stick cooking spray.

To Prepare and Eat Now: Preheat the oven to 350°F. Bake, uncovered, for 20 minutes or until well heated.

To Freeze: Cool to room temperature and wrap, label, and freeze. Recommended freezing time: up to 1 to 2 months.

To Prepare After Freezing: Remove from freezer to defrost. Preheat the oven to 350°F. Bake, covered, for 30 minutes or until well heated.

NUTRITIONAL INFORMATION PER SERVING: *Calories 270, Protein (g) 21, Carbohydrate (g) 32, Fat (g) 6, Calories from Fat (%) 21, Saturated Fat (g) 3, Dietary Fiber (g) 4, Cholesterol (mg) 119, Sodium (mg) 275, Diabetic Exchanges: 2.5 lean meat, 1.5 starch, 2 vegetable*

Seafood

Crawfish Eleganté

I tweaked this classic recipe to create a very tasty and delicious variation. Serve over patty shells or rice for a main course or in a chafing dish with melba rounds for a dip. Whichever serving option you use, this recipe always leaves a lasting impression and an empty pot.

MAKES 6 TO 8 SERVINGS

3	tablespoons butter
1	cup onion, finely chopped
1	bunch green onions (scallions), chopped
½	cup chopped parsley
1	pound crawfish tails rinsed and drained
3	tablespoons all-purpose flour
1	cup skim milk
3	tablespoons sherry
1	teaspoon onion powder
1	teaspoon garlic powder
	Dash cayenne
	Salt and pepper to taste

In medium non-stick skillet, melt butter and sauté onion, green onion, and parsley for about 5 minutes or until very tender. Add crawfish, stirring for one minute. Sprinkle with flour over the mixture, stirring for one minute. Gradually add milk, stirring until well combined, and then add sherry. Add onion powder, garlic powder, cayenne, and salt and pepper. Bring mixture to a boil, lower heat, and stir for 3 to 5 minutes longer.

To Prepare and Eat Now: Eat when ready.

To Freeze: Cool to room temperature, then wrap, label, and freeze. Recommended freezing time: up to 1 to 2 months.

To Prepare After Freezing: Remove from freezer to defrost. Reheat in a non-stick pot over low heat until well heated. May be reheated in the microwave.

NUTRITIONAL INFORMATION PER SERVING: *Calories 166, Protein (g) 19, Carbohydrate (g) 9, Fat (g) 5, Calories from Fat (%) 31, Saturated Fat (g) 3, Dietary Fiber (g) 2, Cholesterol (mg) 133, Sodium (mg) 122, Diabetic Exchanges: 2.5 lean meat, 2 vegetable*

Seafood

Crawfish Fettuccine

This is my southern standby when we have a group coming over or I need to freeze a dish for someone. The fettuccine and crawfish (cooked shrimp may be substituted) in this wonderful cheesy white sauce is a winner every time.

MAKES 8 TO 10 SERVINGS

1	pound fettuccine
3	tablespoons butter
1	large onion, chopped
2	green bell peppers, seeded and chopped
1	red bell pepper, seeded and chopped
1	teaspoon minced garlic
¼	cup all-purpose flour
1½	cups skim milk
½	pound light pasteurized cheese spread
2	pounds crawfish tails, rinsed and drained
2	tablespoons chopped parsley
1	tablespoon Worcestershire sauce
¼	teaspoon cayenne
1	bunch green onions (scallions), chopped

Cook fettuccine according to directions on package, omitting oil and salt. Drain; set aside.

In large non-stick pot, melt butter and sauté onion, green pepper, red pepper, and garlic until tender. Add flour, stirring until mixed. Gradually add milk, stirring until smooth. Add cheese, stirring until melted. Add crawfish, parsley, Worcestershire sauce, and cayenne. Toss with pasta. Sprinkle with green onions.

To Prepare and Eat Now: Eat when ready.

To Freeze: Cool to room temperature and wrap, label, and freeze. Recommended freezing time: up to 1 to 2 months.

To Prepare After Freezing: Defrost to room temperature. Preheat the oven to 350°F. Sprinkle with green onions and cook, covered, for about 40 minutes or until well heated, stirring as needed.

NUTRITIONAL INFORMATION PER SERVING: *Calories 362, Protein (g) 26, Carbohydrate (g) 46, Fat (g) 8, Calories from Fat (%) 20, Saturated Fat (g) 4, Dietary Fiber (g) 2, Cholesterol (mg) 119, Sodium (mg) 272, Diabetic Exchanges: 2.5 lean meat, 2.5 starch, 1 vegetable*

Seafood

Salmon and Asparagus Pasta Toss

Salmon and asparagus pair well in this white sauce tossed with pasta.

MAKES 6 TO 8 SERVINGS

1	(8-ounce) package spinach tortellini
8	ounces bow tie pasta
8	ounce salmon fillet
	Salt and pepper to taste
¼	teaspoon sugar
1	tablespoon all-purpose flour
1	(12-ounce) can fat-free evaporated milk
1	(5-ounce) can fat-free evaporated milk
½	cup skim milk
1	bunch fresh asparagus, cut into 2 inch pieces
½	cup chopped green onions (scallions)
1	teaspoon dried dill weed leaves
3	tablespoons grated Parmesan cheese

In a large pot of boiling water, add the tortellini and cook for about 3 minutes. To the same pot, add the bow tie pasta and continue cooking until the pasta is done, about 8 to 10 minutes. Drain and set aside.

Meanwhile, season the salmon with salt, pepper, and sugar. In a non-stick skillet coated with non-stick cooking spray, cook the salmon on each side, 3 to 5 minutes, until golden brown and cooked through. Remove the skin and cut into chunks; set aside.

In the same non-stick skillet, add the flour, stirring. Gradually add all of the milk, and heat until thick and bubbly, stirring constantly. Reduce the heat and simmer for about 5 minutes. Add the asparagus, cooking for about 3 to 5 minutes or until tender. Add the green onions and dill weed, cooking for 1 minute. Add the cooked pasta. Carefully toss in the salmon. Sprinkle with Parmesan cheese.

To Prepare and Eat Now: Eat when ready.

To Freeze: Cool to room temperature and transfer to a freezer container. Label and freeze. Recommended freezing time: up to 1 month.

To Prepare After Freezing: Remove from freezer to defrost. In a large non-stick skillet coated with non-stick cooking spray heat over medium heat, stirring. If you need more sauce, add evaporated milk or skim milk. This dish also may be reheated in an oven preheated to 350°F. and baked, covered, for about 20 to 30 minutes.

NUTRITIONAL INFORMATION PER SERVING: *Calories 279, Protein (g) 19, Carbohydrate (g) 42, Fat (g) 4, Calories from Fat (%) 13, Saturated Fat (g) 2, Dietary Fiber (g) 3, Cholesterol (mg) 26, Sodium (mg) 199, Diabetic Exchanges: 1 very lean meat, 2 starch, 0.5 skim milk, 1 vegetable*

Seafood

Roasted Salmon with Roasted Fresh Tomato Sauce

When I made this dish, my daughter, who is not a salmon fan, raved about the recipe. Serve some of the salmon for dinner and freeze the remainder for another time. The roasted spicy salmon with a balsamic fresh tomato topping is spectacular.

MAKES 4 SERVINGS

4	(6-ounce) salmon fillets
1 ½	teaspoons paprika
1 ½	teaspoons dried oregano leaves
	Salt and pepper to taste
2	cups tomatoes, cut into chunks
2	tablespoons balsamic vinegar
1	teaspoon minced garlic

Preheat the oven to 450°F.

Sprinkle the salmon with the paprika, oregano, and salt and pepper. Place on a pan lined with foil.

On another pan lined with foil, toss the tomatoes, vinegar, garlic, and salt and pepper and spread out on pan. Place both baking sheets in the oven and bake for about 10 to 15 minutes or until the fish flakes easily with a fork depending on the thickness of the salmon. The tomatoes cook about the same amount or until tender, but not mushy.

To Prepare and Eat Now: Eat when ready with tomatoes over salmon.

To Freeze: If you're preparing this dish to freeze only, undercook the salmon. Cool to room temperature and transfer to a freezer container, then wrap, label, and freeze. Tomato mixture may be made when serving and salmon frozen individually. Recommended freezing time: up to 1 month.

To Prepare After Freezing: Preheat the oven to 350°F. Bake in oven for about 15 minutes or until thoroughly heated. It may also be reheated in the microwave. Serve roasted tomatoes over the salmon if not frozen with the salmon.

NUTRITIONAL INFORMATION PER SERVING: *Calories 226, Protein (g) 35, Carbohydrate (g) 6, Fat (g) 6, Calories from Fat (%) 25, Saturated Fat (g) 1, Dietary Fiber (g) 2, Cholesterol (mg) 88, Sodium (mg) 121, Diabetic Exchanges: 4.5 lean meat, 1 vegetable*

Seafood

Salmon Cakes with Chili Sauce

If you have never tried salmon cakes, you will be surprised how outstanding they are. Using fresh salmon makes such a difference. Serve them for lunch, dinner, or as an appetizer with Chili Sauce on the side.

MAKES 6 TO 8 SERVINGS

1   pound salmon fillets, trimmed

½   cup finely ground cracker crumbs

1   egg

1   teaspoon dried dill weed leaves

1   tablespoon lemon juice

⅓   cup chopped red bell pepper

½   cup chopped green onions (scallions)

Salt and pepper to taste

Dash cayenne pepper

Chili Sauce (recipe follows)

Cut the salmon into 2-inch cubes and place in a food processor or chop coarsely by hand. Chop the salmon the consistency you prefer, I like to taste the salmon chunks in my cakes as opposed to finely chopped salmon.

In a bowl, combine the salmon, cracker crumbs, egg, dill, lemon juice, red pepper, and green onions, mixing gently until blended. Season with salt and pepper and cayenne. Form the mixture into 3-inch patties about 1-inch thick.

To Prepare and Eat Now: Heat a large non-stick skillet coated with non-stick cooking spray over medium heat and cook for about 3 minutes on each side or until golden brown. Do not overcook. Serve with Chili Sauce (see recipe).

To Freeze: Wrap patties individually in plastic wrap and transfer to zip-top freezer bags, label, and freeze. Recommended freezing time: up to 1 month.

To Prepare After Freezing: Remove from freezer to defrost or cook frozen on low heat in non-stick skillet coated with non-stick cooking spray about 5 to 7 minutes on each side until cooked through. Once defrosted, cook on medium to brown sides, but don't overcook the salmon. Serve with Chili Sauce.

NUTRITIONAL INFORMATION PER SERVING: *Calories 102, Protein (g) 13, Carbohydrate (g) 5, Fat (g) 3, Calories from Fat (%) 29, Saturated Fat (g) 1, Dietary Fiber (g) 1, Cholesterol (mg) 56, Sodium (mg) 106, Diabetic Exchanges: 2 very lean meat, 0.5 starch*

Seafood

It's a Fact!

Salmon provides a great supply of Omega-3 fatty acids, which are good for you. It's also a good source of high-quality protein.

Chili Sauce

This sauce is great with these salmon cakes, but don't freeze it!

¼   cup light mayonnaise

⅓   cup chili sauce

1   tablespoon prepared horseradish

1   tablespoon lemon juice

Dash hot sauce

In a small bowl, combine mayonnaise, chili sauce, horseradish, lemon juice, and hot sauce, mixing well.

NUTRITIONAL INFORMATION PER SERVING: *Calories 61, Protein (g) 0, Carbohydrate (g) 3, Fat (g) 6, Calories from Fat (%) 80, Saturated Fat (g) 1, Dietary Fiber (g) 0, Cholesterol (mg) 2, Sodium (mg) 197, Diabetic Exchanges: 1 fat*

Seafood

Seafood and Wild Rice Casserole

Shrimp and crabmeat mixed with wild rice with a light binding sauce makes a tasty one-dish dinner.

MAKES 8 TO 10 SERVINGS

2   (6-ounce) boxes wild rice

1   tablespoon butter

1   onion, chopped

½   pound sliced mushrooms

1   tablespoon lemon juice

2   tablespoons all-purpose flour

1½ cups chicken broth

½   cup skim milk

⅓   cup white wine

    Salt and pepper to taste

3   tablespoons grated Parmesan cheese

1   pound cooked shrimp

1   pound white crabmeat, picked for shells

1   bunch green onions (scallions), chopped

Cook the rice according to package directions; set aside.

In a large non-stick skillet, melt the butter and sauté the onions and mushrooms until tender, about 5 minutes. Add lemon juice. Gradually add the flour, stirring for one minute. Gradually add the chicken broth and milk. Bring the mixture to a boil, reduce heat, and simmer until thickened. Add the wine and continue cooking for 2 minutes. Reserve ¾ cup sauce. Combine the remaining sauce with the rice, Parmesan cheese, shrimp, crabmeat, and green onions, mixing well. Transfer to a 2-quart casserole dish coated with non-stick cooking spray. Pour the reserved sauce on top of the casserole.

To Prepare and Eat Now: Preheat the oven to 350°F. Bake, covered, for 30 minutes or until well heated.

To Freeze: Cool to room temperature, then wrap, label, and freeze. Recommended freezing time: up to 1 to 2 months.

To Prepare After Freezing: Remove from freezer to defrost. Preheat the oven to 350°F. and bake, covered, for 40 to 45 minutes or until well heated.

NUTRITIONAL INFORMATION PER SERVING: *Calories 283, Protein (g) 26, Carbohydrate (g) 31, Fat (g) 5, Calories from Fat (%) 17, Saturated Fat (g) 2, Dietary Fiber (g) 4, Cholesterol (mg) 136, Sodium (mg) 348, Diabetic Exchanges: 2 lean meat, 2 starch*

Seafood

Seafood Stuffed Bell Peppers

Instead of a meat and rice stuffing, I came up with seafood stuffing with seasonings, stuffing mix, and cheese. You might not go back to the basic meat-filled pepper after trying these. The assorted colored peppers give this recipe eye appeal with the flavor to match. The whole pepper may be stuffed for a larger portion or you can serve two halves.

MAKES 12 SERVINGS

6	assorted colored bell peppers, halved and cored
1	cup skim milk
4	cups dry herb stuffing mix
2	stalks celery, chopped
1	large onion, chopped
1½	teaspoons minced garlic
1	bunch green onions (scallions), chopped
½	cup finely chopped parsley
¼	cup grated Parmesan cheese
1	cup shredded, part-skim Mozzarella cheese
1	pound cooked shrimp, peeled
1	pound white crabmeat, picked for shells
	Heavy dose hot sauce
	Salt and pepper to taste

NUTRITIONAL INFORMATION PER SERVING: *Calories 215, Protein (g) 22, Carbohydrate (g) 22, Fat (g) 4, Calories from Fat (%) 16, Saturated Fat (g) 1, Dietary Fiber (g) 4, Cholesterol (mg) 102, Sodium (mg) 862, Diabetic Exchanges: 3 very lean meat, 1 starch, 1.5 vegetable*

Bring a large pot of water to a boil and add the peppers, boiling for 5 minutes. Remove from water, drain.

In a bowl, pour the milk over the stuffing mix and let sit until ready to use, mixing together.

In a large non-stick skillet coated with non-stick cooking spray, sauté the celery, onion, and garlic until tender, about 5 minutes. Remove from heat and add the green onions, parsley, stuffing mix, Parmesan cheese, Mozzarella cheese, shrimp, crabmeat, hot sauce, and season with salt and pepper, mixing well. Stuff the pepper halves with this mixture.

To Prepare and Eat Now: Preheat the oven to 350°F. Place the stuffed pepper halves in a baking dish. Bake for one hour.

To Freeze: Cool to room temperature, then wrap, label, and freeze. Recommended freezing time: up to 1 to 2 months.

To Prepare After Freezing: Remove from freezer to defrost. Preheat the oven to 350°F. Place the stuffed pepper halves in a baking dish. Bake for one hour.

Seafood Stuffed Potatoes

Seafood mixed with Mozzarella, Cheddar, and green onions produces an incredible potato. Great to pull out on those nights when a little something special is desired.

MAKES 6 SERVINGS

6	small baking potatoes (about 4 pounds)
1	tablespoon butter
½	cup fat-free plain yogurt or sour cream
	Salt and pepper to taste
1	bunch green onions (scallions), chopped
⅔	cup shredded, reduced-fat sharp Cheddar cheese
⅔	cup shredded, part-skim Mozzarella cheese
1	pound peeled shrimp (crawfish tails may be used)
1	pound lump crabmeat, picked for shells

Preheat the oven to 400°F.

Wash the potatoes well, and dry thoroughly. Place the potatoes directly on the oven rack, and bake for approximately 1 hour or until soft when squeezed. Cut a thin slice off top of potato lengthwise. Scoop out the inside potato flesh, leaving a thin shell.

In a mixer or by hand, mash the potato flesh with the butter and yogurt, mixing well. Season with salt and pepper. Stir in the green onions, Cheddar, and Mozzarella cheese.

In a small non-stick skillet coated with non-stick cooking spray, sauté the shrimp until done, about 5 minutes. Season to taste. Drain any liquid. Gently fold crabmeat and shrimp into potato mixture. Spoon the mixture into the shells.

To Prepare and Eat Now: Preheat the oven to 350°F. Place on a baking sheet and bake for 15 minutes or until potatoes are heated through.

To Freeze: Wrap stuffed potatoes individually, label, and freeze. Recommended freezing time: up to 1 to 2 months.

To Prepare After Freezing: Remove from freezer to defrost. Preheat the oven to 350°F. and bake for 20 to 25 minutes or until potatoes are heated through. Alternately, you can reheat these in the microwave.

NUTRITIONAL INFORMATION PER SERVING: *Calories 476, Protein (g) 46, Carbohydrate (g) 53, Fat (g) 8, Calories from Fat (%) 16, Saturated Fat (g) 4, Dietary Fiber (g) 5, Cholesterol (mg) 225, Sodium (mg) 662, Diabetic Exchanges: 5 very lean meat, 3.5 starch*

Seafood

Desserts

Freezing, Thawing, and Preparing Desserts

❄ **Fruit:** Frozen fruit can be thawed partially at room temperature and is actually best when served with some ice crystals remaining. If the fruit is to be used in a cooked dish, use it directly from the freezer.

Fruits are 80 percent or more water. When frozen, the water expands, causing a change in the texture. When thawed, the texture will be mushy so defrosted fruit is best served in a recipe and not alone.

Save time thawing fruit or vegetables by running them under cool water in the sink.

❄ **Bananas:** Overripe bananas can be peeled, broken into chunks, and stored in a freezer safe container or bag to help make creamy smoothies in no time.

Smoothies make it easy to get extra fruit into your diet and are a great breakfast or snack in a hurry. Frozen bananas are great for this. Peel bananas, slice, and place on a cookie sheet. Put in freezer and freeze until solid. Remove from freezer and blend.

❄ Fresh pineapple and fresh kiwi fruit should not be frozen because they contain an enzyme that prevents a gel from forming. Canned or frozen pineapple or kiwi fruit, however, can be frozen successfully because they have been heated in processing (heating destroys the enzyme).

❄ **Strawberries, Blueberries, Blackberries, and Raspberries:** Wash and sort, adding sugar if desired. Freeze and label. Recommended freezing for up to one year at 0°F.

❄ **To freeze sweetened berries:** Wash strawberries and drain in a colander. Remove stems and slice berries. Mix ¾ cup sugar to 4 cups sliced berries. Stir and let stand until sugar dissolves (just a few minutes), freeze.

Berries can also be crushed, sweetened, and then frozen.

❄ Freezing whole berries for garnishes: Wash large, select berries, and drain on a paper towel. Flash freeze, transfer to a freezer bag.

❄ **Peaches:** Make a simple syrup of 1¾ cups sugar boiled with 4 cups water and 2 tablespoons lemon juice. Cool. To get peels off easily, dip peaches in boiling water for 30 seconds, and then dip into ice water. Peel peaches and cut into chunks. Pour cooled syrup over cut peaches. Put peaches and syrup into plastic containers, allowing about ½ inch of headspace or freezer bags making sure peaches are completely covered by the syrup to prevent browning.

Desserts

Chocolate-Dipped Frozen Bananas

These easy-to-make dipped bananas are an ideal snack to pull out of the freezer.

MAKES 12

4   bananas

1   cup semisweet or bittersweet chocolate chips

1   tablespoon butter

    Dipping ingredients: granola, chopped nuts, miniature M&Ms

Line a sheet pan with waxed paper. Peel the bananas and cut 1 inch off each end and cut into thirds. Place the bananas on the sheet pan and freeze for 1 hour.

In a microwave-safe container, place the chocolate chips and butter in the microwave for one minute or until melted. Arrange dipping ingredients on a plate. Remove bananas from the freezer and dip into the chocolate, turning to coat completely. Roll the dipped banana in the desired ingredients. Return to pan and repeat with remaining bananas.

To Prepare and Eat Now: Eat when ready.

To Freeze: After freezing on pan, transfer to large freezer zip-top bags to store, label, and freeze. Recommended freezing time: up to 2 months.

To Prepare After Freezing: Serve directly from the freezer.

NUTRITIONAL INFORMATION PER SERVING: *Calories 137, Protein (g) 2, Carbohydrate (g) 21, Fat (g) 6, Calories from Fat (%) 39, Saturated Fat (g) 4, Dietary Fiber (g) 2, Cholesterol (mg) 3, Sodium (mg) 7, Diabetic Exchanges: 0.5 fruit, 1 other carbohydrate, 1 fat*

Desserts

Frozen Surprise S'Mores

These treats look like typical S'Mores, but have a surprise chocolate-peanut butter filling for the chocolate candy and a dollop of whipped topping for the marshmallow.

MAKES ABOUT 29

1 (4 serving) package instant chocolate pudding and pie filling

1½ cups skim milk

½ cup peanut butter

1 pound box graham crackers

1 (8-ounce) container fat-free frozen whipped topping, thawed

In a bowl, whisk together the pudding, milk, and peanut butter. Divide graham crackers in half (2 pieces together) and lay on baking sheet. Spread pudding mixture on half of the graham crackers, and top with whipped topping. Cover with other half of graham cracker, pressing down gently to form a sandwich. Freeze on baking sheet.

To Prepare and Eat Now: Eat as desired when frozen.

To Freeze: Transfer frozen S'Mores to freezer zip-top bags, label and freeze. Recommended freezing time: up to 2 to 3 months.

To Prepare After Freezing: Serve directly from the freezer.

NUTRITIONAL INFORMATION PER SERVING: *Calories 123, Protein (g) 3, Carbohydrate (g) 19, Fat (g) 4, Calories from Fat (%) 28, Saturated Fat (g) 1, Dietary Fiber (g) 1, Cholesterol (mg) 0, Sodium (mg) 174, Diabetic Exchanges: 1 starch, 0.5 other carbohydrate, 0.5 fat*

Desserts

Banana Cheesecake with Caramel Sauce and Walnuts

Combining America's favorite—cheesecake—with bananas and caramel sauce is true indulgence.

MAKES 16 TO 20 SERVINGS

1   cup reduced-fat vanilla wafer crumbs

2   tablespoons butter, melted

2   (8-ounce) packages reduced-fat cream cheese

1   cup sugar

2   tablespoons cornstarch

2   eggs

1   egg white

1½ cups mashed bananas

1   cup fat-free sour cream

1   teaspoon ground cinnamon

1   tablespoon lemon juice

1   teaspoon vanilla extract

¼   cup coarsely chopped walnuts, toasted

2   bananas, sliced

1   (12.25-ounce) jar caramel topping, warmed

Preheat the oven to 350°F. Coat a 9-inch spring form pan with non-stick cooking spray.

In a small bowl, mix together the wafer crumbs and butter and pat into the bottom and up sides of the prepared pan.

In another mixing bowl, beat the cream cheese, sugar, and cornstarch until creamy. Add eggs and egg white, one at a time, beating until blended after each addition. Add the mashed bananas, sour cream, cinnamon, lemon juice, and vanilla, mixing until combined. Transfer the filling to crust lined pan. Bake for 1 hour or until center of cake is just about set. Remove from oven and transfer to a wire rack to cool completely at room temperature.

To Prepare and Eat Now: Refrigerate until chilled and serve with walnuts, sliced bananas and drizzles of caramel sauce.

To Freeze: Cool to room temperature, wrap, label, and freeze. Recommended freezing time: up to 2 to 4 months.

To Prepare After Freezing: Defrost in refrigerator overnight. Serve with walnuts and sliced bananas, and drizzle with caramel sauce.

NUTRITIONAL INFORMATION PER SERVING: *Calories 291, Protein (g) 7, Carbohydrate (g) 44, Fat (g) 10, Calories from Fat (%) 30, Saturated Fat (g) 5, Dietary Fiber (g) 1, Cholesterol (mg) 53, Sodium (mg) 220, Diabetic Exchanges: .5 very lean meat, 3 other carbohydrate, 2 fat*

Desserts

Peanut Butter Cheesecake 🥕

A light cheesecake with a peanut butter flavor topped with chocolate syrup resembles one of our favorite candy bars.

MAKES 12 TO 16 SERVINGS

1   cup graham cracker crumbs

2   tablespoons butter, melted

2   (8-ounce) packages reduced-fat cream cheese

1   cup fat-free sour cream

1   cup dark brown sugar

2   eggs

3   egg whites

1   tablespoon cornstarch

⅓   cup creamy peanut butter

1   teaspoon vanilla extract

3   tablespoons chocolate syrup

Preheat the oven to 325°F.

In a small bowl, combine the graham cracker crumbs and butter. Pat into the bottom and up the sides of a 9-inch spring form pan.

In a large bowl, beat together the cream cheese and sour cream until creamy. Add the brown sugar, eggs, and egg whites, one at a time, beating well after each addition. Add the cornstarch, peanut butter, and vanilla, mixing well. Spoon the mixture into the crust. Bake for 50 to 60 minutes or until set.

To Prepare and Eat Now: Remove from oven and let cool to room temperature. Drizzle chocolate syrup over cheesecake and serve.

To Freeze: Wrap, label, and freeze. Recommended freezing time: up to 2 to 4 months.

To Prepare After Freezing: Defrost in the refrigerator. Serve with chocolate syrup drizzled over the cheesecake.

NUTRITIONAL INFORMATION PER SERVING: *Calories 229, Protein (g) 7, Carbohydrate (g) 24, Fat (g) 11, Calories from Fat (%) 44, Saturated Fat (g) 6, Dietary Fiber (g) 1, Cholesterol (mg) 53, Sodium (mg) 228, Diabetic Exchanges: 0.5 very lean meat, 1.5 other carbohydrate, 2 fat*

Lemon Cheesecake with Raspberry Sauce 🥕

Attention cheesecake and lemon lovers! Here is the ultimate dessert. Serve with Raspberry Sauce and you'll always make room for dessert.

MAKES 12 TO 16 SERVINGS

1 cup gingersnap cookie crumbs

2 tablespoons butter, melted

3 (8-ounce) packages reduced-fat cream cheese

1 cup sugar

2 large eggs

2 large egg whites

3 tablespoons all-purpose flour

1 tablespoon grated lemon rind

1 (8-ounce) container nonfat lemon yogurt

1 teaspoon vanilla extract

Raspberry Sauce (recipe follows)

Preheat the oven to 350°F.

To make crust, combine gingersnap crumbs and butter and pat along bottom of a 9-inch spring form pan coated with non-stick cooking spray.

In a mixing bowl, beat together the cream cheese and sugar until smooth. Add the eggs and egg whites, one at a time, beating until creamy. Add the flour, lemon rind, yogurt, and vanilla. Pour into prepared crust. Bake for 50 to 60 minutes or until center is set. Turn oven off, and let the cheesecake cool to room temperature in the oven.

To Prepare and Eat Now: Cover and refrigerate until chilled. Serve.

To Freeze: After cheesecake is chilled, wrap, label, and freeze. Raspberry Sauce freezes too. Recommended freezing time: up to 2 to 4 months.

To Prepare After Freezing: Defrost in refrigerator. Serve with Raspberry Sauce (see recipe).

NUTRITIONAL INFORMATION PER SERVING: *Calories 220, Protein (g) 7, Carbohydrate (g) 21, Fat (g) 12, Calories from Fat (%) 48, Saturated Fat (g) 7, Dietary Fiber (g) 0, Cholesterol (mg) 61, Sodium (mg) 252, Diabetic Exchanges: .5 lean meat, 1.5 other carbohydrate, 2 fat*

Desserts

It's a Fact!

Remember to use room temperature ingredients whenever you make a cheesecake. And don't overbeat them! It'll help avoid cracks.

Raspberry Sauce

MAKES 1 ¼ CUP

1   (12-ounce) package frozen sweetened raspberries, thawed (about 2 cups)

2   tablespoons lemon juice

1 ½ tablespoons cornstarch

Combine all ingredients in a non-stick saucepan; bring to a boil. Cook over medium heat, stirring until thickened. Remove from heat, cover and chill. If raspberries are unsweetened, add about ⅓ cup sugar.

NUTRITIONAL INFORMATION PER SERVING: *Calories 293, Protein (g) 9, Carbohydrate (g) 28, Fat (g) 16, Calories from Fat (%) 48, Saturated Fat (g) 10, Dietary Fiber (g) 0, Cholesterol (mg) 81, Sodium (mg) 336, Diabetic Exchanges: 1 lean meat, 2 other carbohydrate, 2.5 fat*

Desserts

White Chocolate Cheesecake

What can be better than white chocolate cheesecake in an almond oatmeal crust? One bite of this decadence is all it takes to make this a favorite. More white chocolate may be used in the cheesecake for a richer grand finale.

MAKES 12 TO 16 SERVINGS

1	cup graham cracker crumbs
½	cup old-fashioned oatmeal
2	tablespoons plus ⅔ cup sugar
1	teaspoon almond extract
2	tablespoons butter, melted
3	(8-ounce) packages reduced-fat cream cheese
2	eggs
2	egg whites
¼	cup all-purpose flour
3	ounces white chocolate, melted
1	cup fat-free sour cream
2	teaspoons vanilla extract
	Raspberries, for garnish

Preheat the oven to 325°F.

In a bowl, mix together the graham cracker crumbs, oatmeal, 2 tablespoons sugar, almond extract, and butter. Press into the bottom and up sides of a spring form pan.

In a mixing bowl, blend together the cream cheese and remaining sugar until light and fluffy. Add eggs and egg whites, one at a time, beating well after each addition. Add flour and melted white chocolate, mixing well. Add the sour cream and vanilla, mixing until well combined. Transfer to prepared pan and bake for 55 minutes or until set.

To Prepare and Eat Now: Remove from the oven, cool to room temperature, and refrigerate until well chilled. Serve with raspberries.

To Freeze: To store, wrap, label, and freeze. Recommended freezing time: up to 2 to 4 months.

To Prepare After Freezing: Remove to refrigerator to defrost. Serve with raspberries.

NUTRITIONAL INFORMATION PER SERVING: *Calories 253, Protein (g) 8, Carbohydrate (g) 24, Fat (g) 14, Calories from Fat (%) 49, Saturated Fat (g) 8, Dietary Fiber (g) 0, Cholesterol (mg) 65, Sodium (mg) 258, Diabetic Exchanges: 0.5 very lean meat, 1.5 other carbohydrate, 3 fat*

Desserts

Cheesecake Surprises

These individual luscious cheesecakes have a sweet surprise, a peanut butter cup hidden inside.

MAKES 24

1 ½   cups graham cracker crumbs

2   tablespoons sugar

2   tablespoons butter, melted

2   teaspoons vanilla extract, divided

24   bite-size peanut butter cups

2   (8-ounce) packages reduced-fat cream cheese

1   cup sugar

2   eggs

1   egg white

¼   cup all-purpose flour

1   cup fat-free sour cream

Preheat the oven to 350°F. Line a muffin pan with paper cups.

In a small bowl, combine graham cracker crumbs, sugar, butter, and 1 teaspoon vanilla until crumbs are moistened. Press crust into bottom of each muffin cup. Put 1 peanut butter cup into the center of each cup.

In a mixing bowl, beat the cream cheese and sugar. Add the eggs and egg white, one at a time, beating well after each addition. Add the flour and then mix in the sour cream and remaining vanilla. Spoon cream cheese mixture over peanut butter cups and graham cracker crusts. Bake until just set, about 20 to 30 minutes.

To Prepare and Eat Now: Allow to cool completely before serving. Refrigerate. Serve with grated chocolate, if desired.

To Freeze: Cool to room temperature. Wrap, label, and freeze. Recommended freezing time: up to 2 to 4 months.

To Prepare After Freezing: Remove from freezer to defrost. Serve with grated chocolate on top if desired.

NUTRITIONAL INFORMATION PER SERVING: *Calories 173, Protein (g) 5, Carbohydrate (g) 20, Fat (g) 8, Calories from Fat (%) 42, Saturated Fat (g) 4, Dietary Fiber (g) 0, Cholesterol (mg) 36, Sodium (mg) 158, Diabetic Exchanges: 1.5 other carbohydrate, 1 ½ fat*

Desserts

Tortoni

Toasted almonds mixed with an almond-coffee flavored whipped cream makes a wonderful creation. Try serving in champagne glasses and garnishing with shaved chocolate and toasted almonds.

MAKES 4 TO 6 SERVINGS

1	tablespoon instant coffee, dissolved in 1 tablespoon water
⅓	cup confectioners' sugar
1	teaspoon vanilla extract
⅛	teaspoon almond extract
¼	cup sliced almonds, toasted
1½	cups fat-free frozen whipped topping, thawed

In a bowl, combine the coffee, confectioners' sugar, vanilla, almond extract, and toasted almonds into the whipped topping. Divide the mixture into champagne glasses or paper lined muffin tins. Freeze until serving.

To Prepare and Eat Now: When frozen, serve.

To Prepare After Freezing: Remove from freezer and serve.

To Freeze: Freeze then transfer to freezer zip-top bags. Recommended freezing time: up to 2 to 3 months.

NUTRITIONAL INFORMATION PER SERVING: *Calories 82, Protein (g) 1, Carbohydrate (g) 14, Fat (g) 2, Calories from Fat (%) 23, Saturated Fat (g) 0, Dietary Fiber (g) 0, Cholesterol (mg) 0, Sodium (mg) 10, Diabetic Exchanges: 1 other carbohydrate, 0.5 fat*

Desserts

Two-Minute Banana Tiramisu

Bananas, whipped topping, and chocolate-chunk cookies create this simple and sensational dessert. Even if you aren't a Tiramisu fan, this banana version will quickly win you over. I can't tell you how many times I have made this recipe and my willpower fails me each time.

MAKES 10 TO 12 SERVINGS

⅓ to ½ cup coffee liqueur, depending on taste

14 Pepperidge Farm chocolate chunk cookies

4 bananas, sliced

1 (12-ounce) container fat-free frozen whipped topping, thawed

Cocoa or chocolate shavings

Pour the liqueur into a bowl and quickly dip each cookie, then use seven cookies to line the bottom of a 10-inch square dish. Layer half of the banana slices over the cookies and cover with half of the whipped topping. Repeat layers. Sprinkle with cocoa.

To Prepare and Eat Now: Slice and Serve.

To Freeze: Cover with plastic wrap and freeze.

To Prepare After Freezing: Defrost, slice, and serve.

NUTRITIONAL INFORMATION PER SERVING: *Calories 296, Protein (g) 3, Carbohydrate (g) 47, Fat (g) 9, Calories from Fat (%) 28, Saturated Fat (g) 4, Dietary Fiber (g) 1, Cholesterol (mg) 12, Sodium (mg) 128, Diabetic Exchanges: 3 other carbohydrate, 2 fat*

Desserts

Frozen Fruit Cups

On a warm day, these delicious fruit lemonade cups make a wonderful snack or a light refreshing dessert.

MAKES 14

1 ½ cups pineapple juice

1 (15-ounce) can peaches, drained and coarsely chopped

1 (15-ounce) can apricots, drained and coarsely chopped

1 (6-ounce) can frozen lemonade, thawed

¼ cup sugar

1 (10-ounce) package frozen strawberries, thawed

2 bananas, diced

Line a muffin pan with paper cups.

In a large bowl, mix together the pineapple juice, peaches, apricots, lemonade, sugar, strawberries, and bananas. Pour mixture into the paper-lined cups.

To Prepare and Eat Now: Eat when frozen.

To Freeze: Freeze and when frozen, then transfer to freezer zip-top bags and label. Recommended freezing time: up to 2 to 3 months.

To Prepare After Freezing: Thaw slightly before eating.

NUTRITIONAL INFORMATION PER SERVING: *Calories 98, Protein (g) 0, Carbohydrate (g) 25, Fat (g) 0, Calories from Fat (%) 0, Saturated Fat (g) 0, Dietary Fiber (g) 1, Cholesterol (mg) 0, Sodium (mg) 5, Diabetic Exchanges: 1.5 fruit*

Desserts

Chocolate Peanut Butter Loaf 🥕

Chocolate and peanut butter team up for this indulgent yet light dessert.

MAKES 10 TO 12 SERVINGS

1	cup graham cracker crumbs
1	tablespoon sugar
2	tablespoons chopped almonds
2	tablespoons butter, melted
1/3	cup chocolate syrup
1/2	cup fat-free sweetened condensed milk
1/4	teaspoon instant coffee powder
1	teaspoon vanilla extract
1	(8-ounce) container reduced-fat frozen whipped topping, thawed and divided
3	ounces reduced-fat cream cheese
3/4	cup confectioners' sugar
1/3	cup skim milk
1/3	cup peanut butter

In a small bowl, combine the graham cracker crumbs, sugar, almonds, and butter and press into a 9 x 5 x 3-inch pan lined with plastic wrap.

In a bowl, mix together the chocolate syrup, condensed milk, coffee powder, and vanilla. Fold in half the whipped topping and carefully spread half the chocolate filling over the crust. Freeze for about one hour or until firm (keep remaining chocolate filling in the refrigerator).

In a mixing bowl, beat together the cream cheese and confectioners' sugar. Add the milk and peanut butter, mixing until creamy. Fold in the remaining whipped topping. Top chocolate layer with the entire peanut butter filling and freeze until firm. Carefully spoon remaining chocolate filling into the pan. Return to freezer.

To Prepare and Eat Now: When frozen, slice and serve.

To Freeze: Wrap, label, and freeze. Recommended freezing time: up to 2 to 3 months.

To Prepare After Freezing: Defrost slightly and slice into pieces.

NUTRITIONAL INFORMATION PER SERVING: *Calories 243, Protein (g) 5, Carbohydrate (g) 35, Fat (g) 9, Calories from Fat (%) 34, Saturated Fat (g) 3, Dietary Fiber (g) 2, Cholesterol (mg) 12, Sodium (mg) 139, Diabetic Exchanges: 2.5 other carbohydrate, 2 fat*

Desserts

Ice Cream Crispy Dessert 🥕

Every bite of this vanilla ice cream dessert has a chocolate peanut butter surprise. To go all the way, serve it with whipped topping and berries.

MAKES 16 TO 18 SERVINGS

1¼ cups semisweet chocolate chips

½ cup peanut butter

6 cups crispy rice cereal

1 gallon fat-free vanilla ice cream or yogurt, softened

1 (8-ounce) container fat-free frozen whipped topping, thawed, optional

1 quart fresh strawberries, stemmed and sliced, optional

In microwave-safe dish, microwave chocolate chips and peanut butter for 1 minute, stir, and reheat as needed to melt.

Place cereal in a large bowl and pour melted chocolate mixture over, tossing gently to combine. Spread mixture onto a baking pan lined with wax paper to cool. Once firm, break up into small pieces. Reserve 1 cup of this mixture for topping. Fold remaining cereal mixture into softened ice cream. Transfer to a 10-inch spring form pan. Sprinkle reserved cereal mixture over top and freeze until hard.

To Prepare and Eat Now: Freeze until firm enough to slice.

To Freeze: To store, wrap, label, and freeze. Recommended freezing time: up to 2 to 3 months.

To Prepare After Freezing: Serve directly from the freezer with whipped topping and sliced strawberries.

NUTRITIONAL INFORMATION PER SERVING: *Calories 332, Protein (g) 11, Carbohydrate (g) 60, Fat (g) 8, Calories from Fat (%) 21, Saturated Fat (g) 3, Dietary Fiber (g) 2, Cholesterol (mg) 0, Sodium (mg) 232, Diabetic Exchanges: 4 other carbohydrate, 1.5 fat*

Lemon Almond Blueberry Ice Cream Dessert

Sensational simplicity! This fabulous make-ahead dessert uses ready-made products to create the perfect combination of almond, blueberry, and lemon, with a crunch at the end.

MAKES 10 TO 12 SERVINGS

1 cup graham cracker crumbs

1½ teaspoons almond extract, divided

¼ cup sugar

4 tablespoons butter, melted

½ gallon fat-free frozen vanilla yogurt or ice cream

1½ cups frozen or fresh blueberries

1 (11-ounce) jar lemon curd

¼ cup sliced almonds, toasted

Preheat the oven to 350°F.

In a bowl, mix together the graham cracker crumbs, ½ teaspoon almond extract, sugar, and butter. Press into the bottom of a 9-inch spring form pan coated with non-stick cooking spray. Bake for 10 minutes, cool completely.

Soften frozen yogurt slightly and mix in the remaining almond extract. Spoon half of the ice cream into the crust and top with the blueberries. Carefully cover blueberries with remaining ice cream, spreading evenly. Cover the top with the lemon curd, and with a knife, swirl the curd into the ice cream. Return to freezer until frozen. Sprinkle with almonds and freeze until ready to serve.

To Prepare and Eat Now: Freeze until firm enough to slice.

To Freeze: To store, wrap, label, and freeze. Recommended freezing time: up to 2 to 3 months.

To Prepare After Freezing: Serve frozen or defrost until can slice.

NUTRITIONAL INFORMATION PER SERVING: *Calories 273, Protein (g) 8, Carbohydrate (g) 47, Fat (g) 6, Calories from Fat (%) 21, Saturated Fat (g) 1, Dietary Fiber (g) 1, Cholesterol (mg) 28, Sodium (mg) 174, Diabetic Exchanges: 3 other carbohydrate, 1 fat*

Desserts

Orange Raspberry Ice Cream Dessert

Orange ice cream, lemonade filling, and almond-vanilla ice cream make a most refreshing and outstanding frozen treat.

MAKES 12 TO 16 SERVINGS

2   (3-ounce) packages lady fingers, split

2   quarts fat-free vanilla frozen yogurt or ice cream, softened, divided

1   (6-ounce) can frozen orange juice, defrosted slightly

1   (12-ounce) package frozen raspberries

1   (11-ounce) can mandarin oranges, drained

1   (8-ounce) can crushed pineapple, drained

1   tablespoon frozen lemonade concentrate

1   teaspoon almond extract

Line the bottom and sides of a 9-inch spring form pan with ladyfingers.

In a bowl, mix 1 quart ice cream with orange juice. Spoon over the ladyfingers and freeze until firm.

Place raspberries, oranges, pineapple, and lemonade in a food processor or blender, blending until smooth. Spoon over firm orange layer and return to freezer.

In another bowl, carefully mix almond extract and remaining ice cream and spoon over raspberry layer.

To Prepare and Eat Now: Freeze until firm enough to slice.

To Freeze: Freeze several hours or overnight. To store, wrap, label, and freeze. Recommended freezing time: up to 2 to 3 months.

To Prepare After Freezing: Serve from freezer and slice.

NUTRITIONAL INFORMATION PER SERVING: *Calories 186, Protein (g) 6, Carbohydrate (g) 40, Fat (g) 1, Calories from Fat (%) 3, Saturated Fat (g) 0, Dietary Fiber (g) 1, Cholesterol (mg) 3, Sodium (mg) 92, Diabetic Exchanges: 2.5 other carbohydrate*

Desserts

Lemon Ice

Lemon ice is between an ice cream and a sorbet. No ice cream maker is needed for this outstanding simple-to-make lemon treat.

MAKES 8 SERVINGS

2   cups evaporated fat-free milk

1   cup sugar

2   tablespoons grated lemon rind

⅓   cup lemon juice (fresh is best)

In a bowl, combine the evaporated milk, sugar, lemon rind, and lemon juice, stirring until well mixed. Pour into an 8-inch square pan. Freeze until firm.

To Prepare and Eat Now: Freeze until firm enough to scoop out.

To Freeze: To store, wrap, label, and freeze. Recommended freezing time: up to 2 to 3 months.

To Prepare After Freezing: Scoop out the lemon ice to serve. Garnish with fresh berries and a sprig of mint.

NUTRITIONAL INFORMATION PER SERVING: *Calories 150, Protein (g) 5, Carbohydrate (g) 33, Fat (g) 0, Calories from Fat (%) 0, Saturated Fat (g) 0, Dietary Fiber (g) 0, Cholesterol (mg) 3, Sodium (mg) 74, Diabetic Exchanges: 2 other carbohydrate*

Desserts

Pies, Cookies, and Cakes

Freezing, Thawing, and Preparing Pies, Cookies, and Cakes

❄ **Cookies, Cakes and Frosting:** Baked cookies can be frozen up to 6 months.

❄ **Frostings that freeze well:** fudge frosting or confectioners' sugar icing. Do not freeze seven minute frosting, or frosting made with egg whites.

Frosted or filled cakes should be thawed in the refrigerator. Unfrosted cakes can be thawed in their wrapping at room temperature. Recommended freezing for 3 months.

Angel food cakes can be frozen 4 to 6 months.

❄ **Pies:** Unbaked fruit pies have a better fresh fruit flavor than frozen baked pies, but the bottom crust tends to get soggy. If freezing, the filling should be slightly thicker than usual (can use extra 1 tablespoon flour, ½ tablespoon cornstarch). Do not cut vents in top crust. Bake without thawing, cut slits in upper crust and bake at 375°F. for 40 to 50 minutes or until top crust is brown. Recommended freezing baked fruit pies, mince pies, nut pies for 3 to 4 months. Custard pies recommended for 2 months.

Pie dough freezes well, make some extra to have when needed. Wrap tightly in heavy-duty aluminum foil or freezer-weight plastic wrap and seal in a freezer bag. It should keep for up to 6 months. For added convenience, freeze pie crusts in the pan.

❄ Prepare and bake pastry as usual. Cool, package, and freeze. Thaw in wrapping at room temperature. Recommended freezing for 2 to 3 months.

Maple Nut Tart

This tart just came together one night as I had just flown home and had two bags of honey roasted peanuts from the airplane. It was wonderful with peanuts and toasted pecans, but you can use your choice of nuts. Top with whipped topping for a nice finishing touch.

MAKES 8 TO 10 SERVINGS

1   egg

3   tablespoons buttermilk

½   cup pure maple syrup

1   teaspoon vanilla extract

2   tablespoons butter, melted

½   cup honey roasted peanuts, toasted or honey roasted pecans or combination

1   (9-inch) pie crust

Preheat the oven to 350°F.

In a bowl, mix together the egg, buttermilk, maple syrup, vanilla, and butter. Stir in the nuts. Pour mixture into pie crust. Bake for 25 to 30 minutes or until top of tart is puffed and bubbly and crust is brown.

To Prepare and Eat Now: Cool and serve.

To Freeze: Cool to room temperature, then wrap, label, and freeze. Recommended freezing time: up to 3 to 4 months.

To Prepare After Freezing: Remove from freezer to defrost. Slice and serve.

NUTRITIONAL INFORMATION PER SERVING: *Calories 220, Protein (g) 3, Carbohydrate (g) 23, Fat (g) 13, Calories from Fat (%) 52, Saturated Fat (g) 5, Dietary Fiber (g) 1, Cholesterol (mg) 31, Sodium (mg) 156, Diabetic Exchanges: 1.5 other carbohydrate, 2.5 fat*

Pecan Caramel Pie

Toasted pecans and caramels make this the ultimate decadence. Everyone who has a piece asks immediately for the recipe!

MAKES 8 TO 10 SERVINGS

24	caramels
¼	cup butter
¼	cup water
⅓	cup sugar
2	eggs
1	teaspoon vanilla extract
½	cup coarsely chopped pecans, toasted
1	(9-inch) pie crust

Preheat the oven to 400°F.

In a large non-stick saucepan, combine the caramels, butter, and water. Cook, stirring constantly, about 5 minutes or until caramels are melted. Remove from heat.

In a bowl, mix the sugar, eggs, and vanilla; stir into caramel mixture. Add pecans. Pour pecan caramel filling into prepared crust. Bake for 10 minutes, reduce heat to 350°F. and continue baking for 20 more minutes or until filling is set.

To Prepare and Eat Now: Slice and serve.

To Freeze: Cool to room temperature, then wrap, label, and freeze. Recommended freezing time: up to 3 to 4 months.

To Prepare After Freezing: Remove from freezer to defrost. Slice and serve.

NUTRITIONAL INFORMATION PER SERVING: *Calories 310, Protein (g) 4, Carbohydrate (g) 37, Fat (g) 17, Calories from Fat (%) 49, Saturated Fat (g) 7, Dietary Fiber (g) 1, Cholesterol (mg) 60, Sodium (mg) 185, Diabetic Exchanges: 2.5 other carbohydrate, 3.5 fat*

Chess Pie

Sometimes, a plain chess pie just hits the spot.

MAKES 8 TO 10 SERVINGS

2	eggs
1	cup sugar
⅔	cup buttermilk
2	tablespoons butter, melted
2	tablespoons all-purpose flour
1	teaspoon vanilla extract
1	(9-inch) pie crust

Preheat the oven to 350°F.

In a bowl, whisk the eggs, sugar, buttermilk, butter, flour, and vanilla. Pour into pie crust and bake for 35 to 40 minutes.

To Prepare and Eat Now: Serve warm or room temperature.

To Freeze: Cool to room temperature, then wrap, label, and freeze. Recommended freezing time: up to 2 to 3 months.

To Prepare After Freezing: Remove from freezer to defrost. Slice and serve.

NUTRITIONAL INFORMATION PER SERVING: *Calories 220, Protein (g) 3, Carbohydrate (g) 32, Fat (g) 9, Calories from Fat (%) 36, Saturated Fat (g) 4, Dietary Fiber (g) 0, Cholesterol (mg) 53, Sodium (mg) 126, Diabetic Exchanges: 2 other carbohydrate, 2 fat*

Apple Crumble Custard Pie

The cinnamon apple mixture on the bottom, custard filling, and a cinnamon crumble topping make this Apple Pie one of the very best I have ever made.

MAKES 8 TO 10 SERVINGS

3   tablespoons butter, divided

2   tart baking apples, peeled and sliced

¼   cup plus ½ cup sugar

½   teaspoon cinnamon

2   eggs

3   egg whites

2   tablespoons all-purpose flour

1   teaspoon vanilla extract

¾   cup buttermilk

1   (9-inch) pie crust

Crumble Topping (recipe follows)

Preheat the oven to 325°F.

In a non-stick skillet, melt 1 tablespoon butter and add the apples, ¼ cup sugar, and cinnamon. Cook, stirring occasionally, 3 to 5 minutes or until apples are tender; set aside.

In a large bowl, beat together remaining butter and sugar until creamy. Add eggs and egg whites, one at a time, beating after each addition. Add the flour and vanilla, beating until blended. Add the buttermilk, beating until smooth. Spoon apple mixture into the pie crust and pour buttermilk mixture over the apple mixture. Bake for 30 minutes and top with Crumble Topping. Continue baking for 40 minutes longer or until a knife inserted in the center comes out clean.

To Prepare and Eat Now: Serve warm or room temperature

To Freeze: Cool to room temperature, then wrap, label, and freeze. Recommended freezing time: up to 2 to 3 months.

To Prepare After Freezing: Defrost and serve room temperature or heat in the oven until warm. Alternately, you can reheat slices in the microwave to serve warm.

NUTRITIONAL INFORMATION PER SERVING: *Calories 286, Protein (g) 4, Carbohydrate (g) 39, Fat (g) 12, Calories from Fat (%) 39, Saturated Fat (g) 6, Dietary Fiber (g) 1, Cholesterol (mg) 62, Sodium (mg) 171, Diabetic Exchanges: 2.5 other carbohydrate, 2.5 fat*

It's a Fact!

To keep your pie crust from browning too quickly, cover the edges with strips of foil and keep baking.

Crumble Topping

2	tablespoons butter
¼	cup light brown sugar
⅓	cup all-purpose flour
¼	teaspoon ground cinnamon
½	teaspoon vanilla extract

Stir together the butter, brown sugar, flour, cinnamon, and vanilla until crumbly. Sprinkle over pie.

Banana Split Pie

This dessert appeals to everyone. Use your favorite flavored frozen yogurt to create your own fabulous frozen wonder.

MAKES 16 SERVINGS

1½ cups chocolate wafer crumbs

¼ cup sugar

3 tablespoons butter, melted, divided

3 teaspoons vanilla extract, divided

½ gallon nonfat frozen vanilla yogurt, softened

3 bananas, mashed

2 tablespoons cocoa

⅔ cup confectioners' sugar

2 tablespoons hot water

1 cup raspberries, strawberries, or seasonal fruit

Preheat the oven to 375°F. In an oblong 3-quart glass dish (13 x 9 x 2-inch), mix together chocolate crumbs, sugar, 2 tablespoons butter and 1 teaspoon vanilla. Pat into the bottom of the dish. Bake for 10 minutes. Cool completely.

In a large bowl, mix together the yogurt, bananas, and 1 teaspoon vanilla. Quickly spread on top of cooled crust. Place in the freezer until the yogurt layer is set.

In a small bowl, mix together the remaining butter and vanilla, and the cocoa, confectioners' sugar, and hot water, stirring until smooth. Remove partially frozen dessert from freezer and quickly drizzle with chocolate sauce. Return to freezer.

To Prepare and Eat Now: Return to freezer for several hours or overnight. Top with fresh fruit and serve.

To Freeze: Freeze for several hours or overnight. Wrap, label, and freeze. Recommended freezing time: up to 2 to 3 months.

To Prepare After Freezing: Serve directly from the freezer and top with fresh fruit.

NUTRITIONAL INFORMATION PER SERVING: *Calories 209, Protein (g) 6, Carbohydrate (g) 39, Fat (g) 4, Calories from Fat (%) 15, Saturated Fat (g) 2, Dietary Fiber (g) 1, Cholesterol (mg) 7, Sodium (mg) 126, Diabetic Exchanges: 2.5 other carbohydrate, 1 fat*

Frozen Pistachio Pie

This pie, laced with nuts in a chocolate crust and topped with hot fudge, is refreshingly indulgent.

MAKES 8 TO 10 SERVINGS

1½   cups crushed chocolate graham crackers

2   tablespoons sugar

3   tablespoons butter, melted

¼   cup chopped pistachios or cashews

1   quart fat-free vanilla ice cream or yogurt, softened

1   (4-serving) instant pistachio-flavored pudding and pie filling

½   cup fat-free chocolate fudge topping, warmed

Preheat the oven to 375°F.

In a 9-inch pie plate, stir together the graham cracker crumbs, sugar, and butter and press on the bottom and up the sides. Bake for 8 to 10 minutes. Cool completely.

Meanwhile, in a large bowl, quickly combine the pistachios, ice cream, and pudding until well mixed. Transfer mixture into cooled crust.

To Prepare and Eat Now: Freeze, covered, for at least 4 hours or until firm. Serve with warmed chocolate fudge topping on each slice.

To Freeze: Freeze, covered, for at least 4 hours or until firm. Recommended freezing time: up to 2 to 3 months.

To Prepare After Freezing: Serve from the freezer. Drizzle warmed chocolate topping on each piece when serving.

NUTRITIONAL INFORMATION PER SERVING: *Calories 272, Protein (g) 5, Carbohydrate (g) 50, Fat (g) 6, Calories from Fat (%) 21, Saturated Fat (g) 3, Dietary Fiber (g) 1, Cholesterol (mg) 9, Sodium (mg) 353, Diabetic Exchanges: 3.5 other carbohydrate, 2 fat*

Frozen Piña Colada Pie

If you are looking for a spectacular and refreshing dessert, this simple make ahead pie with pineapple and coconut flavors will have your friends asking for seconds.

MAKES 8 TO 10 SERVINGS

1	cup graham cracker crumbs
2	tablespoons light brown sugar
5	tablespoons flaked coconut, divided
1	tablespoon butter, melted
1	quart pineapple sherbet
1	(8-ounce) container fat-free frozen whipped topping, thawed
1	teaspoon coconut extract
3	tablespoons coconut, toasted

Preheat the oven to 350°F.

In a small bowl, combine the graham cracker crumbs, brown sugar, coconut, and butter. Pat into a 9-inch pie plate. Bake for about 8 to 10 minutes or until golden brown. Remove from oven and cool completely.

Carefully spread pineapple sherbet over the cooled crust. Mix the whipped topping and coconut extract and spread on top of the pineapple sherbet. Sprinkle with toasted coconut.

To Prepare and Eat Now: When frozen, slice and serve.

To Freeze: Wrap, label, and freeze. Recommended freezing time: up to 2 to 3 months.

To Prepare After Freezing: Serve directly from the freezer or defrost until soft enough to cut.

NUTRITIONAL INFORMATION PER SERVING: *Calories 191, Protein (g) 1, Carbohydrate (g) 36, Fat (g) 4, Calories from Fat (%) 19, Saturated Fat (g) 2, Dietary Fiber (g) 2, Cholesterol (mg) 3, Sodium (mg) 106, Diabetic Exchanges: 2.5 other carbohydrate, 1 fat*

Frozen Strawberry Margarita Pie

Strawberry margarita in a pie with a pretzel crust. What more could you want?

MAKES 8 TO 10 SERVINGS

1¼ cups finely crushed pretzels

2 tablespoons sugar

5 tablespoons butter, melted

1 (21-ounce) can strawberry fruit filling

½ cup frozen margarita mix, thawed

1 (8-ounce) container fat-free frozen whipped topping, thawed

Fresh strawberries, garnish

Preheat the oven to 350°F.

In a 9-inch glass pie, combine the pretzels, sugar, and butter and press evenly onto bottom and up sides of pan. Bake for 8 to 10 minutes or until lightly brown. Remove from oven and cool completely.

In a bowl, combine the strawberry filling and margarita mix. Fold in the whipped topping and spoon into crust.

To Prepare and Eat Now: Freeze for 4 hours or until firm and can slice.

To Freeze: To store, wrap, label, and freeze. Recommended freezing time: up to 2 months.

To Prepare After Freezing: Before serving, remove pie from freezer and let stand at room temperature to soften slightly. Slice and serve.

NUTRITIONAL INFORMATION PER SERVING: *Calories 228, Protein (g) 2, Carbohydrate (g) 39, Fat (g) 6, Calories from Fat (%) 25, Saturated Fat (g) 4, Dietary Fiber (g) 1, Cholesterol (mg) 15, Sodium (mg) 252, Diabetic Exchanges: 2.5 other carbohydrate, 1 fat*

Peanut Butter Pie

This enticing, no-bake, creamy, dreamy peanut butter pie makes a quick dessert in a pinch. Purchase a prepared reduced-fat graham cracker crust for an even shorter cut.

MAKES 8 TO 10 SERVINGS

1½   cups graham cracker crumbs or chocolate wafer crumbs

2   tablespoons butter, melted

4   ounces reduced-fat cream cheese

1   cup confectioners' sugar

½   cup crunchy peanut butter

½   cup skim milk

1   (8-ounce) container fat-free frozen whipped topping, thawed

2   tablespoons chocolate syrup

     Chopped peanuts, optional

In a 9-inch pie plate, combine the graham cracker crumbs and butter. Press the mixture into the bottom and up the sides of the pie plate.

In a mixing bowl, mix together the cream cheese and confectioners' sugar until creamy. Add peanut butter, mixing well. Gradually add milk beating until smooth and thickened. Fold in whipped topping and pour into prepared crust.

To Prepare and Eat Now: When frozen, serve with chocolate syrup and top with peanuts.

To Freeze: Freeze for at least 2 hours. To store, wrap, label, and freeze. Recommended freezing time: up to 2 to 3 months.

To Prepare After Freezing: Serve from freezer, drizzle with chocolate syrup and sprinkle with chopped peanuts.

NUTRITIONAL INFORMATION PER SERVING: *Calories 276, Protein (g) 6, Carbohydrate (g) 35, Fat (g) 12, Calories from Fat (%) 41, Saturated Fat (g) 4, Dietary Fiber (g) 1, Cholesterol (mg) 14, Sodium (mg) 213, Diabetic Exchanges. 0.5 lean meat, 2.5 other carbohydrate, 2 fat*

Pies, Cookies, and Cakes

Raspberry Dream Pie

This quick five-ingredient dessert highlights raspberries in a creamy pie.

MAKES 8 SERVINGS

1   (10-ounce) bag large marshmallows

½   cup skim milk

1   (12-ounce) package frozen raspberries

1   (8-ounce) container fat-free frozen whipped topping, thawed

1   (l0-inch) prepared reduced-fat graham cracker crust

In a large microwave-safe bowl, heat marshmallows and milk for 1 minute, stir, and return to microwave if needed, stirring until smooth. Stir in raspberries and syrup. Gently fold in the whipped topping. Pour into the crust.

To Prepare and Eat Now: Freeze for four hours or firm enough to cut slices.

To Freeze: Freeze for 4 hours or until firm. To store, wrap, label, and freeze. Recommended freezing time: up to 2 to 3 months.

To Prepare After Freezing: Remove from freezer and serve.

NUTRITIONAL INFORMATION PER SERVING: *Calories 290, Protein (g) 3, Carbohydrate (g) 61, Fat (g) 3, Calories from Fat (%) 11, Saturated Fat (g) 1, Dietary Fiber (g) 3, Cholesterol (mg) 0, Sodium (mg) 157, Diabetic Exchanges: 4 other carbohydrate, 0.5 fat*

German Chocolate Angel Pie

This incredibly luscious pie in a meringue shell melts in your mouth. When we made this recipe, we hid it in the freezer for ourselves, not giving any away it was so good.

MAKES 8 SERVINGS

3	egg whites, room temperature
¼	teaspoon salt
¼	teaspoon cream of tartar
¾	cup sugar
1	tablespoon plus 1 teaspoon vanilla extract, divided
1	(4-ounce) bar German Sweet Chocolate
3	tablespoons water
1	(8-ounce) container fat-free frozen whipped topping, thawed

Preheat the oven to 300°F.

In mixing bowl, beat the egg whites with salt and cream of tartar until foamy. Add sugar, 2 tablespoons at a time, beating well after each addition. Continue beating until stiff peaks form. Fold in 1 tablespoon vanilla. Spoon into a 9-inch pie plate coated with non-stick cooking spray and form a nest-like shell. Bake for 45 minutes. Cool.

In a microwave-safe cup, melt the chocolate in the water for 1 minute, stir until melted. Cool. Add remaining vanilla. Fold whipped topping into cooled chocolate. Spoon into meringue shell.

To Prepare and Eat Now: Freeze until firm enough to slice.

To Freeze: Wrap, label, and freeze. Recommended freezing time: up to 2 to 3 months.

To Prepare After Freezing: Thaw slightly to serve.

NUTRITIONAL INFORMATION PER SERVING: Calories 198, Protein (g) 2, Carbohydrate (g) 37, Fat (g) 4, Calories from Fat (%) 17, Saturated Fat (g) 2, Dietary Fiber (g) 1, Cholesterol (mg) 0, Sodium (mg) 110, Diabetic Exchanges: 2.5 other carbohydrate, 1 fat

Ice Cream Pie 🥕

I created this ice cream dessert for my daughter when she had her wisdom teeth out. The light banana flavor and chocolate trickling throughout really helped put a smile on her face.

MAKES 12 TO 16 SERVINGS

2 cups chocolate sandwich cookie crumbs or chocolate wafer crumbs

½ gallon nonfat vanilla frozen yogurt or fat-free ice cream, softened

1 cup mashed bananas

¼ cup orange juice

1 tablespoon vanilla extract

1 cup semisweet chocolate chips

1 (8-ounce) container fat-free frozen whipped topping, thawed

In a 3-quart oblong glass dish, spread the chocolate crumbs.

In a large bowl, combine the frozen yogurt, bananas, orange juice, and vanilla, mixing well and working quickly.

In a microwave-safe dish, melt the chocolate chips for one minute, stir. Drizzle the melted chocolate in a thin layer into the frozen yogurt mixture, stirring to mix well. Carefully spread on top of the chocolate crust mixture. Freeze until yogurt mixture is firm and top with whipped topping.

To Prepare and Eat Now: Freeze until firm enough to cut pieces.

To Freeze: To store, wrap, label, and freeze. Recommended freezing time: up to 2 to 3 months.

To Prepare After Freezing: Serve from the freezer and cut pieces.

NUTRITIONAL INFORMATION PER SERVING: *Calories 280, Protein (g) 6, Carbohydrate (g) 52, Fat (g) 7, Calories from Fat (%) 20, Saturated Fat (g) 3, Dietary Fiber (g) 2, Cholesterol (mg) 0, Sodium (mg) 203, Diabetic Exchanges: 3.5 other carbohydrate, 1.5 fat*

Slice and Bake
Chocolate Chip Cookies 🥕

Homemade slice and bake cookies are the best. Make the dough and have it ready for that craving for hot, freshly baked cookies.

MAKES 3½ DOZEN

½	cup butter
¾	cup dark brown sugar
¾	cup confectioners' sugar
1	egg
1	teaspoon vanilla extract
2¼	cups all-purpose flour
1	teaspoon baking soda
⅔	cup semisweet chocolate chips
½	cup chopped pecans, optional

In a mixing bowl, beat together the butter, brown sugar, and confectioners' sugar. Add the egg and vanilla, beating until fluffy.

In a small bowl, combine the flour and baking soda; add to creamed mixture. Stir in chocolate chips and pecans. Shape dough into two 12-inch logs.

To Prepare and Eat Now:
Wrap each log in plastic wrap, refrigerator for one hour. Preheat the oven to 350°F. Slice dough into about ½-inch thick slices. Place on non-stick cookie sheet coated with non-stick cooking spray and bake for 8 to 10 minutes or until golden.

To Freeze: Wrap dough, label, and freeze. Recommended freezing time: up to 6 months.

To Prepare After Freezing:
Defrost dough from the freezer. Preheat the oven to 350°F. Slice dough into about ½-inch thick slices onto baking sheet coated with non-stick cooking spray. Bake for 8 to 10 minutes or until lightly brown.

NUTRITIONAL INFORMATION PER SERVING: *Calories 86, Protein (g) 1, Carbohydrate (g) 13, Fat (g) 3, Calories from Fat (%) 34, Saturated Fat (g) 2, Dietary Fiber (g) 0, Cholesterol (mg) 11, Sodium (mg) 49, Diabetic Exchanges: 1 other carbohydrate, 0.5 fat*

Old-Fashioned Peanut Butter Cookies 🥕

This basic peanut butter cookie is wonderful as is, although chopped peanuts or chocolate chips do make it nice, as well! Sometimes I add 1 cup old fashioned oatmeal for Oatmeal Peanut Butter Cookies.

MAKES 36

6	tablespoons butter
½	cup reduced-fat peanut butter
½	cup sugar
⅓	cup light brown sugar
1	egg
1⅓	cups all-purpose flour
½	teaspoon baking soda
½	teaspoon baking powder
1	teaspoon vanilla extract

Preheat the oven to 350°F.

In a mixing bowl, cream the butter, peanut butter, sugar, and brown sugar until light and fluffy. Add the egg, mixing well.

In a small bowl, combine the flour, baking soda, and baking powder. Add to the sugar mixture, mixing. Add vanilla.

Note:
Most cookies freeze well, therefore, use this recipe as a guide to freeze cookies.

Drop by teaspoonful onto a baking sheet coated with non-stick cooking spray. Bake for 10 minutes or until golden brown.

To Prepare and Eat Now: Eat when ready.

To Freeze: Cool to room temperature and transfer to freezer zip-top bags, label, and freeze. Recommended freezing time: up to 6 months.

To Prepare After Freezing: Defrost or enjoy eating frozen from the freezer.

NUTRITIONAL INFORMATION PER SERVING: *Calories 76, Protein (g) 2, Carbohydrate (g) 10, Fat (g) 3, Calories from Fat (%) 40, Saturated Fat (g) 2, Dietary Fiber (g) 0, Cholesterol (mg) 11, Sodium (mg) 67, Diabetic Exchanges: 0.5 other carbohydrate, 0.5 fat*

Basic Oatmeal Cookies

I couldn't decide whether to include white chocolate chips and cranberries or chocolate chips to this oatmeal cookie, so instead, here is the basic recipe for the best oatmeal cookie you'll ever have. You can add whatever extras you want.

MAKES 3 TO 3½ DOZEN

⅓ cup canola oil

1 cup light brown sugar

½ cup sugar

1 tablespoon vanilla extract

1 teaspoon butter extract

1 egg

1 egg white

1½ cups all-purpose flour

1 teaspoon ground cinnamon

1 teaspoon baking soda

1½ cups old-fashioned oatmeal

½ cup chopped pecans

Preheat the oven to 350°F.

In a large bowl, mix the oil, brown sugar, sugar, vanilla, butter extract, egg, and egg white until smooth and creamy.

In a separate bowl, combine the flour, cinnamon, and baking soda. Gradually add the dry mixture to the sugar mixture. Stir in the oatmeal and pecans. Drop dough by rounded teaspoons onto a baking sheet coated with a non-stick cooking spray; bake for 10 to 12 minutes.

Note:

Butter extract, which is sold in the same aisle as vanilla extract, gives these cookies a rich buttery flavor without all the fat that comes with real butter.

To Prepare and Eat Now: Eat when ready.

To Freeze: Cool to room temperature, transfer to freezer zip-top bags, label, and freeze. Recommended freezing time: up to 6 months.

To Prepare After Freezing: Defrost or enjoy eating frozen from the freezer.

NUTRITIONAL INFORMATION PER SERVING: *Calories 85, Protein (g) 1, Carbohydrate (g) 13, Fat (g) 3, Calories from Fat (%) 33, Saturated Fat (g) 0, Dietary Fiber (g) 1, Cholesterol (mg) 5, Sodium (mg) 35, Diabetic Exchanges: 1 other carbohydrate, 0.5 fat*

Raspberry Coconut Bars

Begin with a yellow cake mix and raspberry jam to create these incredible Viennese-type cookies. This recipe makes a ton of bars, which makes it very freezer friendly!

MAKES 60 BARS

1	(18.25-ounce) yellow cake mix
8	tablespoons butter, divided
4	eggs, divided
1	(10-ounce) jar seedless raspberry spread
1	cup sugar
¼	teaspoon baking powder
1	teaspoon coconut extract
½	cup flaked coconut

Preheat the oven to 350°F.

In a mixing bowl, mix together the cake mix, 6 tablespoons butter and 1 egg until crumbly and mixed. Pat mixture into the bottom of a 15 x 10 x 1-inch baking pan coated with non-stick cooking spray. Bake for 10 minutes. Remove from oven and carefully spread with fruit.

Note:

Most bar cookies freeze well, therefore, use this recipe as a guide to freeze bar cookies.

In a mixing bowl, beat the remaining 3 eggs, sugar, baking powder, remaining 2 tablespoons butter, and coconut extract. Stir in coconut and pour over raspberry layer. Return to oven and continue baking for 15 to 20 minutes or until filling is set.

To Prepare and Eat Now: Refrigerate before cutting to make easier to cut.

To Freeze: Cool to room temperature, wrap, label, and freeze. Recommended freezing time: up to 6 months.

To Prepare After Freezing: Defrost and serve or cut into bars, if needed.

NUTRITIONAL INFORMATION PER SERVING: *Calories 78, Protein (g) 1, Carbohydrate (g) 13, Fat (g) 3, Calories from Fat (%) 30, Saturated Fat (g) 2, Dietary Fiber (g) 0, Cholesterol (mg) 18, Sodium (mg) 75, Diabetic Exchanges: 1 other carbohydrate, 0.5 fat*

Chocolate Buttermilk Brownies

Our family reputation is based on these simple yet rich-tasting brownies with a chocolate icing, fulfilling any chocoholic's craving. Top with some toasted nuts, or mix the nuts in the icing for the deluxe version. This recipe makes a ton, so I find myself making these brownies for all sorts of occasions.

MAKES 5½ TO 6 DOZEN

2	cups all-purpose flour
1¾	cups sugar
¼	cup cocoa
1	cup water
⅓	cup canola oil
½	cup buttermilk
1	teaspoon baking soda
1	egg, beaten
	Chocolate Icing (recipe follows)

Preheat the oven to 400°F. Coat a 15 x 10 x 1-inch baking pan with non-stick cooking spray.

In a large bowl, combine the flour, sugar, and cocoa.

In a small non-stick pot, combine water and oil; bring to a boil. Add water mixture to the flour mixture, and stir well.

In a small bowl, mix the buttermilk and baking soda, stirring until the baking soda dissolves. Add buttermilk mixture and egg to batter, stirring well. Transfer the batter to the prepared baking pan. Bake for 15 minutes, or just until the top springs back when touched. Remove from oven and immediately pour Chocolate Icing (see recipe) on top and spread. Cool the brownies completely at room temperature, and cut into squares.

To Prepare and Eat Now: Cut into squares and serve.

To Freeze: Cool to room temperature and transfer to a freezer container, or wrap, label, and freeze. Recommended freezing time: up to 1 to 2 months.

To Prepare After Freezing: Defrost and serve.

NUTRITIONAL INFORMATION PER SERVING: *Calories 78, Protein (g) 1, Carbohydrate (g) 14, Fat (g) 2, Calories from Fat (%) 25, Saturated Fat (g) 1, Dietary Fiber (g) 0, Cholesterol (mg) 6, Sodium (mg) 28, Diabetic Exchanges: 1 other carbohydrate, 0.5 fat*

It's a Fact!

If you don't have buttermilk, mix 1 tablespoon distilled vinegar or lemon juice with 1 cup of milk.

Chocolate Icing

6	tablespoons butter
⅓	cup buttermilk
¼	cup cocoa
1	(16-ounce) box confectioners' sugar
1	teaspoon vanilla extract

In a medium non-stick pot, combine butter, buttermilk, and cocoa, and bring to a boil. Add confectioners' sugar and vanilla, mixing until smooth. Pour over hot brownies.

Ooey Gooey Squares

My daughter, Haley, insisted that I include this recipe here. These squares are all of her friends' favorite and her most requested recipe. For a variation, she includes a combination of white and chocolate chips.

MAKES 48 SQUARES

1	(18.25-ounce) box yellow cake mix
½	cup butter, melted
1	egg
1	tablespoon water
1	(8-ounce) package reduced-fat cream cheese
1	(16-ounce) box confectioners' sugar
2	egg whites
1	teaspoon vanilla extract
1	cup semisweet chocolate chips

Preheat the oven to 350°F.

In a mixing bowl, beat together the cake mix, butter, egg, and water until well mixed. Spread the batter into the bottom of a 13 x 9 x 2-inch baking pan coated with non-stick cooking spray.

In a mixing bowl, beat together the cream cheese, confectioners' sugar, egg whites, and vanilla. Stir in the chocolate chips. Pour this mixture over the batter in the pan. Bake for 40 to 50 minutes or until the top is golden brown.

To Prepare and Eat Now: Cool to room temperature and cut into squares.

To Freeze: Wrap, label, and freeze. Recommended freezing time: up to 4 to 6 months.

To Prepare After Freezing: Defrost and serve.

NUTRITIONAL INFORMATION PER SERVING: *Calories 134, Protein (g) 1, Carbohydrate (g) 21, Fat (g) 5, Calories from Fat (%) 34, Saturated Fat (g) 3, Dietary Fiber (g) 0, Cholesterol (mg) 13, Sodium (mg) 108, Diabetic Exchanges: 1.5 other carbohydrate, 1 fat*

White Chocolate Bundt Cake

Keep these ingredients in your pantry to whip up this unbelievable cake in a pinch. This is another standby favorite I frequently make when I need to take a cake somewhere or to satisfy my craving.

MAKES 16 SERVINGS

1   (18.25-ounce) box yellow cake mix

1   (4-serving) box instant white chocolate pudding and pie filling

1   cup fat-free sour cream

¼   cup canola oil

⅔   cup skim milk

1   egg

3   egg whites

½   cup white chocolate chips

½   cup chopped pecans

1½   cups confectioners' sugar

¼   cup skim milk

1   tablespoon almond extract

Preheat the oven to 350°F. Coat a 10-inch non-stick Bundt pan with non-stick cooking spray.

In a mixing bowl, combine the cake mix, pudding, sour cream, oil, milk, egg, and egg whites, mixing until well mixed. Stir in the white chocolate chips and pecans. Pour in the Bundt pan and bake for 40 to 50 minutes or until wooden toothpick inserted comes out clean.

Meanwhile, in a small bowl, mix confectioners' sugar, milk, and almond extract; set aside.

Cool cake on rack for 10 minutes before inverting on serving plate. Drizzle glaze over warm cake.

Note:
Different shaped Bundt pans allow for fun types of cakes.

To Prepare and Eat Now: Slice and serve.

To Freeze: Cool to room temperature, then wrap, label, and freeze. Recommended freezing time: up to 4 to 6 months.

To Prepare After Freezing: Defrost, slice, and serve.

NUTRITIONAL INFORMATION PER SERVING: *Calories 318, Protein (g) 4, Carbohydrate (g) 51, Fat (g) 11, Calories from Fat (%) 31, Saturated Fat (g) 3, Dietary Fiber (g) 0, Cholesterol (mg) 18, Sodium (mg) 338, Diabetic Exchanges: 3.5 other carbohydrate, 2 fat*

Chocolate Fudge Cake with Fudgy Peanut Butter Frosting

Rich, moist cake with a thick fudgy frosting makes this a chocoholic favorite.

MAKES 24 TO 28 SERVINGS

2	cups all-purpose flour
2	cups sugar
1	teaspoon baking soda
1	cup water
½	cup butter
¼	cup cocoa
½	cup buttermilk
2	eggs
1	teaspoon vanilla extract
	Fudgy Peanut Butter Frosting (recipe follows)

Preheat the oven to 350°F.

In a large bowl, mix together flour, sugar, and baking soda.

In a small non-stick saucepan, combine the water, butter, and cocoa, bringing to a boil, stirring. Remove from heat and add to flour mixture with buttermilk, eggs, and vanilla, stirring until mixed. Transfer to a 13 x 9 x 2-inch pan coated with non-stick cooking spray. Bake for 25 to 30 minutes or just until wooden toothpick inserted in center comes out clean. Ice with Fudgy Peanut Butter Frosting (see recipe).

To Prepare and Eat Now: Cut into squares and serve.

To Freeze: Cool to room temperature, then wrap, label, and freeze. Recommended freezing time: up to 1 to 2 months.

To Prepare After Freezing: Defrost and serve.

NUTRITIONAL INFORMATION PER SERVING: *Calories 205, Protein (g) 3, Carbohydrate (g) 34, Fat (g) 7, Calories from Fat (%) 28, Saturated Fat (g) 3, Dietary Fiber (g) 1, Cholesterol (mg) 25, Sodium (mg) 105, Diabetic Exchanges: 2.5 other carbohydrate, 1.5 fat*

It's a Fact!

Whenever you measure flour, don't just use the measuring cup to scoop the flour out of the canister. Lightly spoon the flour into a dry measuring cup and level it with a knife for a more accurate measurement.

Fudgy Peanut Butter Frosting

½   cup peanut butter

1   tablespoon butter

⅓   cup buttermilk

¼   cup cocoa

2½ cups confectioners' sugar

1   tablespoon vanilla extract

In a non-stick saucepan, combine peanut butter, butter, buttermilk, and cocoa, cooking over a low heat until mixture is smooth. Remove from heat and add confectioners' sugar and vanilla, blending until creamy and smooth. Frost warm cake.

Italian Cream Cake 🥕

Since most cakes freeze well, I decided to include my very favorite cake to use as a guide for freezing layered cakes. This recipe was featured as the *Cooking Light Magazine* Best Cake Ever in their 10 Year Anniversary Issue and I agree with them! Toast coconut and pecans to cover the top of the cake for a real beauty shot and added flair.

MAKES 16 TO 20 SLICES

½   cup butter

¼   cup canola oil

2   cups sugar

2   eggs, separated

2   cups all-purpose flour

1   teaspoon baking soda

1   cup buttermilk

1   teaspoon vanilla extract

1   teaspoon butter extract

1   teaspoon coconut extract

½   cup chopped pecans

4   egg whites

    Cream Cheese Icing (recipe follows)

Preheat the oven to 350°F. Coat three 9-inch non-stick round cake pans with non-stick cooking spray.

In a mixing bowl, cream the butter and oil. Gradually add the sugar and beat until light and fluffy. Add the 2 egg yolks, one at a time, beating well after each addition.

Mix the flour and baking soda together. Add the flour to the sugar mixture, alternating with the buttermilk and ending with the flour. Beat after each addition. Add the vanilla, butter, and coconut extracts and the pecans.

> **Note:**
>
> **I sometimes add a small amount of coconut to the batter, as I like the coconut texture. The coconut flavoring already gives the illusion of coconut being in the cake.**

In a mixing bowl, beat all 6 egg whites until stiff peaks form. Fold the beaten egg whites into the batter mixture. Pour the batter evenly into the cake pans. Bake for 20 to 25 minutes, until the tops spring back when touched. Cool the cakes in the pans for 10 minutes and then turn onto racks to cool thoroughly. Frost the layers and sides with Cream Cheese Icing (see recipe).

Cream Cheese Icing

1   (8-ounce) package reduced-
    fat cream cheese, softened

3   tablespoons butter

1   (16-ounce) box
    confectioners' sugar

1   teaspoon vanilla extract

In mixing bowl, beat the cream cheese and butter until smooth. Add the confectioners' sugar and beat until light. Blend in the vanilla.

To Prepare and Eat Now: Slice and serve.

To Freeze: You can freeze the cake layers separately, and ice the cake when you've defrosted the cake later. Alternately, you can freeze the cake after it's been iced, but place it in the freezer without wrapping. Once the icing has hardened, wrap, label, and freeze until you're ready to eat. Recommended freezing time: up to 4 to 6 months, unfrosted; 1 to 3 months, frosted.

To Prepare After Freezing: Defrost layers and prepare icing as directed if layers frozen separately. If whole cake is frozen, remove wrapping, defrost, and cover.

NUTRITIONAL INFORMATION PER SERVING: *Calories 359, Protein (g) 5, Carbohydrate (g) 54, Fat (g) 14, Calories from Fat (%) 35, Saturated Fat (g) 6, Dietary Fiber (g) 1, Cholesterol (mg) 46, Sodium (mg) 187, Diabetic Exchanges: 3.5 other carbohydrate, 3 fat*

Diet Sprite Paradise Cake 🥕

With one bite of this cake, you will understand the ultimate indulgence outside of the chocolate world. This trip to paradise is made with everyday ingredients and will be the talk of your evening.

MAKES 16 SERVINGS

1   (18.25-ounce) box yellow cake mix

1   (4-serving) box instant coconut cream pudding mix

1   cup nonfat plain yogurt or fat-free sour cream

⅓   cup canola oil

1   cup diet Sprite

1   egg

3   egg whites

⅓   cup flaked coconut

1   (15.25-ounce) can crushed pineapple, well drained

1½   cups confectioners' sugar

1   teaspoon coconut extract

2 to 3 tablespoons skim milk

Preheat the oven to 350°F. Coat a 10-inch non-stick Bundt pan with non-stick cooking spray.

In a mixing bowl, combine cake mix, pudding, sour cream, oil, Sprite, egg, and egg whites, blending until mixed. Stir in coconut and pineapple. Pour into Bundt pan and bake for 40 to 45 minutes or until wooden toothpick inserted comes out clean.

Meanwhile, in small bowl, mix confectioners' sugar, coconut extract, and enough milk to make glaze.

Cool cake for 10 minutes before inverting on serving plate. With a toothpick, poke holes over the top of the cake and spoon glaze over.

Note:

Coconut extract adds the coconut flavor without the fat. Coconut extract is found in the grocery store with flavorings and spices.

To Prepare and Eat Now: Slice and serve.

To Freeze: Wrap, label, and freeze. Recommended freezing time: up to 6 months.

To Prepare After Freezing: Defrost, slice, and serve.

Note: Slice some strawberries or serve berries with a piece of cake for added nutrition, flavor, and color.

NUTRITIONAL INFORMATION PER SERVING: *Calories 279, Protein (g) 3, Carbohydrate (g) 49, Fat (g) 8, Calories from Fat (%) 27, Saturated Fat (g) 3, Dietary Fiber (g) 1, Cholesterol (mg) 14, Sodium (mg) 312, Diabetic Exchanges: 3 other carbohydrate, 1.5 fat*

Suggested Menus

Lasagna

Traditional Lasagna 237
Southwestern Lasagna 239
Mexican Lasagna 238
Chicken Salsa Lasagna 187
Quick Chicken Lasagna 188
Chicken Artichoke and
    Spinach Ravioli Lasagna 189
Spinach Lasagna 155

Breakfast on the Run

Mini Sticky Cinnamon Rolls 62
Mini Muffin Rancheros 66
Florentine English Muffins 65
Raspberry Surprise Bran Muffins 48
Banana Orange Bran Muffins 49
Oatmeal Pancakes 63

Elegant Dining

Almond Glazed Brie 24
Shrimp and Portabella 36
Sirloin Strips and Asparagus 215
Pork Tender Wellington 219
Crabmeat au Gratin 251
Veal Paprika 246
Seafood Stuffed Potatoes 272
Sun Dried Tomato Bread 70
German Chocolate Angel Pie 306
Italian Cream Cake 318
Lemon Almond Blueberry Ice Cream
    Dessert 289
Two-Minute Banana Tiramisu 285

Freezer Fast Food

Barbecue Chicken Pizza 168
White Spinach Pizza 151

Beef Tenderloin Pizza
    with Horseradish Cream 150
Italian Pizza Rolls 33
Stuffed Meaty Pizza 244
Make Ahead Patties 245
Shrimp Loaf 262

New Year's Day

Black-Eyed Pea Dip 38
Black-Eyed Pea Soup 92
Cabbage Roll Casserole 243
Marinated Pork Tenderloin 220
Pulled Pork Chili 81

Holiday Dining

Maple Dijon Glazed Turkey Breast 211
Chicken Cherries Jubilee 174
Pork Chops with Dark Cherry Sauce 222
Cornbread and Rice Dressing 147
Old-Fashioned Cornbread Dressing 148
Sweet Potato Casserole with
    Crumbly Praline Topping 164
Apple Crumble Custard Pie 298
Pecan Caramel Pie 296

Southwestern Favorites

Stuffed Crab Poblano Peppers 43
Stuffed Chicken Breasts with
    Enchilada Sauce 170
Southwestern Lasagna 239
Easy Beef Enchiladas 225
Empanadas 32
Southwestern Shrimp and
    Black Bean Chili 80
Shrimp Enchiladas 259
Frozen Strawberry Margarita Pie 303
Pecan Caramel Pie 296

Barbecue Feasts

Best Beef Brisket 217

Barbecued Pot Roast 218

Southwestern Rice 138

Baked Beans 137

Easy Potato Casserole 159

Triple Corn Pudding 142

Ice Cream Pie 307

Old-Fashioned
    Peanut Butter Cookies 309

Italian Favorites

Meatball Soup 89

Meat Sauce Bolognese 233

Meatballs and Tomato Sauce 234

Italian Stuffed Meat Loaf 229

Chicken Cacciatore 175

Italian Macaroni and Cheese 144

Tortoni 284

Two-Minute Banana Tiramisu 285

Louisiana

Shrimp Creole 254

Crawfish Fettuccine 265

Crabmeat au Gratin 251

Comfort Food

Cheddar Cheese Potato Soup 96

Italian Stuffed Meat Loaf 229

Chicken Pot Pie 182

Macaroni and Cheese 143

Mashed Potatoes 160

Green Bean Casserole 139

Banana Split Pie 300

Southern Comfort

Shrimp Casserole 256

Ham and Sweet Potato Pot Pie
    with Pecan Crust 224

Chicken and Dumplings 173

Smothered Okra 146

Chess Pie 297

Souper Suppers

Chicken Tortilla Soup 116

Beef Stew with Dumplings 85

Different Twist Pork Stew 86

Meatball Soup 89

Roasted Vegetable Minestrone 128

Kids' Favorites

Italian Pizza Rolls 33

Meaty Biscuit Cups 34

Meat and Macaroni Casserole 232

Chicken Pot Pie 182

Salsa Chicken 186

Triple Corn Pudding 142

Ooey Gooey Squares 314

Chocolate-Dipped Frozen Bananas 276

Frozen Surprise S'Mores 277

Cheesecake Surprises 283

Individual Pull Outs

Stuffed Chicken Breasts with Feta,
    Spinach, and Ham 169

Make Ahead Meat Patties 245

Crab Cakes with Dill Sauce 252

Salmon Cakes with Chili Sauce 268

Stuffed Potatoes Primavera 161

Stuffed Sweet Potatoes 163

Seafood Stuffed Potatoes 272

Seafood Stuffed Bell Peppers 271

Family Favorites

Cheddar Cheese Potato Soup 96
Jumbo Stuffed Shells 230
Meat Sauce 236
Chicken Caesar Casserole 181
Mexican Chicken Casserole 209
Shrimp Casserole 256
Basic Beef Stew 84
Best Chili 77
Ice Cream Crispy Dessert 288
Chocolate Buttermilk Brownies 312

Tropical Treats

Toasted Coconut Banana Bread 59
Crab and Goat Cheese Empanadas
   with Mango Salsa 30
Different Twist Pork Stew 86
Marinated Pork Tenderloin 220
Stuffed Sweet Potatoes 163
Diet Sprite Paradise Cake 320
Frozen Piña Colada Pie 302

Hearty Football Party

Shrimp and Sausage Cheesecake 28
Chili Dip 42
Chili Rolls 29
Spinach and Brie Dip 40
Taco Soup 117
Any of the Chili recipes 77-81
Italian Stuffed Bread 72
Cornbread 69

Summer Sweets

Frozen Fruit Cups 286
Lemon Ice 291
Raspberry Dream Pie 305

Frozen Strawberry Margarita Pie 303
Orange Raspberry
   Ice Cream Dessert 290

Feeding Sick Friends

Sweet Potato Praline Coffee Cake 60
Banana Bread 55
Quick Breakfast Swirl Cake 61
Quick Chicken Lasagna 188
Chicken Tortilla Soup 116
Southwestern Chicken Soup 115
Roasted Vegetable Minestrone 128
White Chocolate Bundt Cake 315
Slice and Bake
   Chocolate Chip Cookies 308

Potluck Casseroles

Crawfish Fettuccini 265
Enchilada Casserole 226
Chicken Vermicelli 184
Mexican Chicken Casserole 209
Cheesy Shrimp and Rice 258
Seafood and Wild Rice Casserole 270
Any of the Lasagna recipes 155,
   187-189, 237-240

Something Sweet

White Chocolate Bundt Cake 315
Chocolate Buttermilk Brownies 312
Banana Cheesecake with
   Caramel Sauce and Walnuts 278
Ooey Gooey Squares 314
Pecan Caramel Pie 296

Appetizers

Almond-Glazed Brie 24
Spinach and Artichoke Dip 41
Caramelized Onion Cheesecake 27

Cookware Tips

Preparing delicious, healthy meals often starts with cookware. I recommend using cookware with Teflon® non-stick coating. It is convenient, easy to clean and limits the amount of cooking fats needed so meals are healthy and you can stay Trim & Terrific.

It is also important to properly use and care for any type of cookware so you get the most flavor out of your meals and to help prevent kitchen accidents or fires.

Here are some important things to keep in mind about kitchen safety and cookware care:

Never leave any heated cookware unattended.

- Unattended cooking is the number one contributor to cooking fires—the leading cause of fires in homes across America.

Don't let your pans get too hot.

- Temperatures can rise very quickly in an empty pan left on high heat. High temperatures can lead to intense spattering when food is added, which can be a burn hazard.
- Avoid preheating empty cookware on high heat. Low or medium heat is sufficient.

Learn how to tell when your pan is properly preheated.

- If you are using a non-stick or empty pan, flick a few drops of water onto the pan from your wetted hand. Once the water droplets begin to sizzle and dance in the pan, it is sufficiently preheated.
- If the pan has a small quantity of oil or fat in it, place a small crouton or piece of onion in the pan. When the food is browning on the edges, the pan is ready for cooking.
- Never flick water into hot oil—it will spatter intensely and be a burn hazard!
- Always turn on the exhaust fan or open a window before cooking.
- If accidentally overheated, usually by leaving a preheating pan unattended, some types of cookware, including non-stick, can emit fumes that are harmful to pet birds. Always move your birds out of the kitchen before cooking.

Prolong the life of non-stick cookware through proper care and handling.

- Properly clean non-stick cookware by simply washing with hot, soapy water after each use. A sponge or dishcloth is usually all it takes to get the surface thoroughly clean.
- Try not to use abrasive cleaners or scouring pads. If you've got stubborn food residue, use a non-abrasive cleaner such as soft scrub.
- Generally, using plastic, nylon, or wooden utensils is best since they prevent marring. Avoid using knives and cutting food in the pan to prevent scratching.
- For best performance use cookware that isn't scratched. But non-stick coatings are pretty resilient and cooking with scratched cookware won't affect the safety of your food. And, even if you do ingest any particles, they are not harmful to your health.

Brought to you
by DuPont™ Teflon®
non-stick coatings

The miracles of science™